William Houston joined the N[...] II. Having served as a specia[...] qualified as a chartered eng[...] experience which stood him in[...] new career as a company 'doctor', advising a large range of companies on turnaround and the restructuring of unprofitable businesses.

His first book, *Avoiding Adversity*, was published in 1989 and warned businessmen of the coming recession, suggesting ways to maintain solvency or help rescue an ailing firm. He has also written about independent directors in association with the venture capital house 3i, and is the author of *Meltdown*, also published in Warner paperback, which outlines business strategies for the 1990s.

Also by William Houston

MELTDOWN

RIDING THE BUSINESS CYCLE

How Six Climatic and Economic Cycles Are Changing Our Lives

William Houston

WARNER BOOKS

A *Warner* Book

First published in Great Britain in 1995
by Little, Brown and Company
This edition published in 1996 by Warner Books

Copyright © William Houston 1995

A CIP catalogue record for this book
is available from the British Library.

ISBN: 0 7515 1618 X

Typeset by M Rules
Printed and bound in Great Britain by
Clays Ltd, St Ives plc

Warner Books
A Division of
Little, Brown and Company (UK)
Brettenham House
Lancaster Place
London WC2E 7EN

To Averil, Geraldine,
Carolyn and Evelyn

ACKNOWLEDGEMENTS

Many people have helped with this book but none more than Richard Mogey and his colleagues Steve Bush and Chester Joy at the Foundation for the Study of Cycles, Wayne, Pennsylvania. For two weeks I received every possible help in researching and copying documents: my only contribution was to introduce them to herb tea and temporarily to improve their potassium levels with some good banana deals from the nearby store.

It is not possible to write a book covering such a wide range of subjects without consulting references; these I have either listed under documents for further reading or acknowledged in the text. I am very grateful for this resource. My thanks also are due to a number of people who gave of their time and wisdom. I am particularly indebted to: Martin Armstrong, Stephen Bamford, Teddy Butler-Henderson, James Davidson, Willem Foks, Evelyn Browning Garriss, John Gillum, Terrence Goddard, Charles Houston, Simon Hunt, Jeordie Kidston, Hubert Lamb, Stephen Lewis, Rupert Lowe, Jane Malcomson, David Quinion, Alan Robertson, Peter Spence, John Taylor, Louis Thompson, Peter Warburton, David Whately and Michael White. I hope I have done justice to their contribution; any errors are entirely mine.

I am also very grateful to William Rees-Mogg for writing the preface and to Richard Fox for the introduction; both have added considerably to the scope of the book. It is also good of Basil Denning, Michael Jordan, Brian Pearse, Christopher Woodward, and others I have mentioned earlier to endorse the work. I am grateful for the guidance of my agents Doreen and Caroline Montgomery and Alan Samson who suggested a book on cycles in the first place; he and Julia Charles have been very helpful in advice on organising the contents. Finally, I am deeply indebted to my wife Averil who has painstakingly worked through my draft and helped me improve the meaning of the book, despite the demands of her own work and our nine grand-children.

William Houston,
Datchworth, August 1994

CONTENTS

PREFACE
BY LORD REES-MOGG

The existence of business cycles and their possible connection with climate has been known for a long time. Perhaps the greatest of the late-nineteenth-century English economists, William Stanley Jevons, associated an eleven-year cycle with the effect of sunspots on harvests. Most of us have the instinctive feeling that business has a rhythm like that of the seasons: winter will be followed by spring, high summer will be followed by autumn. As we grow older, we recognise that our own lives have passed through a number of business cycles of that kind.

There is, however, another kind of cycle which does not resemble the benign progress of the seasons – though some winters can be very cold – so much as the build-up and release of tension in an avalanche. Gradually, snowflake by snowflake, an overhang is built up on the mountainside. So long as the build-up continues, nothing changes in the valley below, and everyone goes about ordinary business: the farmer feeds his cattle; the milkmaid milks the cows; all in complete security. Then one day the last snowflake falls, or a boy fires a gun to scare the birds, and the whole weight of snow crashes down into the peaceful valley.

The businessman may be lucky. He may never see an avalanche in his business life. If so, he may believe, as many people did in the 1960s, that the worst problems of the business economy have all been solved, that no great panic or slump will ever happen again; no 1720, no 1929, because we know so much better than our ancestors who lived in the same valley. Those of us who have survived to the mid-1990s are more likely to recognise that the main cycles of business and politics are outside our control, and that we have to adjust to multiple cycles, some regular and some catastrophic, which interact with each other in an unstable environment.

William Houston's book is an invaluable introduction to the understanding of these cycles. He is cautious about his conclusions – cyclical theory can improve one's understanding of the possibilities of the economic future, but is not an Ordnance Survey map of what is going to happen. With all analysis which involves more than one factor, prediction becomes difficult, and the interaction of economic cycles is as multi-factoral as weather forecasting. However, one can look for patterns, and can hope to distinguish the strong trends of long-term cycles, from the weaker movements of the more regular short-term cycles.

The political philosophers of the ancient world, including Aristotle, thought that there was an inherent instability in all political constitutions, which naturally led from dictatorship to oligarchy, from oligarchy to democracy and from democracy back to dictatorship, an ever-turning wheel. In the eighteenth century, British political philosophers believed that they had stopped the wheel turning by developing a mixed constitution, with its dictatorial element in the monarchy, its oligarchic element in the House of Lords, and its democratic element in the House of Commons. Modern Britain, in common with most advanced societies, has become something like a pure democracy, at least in constitutional theory. The European Union has a strong element of meritocratic (and bureaucratic) oligarchy in its constitution.

The reason democracy is unstable is that people want to vote themselves more benefits than they wish to pay taxes. Democracy can self-destruct because it creates unsustainable budget deficits through the mismatch of social entitlements and inadequate tax receipts. The gap has to be filled by debt, and the debt is liable to be liquidated by inflation. We have seen this process clearly enough in the twentieth century, but it has remained comparatively stable, at least in social terms, because the erosion of debt through inflation has usually occurred at a moderate rate, just enough to avoid intolerable debt levels, but slow enough to continue an illusion of price stability.

William Houston explores the likely future development of this debt overhang, which looks particularly threatening in the United States. Present entitlement and financial policies in America are only sustainable for a limited time, and will become unsustainable quite early in the next century.

This is an important book. It deals with real movements of the world economy, and helps provide an understanding of the different economic, climatic and political cycles which interact to determine the future of mankind. Some of them take centuries to evolve, others are short term, but they are fascinating, they are real and they are important.

INTRODUCTION
BY RICHARD J. FOX

From the very beginning of human history, mankind has looked for explanations to provide reasonable cause and effect answers to the natural phenomena which surround us and affect our lives. The question of whether there is 'order in the universe' was hotly debated by Albert Einstein and the leading quantum physicists of his time. Einstein refused to accept the notion that we are at the mercy of 'a God who rolls dice'. Through his studies of cycles and their continuing impact on all life on earth, Bill Houston has given us significant insights into the order of the universe and those forces which may enable us to pull back the veil obscuring the future.

All living things on earth are affected by the forces of the sun, the moon, and the movement of the planets in our solar system. Since these forces and movements are predictable, it is logical to conclude that their impact on earth and living systems is also predictable. The recurrence of sunspots, tidal forces and planetary forces is related to natural phenomena which recurs on earth, so the timing of these forces can be related to recurring cycles identified with them. Over the years, a number of researchers have identified the cycles of economic, social and political events on earth. The author has taken these studies of cycles and provided us with tools to project our thinking into the future. Focusing on the 1990s, Bill Houston has found a coincidence of a number of significant cycles which will occur in this decade. He has studied what massive changes affecting all life on earth took place in the past when this unique convergence of cycles occurred. If the future is similar to the past, this last decade of this century and this millennium will be one of the most tumultuous of all recorded history. What we have seen so far – extraordinary changes in politics, science and economics – will pale compared to what will occur during the next few years.

The author takes us on a voyage through history, pointing out the correlations of climate, economics, movements of people, wars, and the impact these had on those who lived during similar periods of massive change. With skill and amazing insight, he has brought together in this book an overview of the forces that shaped the past and will impact the future.

Bill Houston, in this remarkable book, *Riding the Business Cycle*, has parted the curtain and given us a look into the future.

CHAPTER 1

THE UNEXPECTED IS THE HISTORY YOU HAVE NOT READ

On 20 April 1990 something happened which, if history repeats itself, will commit the world to two or three decades of much cooler weather, civil unrest, food shortages and the collapse of many institutions. What event was this? If it was so important, why were the newspapers not full of it and politicians available to give instant answers? It was a little-reported fact that the sun was disturbed on that day by out-of-balance forces in the solar system – something which has cropped up every 179 years for the last millennium.

It seems that every 179 years the giant planets Jupiter and Saturn cause an imbalance in the solar system; this upsets the powerful magnetic forces working in the upper layers of the sun whose output could fall by as much as 2%. This may not sound much but a drop in the average temperature of 1°F is like living some 300 miles further north – all right for those in Spain perhaps, but tough for people living in Scotland, Canada, Scandinavia or Russia. But this is exactly what happened in 1630 and 1810. When it became extremely cold in the 17th century, masses of people migrated from the Scottish famine and it became even too cold for cod around the Norwegian coasts. During this period, known as the 'little ice age', there were civil wars, dynasties were overthrown and people experienced food shortages as crops could not be harvested.

Recurring events are part of our daily lives guiding such natural events as the seasons, eclipses, night and day, and the tides. Cycles are also about the probability that history will repeat itself and a large number of cycles of varying importance ranging from 500 to 6.4 years all reach their low point in the 1990s. This is why this decade is probably the most singular since the early 1500s when a similar number of cycles converged. With all our technology there is little we can do to escape – though we can be guided by how these cycles have operated in the past.

After he left office Harry S. Truman, one of the most historically aware presidents, said that in his experience the unexpected stemmed from the history he had not read. By this he meant that as people had responded to given situations in the past, there was a good chance that others would react similarly in the future. When the unexpected occurred, his later research almost invariably found parallels in the history he had not previously read.

Whether Truman was a student of cycles is not recorded. However, some forty years later we can be quite selective in our reading of human behaviour because we have a much greater knowledge of cycles and the way people behave in relation to their environment. Of course, history never quite repeats itself but with the knowledge of how cycles work and their duration, we can piece together whether these rhythms will be working either in concert or in opposing directions. Thus we can go some way towards not only anticipating events but also estimating what they might mean in the future.

It is for this reason that a knowledge of cycles is essential for those in authority – whether in politics, business, the media, in the professions – or indeed for individuals. They can then pinpoint particular years or decades when changes are likely to occur so that at least they can make contingency plans which could be implemented if necessary. On a practical level this knowledge will enable providers of goods and services to anticipate customers' needs, and shape political policies.

That is the purpose of this book. The early chapters explain the almost wholly natural causes that drive cycles, then the practical results of matters such as climatic changes and their likely influence on individuals. There are then several chapters on how cycles with a duration varying from 500 years to forty months have worked in the past, and how climatic changes explain many of the seeming irrationalities in human behaviour. This is followed by some practical examples of how cycles explain changes in commodities, bond yields, interest rates and real-estate prices. Some items are covered in detail such as wheat and gold.

The cluster of seven cycles all reaching a significant level during the 1990s makes this decade one of the most interesting for at least 500 years. If the future is to resemble the past we may be faced with a discontinuity in the affairs of mankind; this could profoundly shape our lives, requiring many of us to question the validity and continuity of institutions, practices, principles and values that were previously accepted. The final chapter examines some of these alternatives and suggests some decisions we might be forced to take.

By the end of the 15th century, Europeans had suffered from the Great Famine of 1317–18, the Great Plague twenty years later and the Hundred Years' War; others, including the Chinese, had endured the scourge of Genghis Khan's Golden Hordes. Hardly surprising that many believed they had been visited by the Four Horsemen of the Apocalypse: war, famine, plague and death which had depleted the population by at least one third. It is to be hoped that we will not suffer the same scourges today. But now, 500 years later, can this unusual combination of cycles provide the catharsis which will purge the artificiality, corruption, sleaze and sheer triviality – to say nothing of the decline in faith – that is plaguing much of public and private life today?

Just as previously, a cool and dry period would play havoc with harvests all over the world but particularly in the northern hemisphere, imposing high commodity prices on over-borrowed countries, companies and individuals. The impact on the existing man-made chaos could be devastating – particularly as it would be largely unexpected. Unfortunately politicians could make it even worse. Instead of damping down a troublesome spell, as would have been the practice in the 19th century, our rulers could well inject even more money into the system to avoid a deflationary collapse. The result could be two years of spiralling inflation before the biggest crash ever. Then it could really be like the 17th century . . .

The good news is that any return to the cool-dry climate of the 1500s would bring a new vigour to people who have historically become more independent and self-assured. Power will move away from politicians and bureaucrats back to the individual; but we will have to work hard for it.

CHAPTER 2

BLAME THE SUN AND MOON, JUPITER AND SATURN . . .

We live in a world dominated by cycles. They decide the course of day and night, the seasons of the year, the tides and, as this chapter will explain, our attitude to life. Thankfully, the majority of the cycles featured in this book can be explained not by the manoeuvring of politicians but by events in a highly regulated and predictable planetary system based around the sun. Although the earth owes its life to the sun, it is only an average member of the 200 billion stars that make up the vast Milky Way galaxy – itself part of a much larger cosmos.

The earth benefits from the sun in many ways, but three factors are particularly important:

Firstly, the sun's relatively huge mass (99.9% of the solar system) provides the earth with a predictable orbit called the 'plane of the ecliptic' around which we can calculate our position with great accuracy relative to our sister planets and other stars. It takes the earth 365.24 days to complete the circuit.

Secondly, the earth's tilt at 23.5 degrees from the orbit gives us seasons enabling us to live as far north and south as the Arctic and Antarctic – something not possible if the earth had no tilt.

Thirdly, the sun is very hot, generating its energy by a process of fusion which releases huge quantities of heat while converting hydrogen into helium – just like a hydrogen bomb; the interior of the sun is so hot that a grain of sand at that temperature would frazzle a man 150 kilometres away. Although we are ninety-three million miles away, the sun's energy is enough to drive plant life, and to make it tolerable for humans and animals to live on most of the land masses except those impossibly too dry or cold. The sun's power is not consistent; there are patches on the surface called sunspots which vary the heat output and affect people directly.

Two other planets are nearer to the sun than the earth. Mercury is thirty-six million miles away but, having no atmosphere, has huge extremes of temperature between the hot and cool sides. Venus, the next one out, is sixty-seven million miles from the sun, but its atmosphere keeps the planet at a steady 462°C. Two other planets are important to us: although Jupiter is 484 million miles from the sun its very mass (larger than all the other planets combined) is sufficiently important to unbalance slightly the mass and angular velocity of the solar system. The icy Saturn is also important, at 887 million miles from the sun.

Apart from the sun, the moon is the most important planet to the earth because the gravitational pull – double that of the

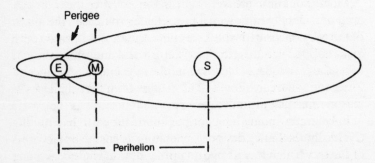

8.85 YEAR TIDAL FORCE CYCLE

Condition of maximum tidal pull
Perihelion: sun's closest orbital position
Perigree: moon's closest orbital position

Perigee

E M   S

Perihelion

Figure 1. Alignment of the earth, sun and moon at the closest point in their orbits.

sun – causes the seas and oceans to be deflected according to the relative positions of the sun, moon and earth. The tides affect every open sea and ocean in a near two-week cycle consisting of the 'spring tides' when the moon and sun are in line and the attraction is at a maximum; the 'neap tides' occur when the pull is minimal. The tidal cycle is completed when the moon has concluded its 29.5-day orbit – the lunar month – around the earth which is tilted at five degrees to the equator.

Although the sun and moon are regularly aligned with the earth every month, there is a point every 8.85 years when they are not only in line but their orbits are closest together, as shown in Figure 1: the point at which the earth is the nearest to the sun in its elliptical orbit is called the 'perihelion' and moon's closest point is called the 'perigee'. As we shall see in the next chapter this alignment can cause considerable strains in the earth's crust where, at its weakest, it can cause earthquakes and volcanoes.

There is a further important alignment of the earth, sun and moon which happens every 18.6 years when ellipses may be expected. Figure 2 shows the earth spinning at nearly 23.5 degrees to the plane of the ecliptic and the moon's orbit is some five degrees to the ecliptic. This means that, relative to the equator, the maximum distance the moon can move north and south is 23.5 + 5 = 28.5 degrees and 23.5 – 5 = 18.5 degrees. Taken in combination, there is a complete alignment of the earth, sun and moon when all are at their closest point every 179.3 years.

Moving out from the sun, earth and moon, there is a 179-year cycle from the rotation of the planets, particularly Jupiter, Saturn, Uranus and Neptune around the sun. Although their mass is tiny relative to the sun, Saturn and Jupiter contribute 86% of the 'torque', or turning motion – enough imbalance to force the centre of gravity of the solar system (called the 'barycentre') away from the centre of the sun.

In his prizewinning essay for the Foundation for the Study of Cycles, James Shirley describes the solar system as a sort of out-of-balance dumbell with a heavy weight one end and a much lighter one at the other. If this dumbell is thrown, the ends will turn unevenly round and round its centre of gravity (the

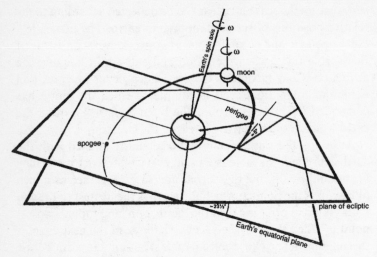

Figure 2. Comparative orbits of the earth, sun and moon.

barycentre) which itself travels in a perfect parabola. Figure 3, taken from T. Landsheidt's book *Sun-Earth-Man*, shows this movement from 1945 to 1994 with the barycentre orbiting three times before passing very close and *inside* its loop. This is known as 'retrograding'.

The planets could also be responsible for disturbance within the earth called the Chandler Wobble. In a paper published by the Foundation for the Study of Cycles, Goran Windelius of the Solaris Research Centre in Hagfors, Sweden explains how the structure of the globe is made up of several parts; there is a molten inner core, a semi-molten thick layer called the mantle and an outer crust which is partly land and partly ocean and the atmosphere. It seems that all the parts are working on slightly different rhythms causing a wobble or disturbance which beats every 6.2 years.

All this could be very unsettling for the highly sensitive parts of the earth where, as the next chapter explains, earthquakes and volcanoes are most likely. In a table of these phenomena going back to 1889 and 1629 respectively, Windelius shows there to be a very high statistical probability that major earthquakes

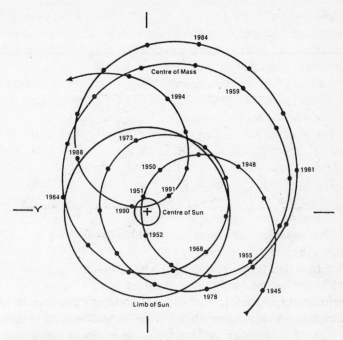

CENTRE OF MASS OF SOLAR SYSTEM
RELATIVE TO SUN'S CENTRE 1945-1995

Figure 3. Movement of the Barycentre around the centre of mass of the sun. Note that instead of the barycentre going round the sun's centre of mass in 1990, it actually turned inside, a condition known as 'retrograding'

and eruptions occur within a short time either before or after the wobble is expected. As the next wobble is due early in 1995, there is a strong probability of a major disturbance to the earth's crust from 1994 through to 1996 and beyond.

How the 179-year cycles have worked in the past
A paper written by Rhodes Fairbridge, Professor Emeritus at Colombia University, and James Shirley shows how nine circuits of the barycentre around the sun as in Figure 3 are made every 178.7 years taking nine to fourteen years to complete one

revolution. At some point in the latter half of the cycle the barycentre becomes close to the sun's centre of mass to create powerful solar activity which coincides with a prolonged reduction in sunspots and reduced heat felt on earth.

All these periods of minimum sunspots are very interesting points in history, as we will discover in later chapters. They are named after their originators:

The Wolf minimum: Sunspots were unusually low from 1275 to 1337, a time that included the Great Famine of 1317–18, then followed the Black Death and the Hundred Years' War.

The Sporer minimum: A particularly cool period with low sunspots during the turbulent times in Europe from 1394 to 1516 ending with the Reformation.

The Maunder minimum: This occurred from 1646 to 1712, taking in the English Civil War, the Thirty Years' War and the food riots that toppled the Ming Dynasty in China.

The Sabine minimum: This occurred from 1798 to 1823, a period that included the French Revolution, the rise and fall of Napoleon and the independence of Latin American republics.

Note: The 'little ice age' is a broad term describing the particularly cool period from around 1560 to 1850, taking in the Maunder and Sabine minimums. As we shall see in later chapters, each minimum led to a considerable release of individual freedom which changed the nature of the next warm cycle.

The message for the present

Fairbridge and Shirley explain what could be in store for us. The barycentre retrograded on 20 April 1990, suggesting a prolonged cool period not dissimilar to the other anniversaries described earlier, but this one to last from 1990 to 2013. By 1994, sunspots (varying dark patches on the sun whose impact is explained in due course) were declining after peaking in 1989 and remained unusually strong until early 1992 when they declined sharply, and are due to reach a minimum in 1995 – over five years before the next expected maximum in 2000. However, if they behave similarly to other 179-year anniversaries, the length of the cycle could increase and the sunspot level remain unusually low.

James Shirley's paper explains how the air flows around the world can be distorted when the sun's power is less than usual. Normally the areas of low pressure at the north and south poles attract the warm moist air from the mid-latitudes which flows towards the poles. The warm air from the south then meets the cooler northern currents at a point known as the 'jet stream'.

This collision of the warm and cool airstreams is marked by a line of considerable storminess, generating a strong localised wind of around sixty knots which flows around the world in an easterly direction; it is usually around 35,000 feet and pilots flying east can add at least 10% to their speed if they fly within it. Normally the jet stream flows continuously around the world, as in Figure 4, which shows the earth from above the North Pole, with the points of high and low pressure marked.

Note: The jet stream was first discovered during the First World War when a Zeppelin bomber over Britain was forced high to evade attacking fighters; the unfortunate crew found themselves trapped in a jet stream which eventually deposited them in Poland frozen to death.

When sunspots are unusually low, the cool air sets up blocks of almost permanent low pressure over the land masses of Eurasia and North America, and areas of high pressure over the warmer oceans. Instead of the jet stream appearing as a more or

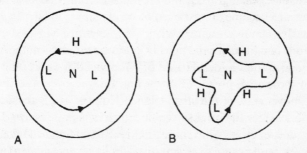

Figure 4. Comparison of the jet stream's position and areas of high and low pressure in the northern hemisphere. 'A' shows a normal pattern with a continuous westerly jet stream; 'B's' pattern becomes meridional, with blocking areas of high and low pressure. (After J. Shirley.)

less regular ring around the globe, it becomes distorted because the prolonged high and low pressure areas force it to loop, as shown in Figure 4B. Instead of the winds flowing westerly they are more inclined to flow north or south in what is known as a 'meridional pattern'. As the cold persists, the snow cover increases in the centre of the great continents, the glaciers advance and any warmth received by the sun is reflected, making the land masses cooler. Even during the summer months, the continents receive less rain than usual, creating droughts and poor crop yields, while those areas with a maritime climate are sometimes warmer than usual with damp southerly winds.

Some historical comparisons with previous cool periods are described in the next chapter; it is as if people were living several hundred miles further north – a fall of 1°F is equivalent to 300 miles. Although the average temperature is cooler than usual, it could fluctuate rapidly as it did during the sweltering summers of 1665 and 1666, preceding the Great Fire of London, before returning to biting cold. Cool periods do not just affect northern latitudes; it seems that all the climatic belts were shifted further south during what was described earlier as the Little Ice Age.

We could be entering an unhappy period. Prolonged areas of drought and cooler weather shorten the growing season; this causes land that is normally productive to become unusable for anything other than grazing and the lands normally occupied by herdsmen to become almost barren. As explained in later chapters, a dry, cool climate makes people more vigorous, a dangerous condition for the fiercely independent Huns in the 5th century, and the Golden Horde of Mongols 800 years later – both of these races invaded Europe and China.

The movements of the larger planets, Jupiter and Saturn, set the time scale for the solar system, a 'clock' which is responsible for the sunspot cycles which have an average duration of 11.2 and 22.4 years. It seems that the sun operates like a sort of dynamo with an inner and outer layer in its construction varying in speed and affected by the gravitational force and momentum of the great planets. It is thought that as the speed of rotation changes, lines of magnetic force are wound up (like ropes) coming to the surface as powerful areas of high magnetism, behaving rather like a horseshoe magnet with the two poles protruding outwards.

In his book *Sun-Earth-Man*, Landsheidt comes to conclusions similar to those of Fairbridge and Shirley, although he approaches the subject from a different viewpoint. He shows how terrestrial events, such as the lynx population, the output of Germany and the Stock Market could be affected when the sun, barycentre and Jupiter are in line – what is called a 'conjunction'. At this point the torque exerted by Jupiter on the sun reduces to zero, changes direction, then increases – just as in the retrograde position in Figure 3. This generates powerful sunspot activity at the time, with the emissions declining rapidly a few years later.

The most recent retrograde was on 20 April 1990, which was marked by particularly strong sunspot activity – some analysts suggesting the highest since the 17th century before the Maunder minimum. Landsheidt agrees with Fairbridge that the instability created by the retrograde could have a corresponding effect on earth. He also believes the present sunspot minimum was triggered in 1990 and will reach its deepest point in around 2030 – seventeen years later than Fairbridge's estimate of 2013.

Landsheidt shows how the number of lynx trapped in North America varied between the years 1730 to 1980 on around a nine-year cycle, with the start of most rhythms coinciding with the sun-barycentre-Jupiter conjunction. However, the phases can change and there are several years when the conjunction marks not the beginning of a trapping upturn but the downturn. A further example shows a nine-year cycle in the German Federal Republic, with the main turning points marked by the sun-barycentre-Jupiter conjunction; the chart shows how there was major instability in 1968, which changed the phase of the turning points, and it is interesting that the next downturn is marked for 1994.

Sunspots may be warm but they may not be good for you
The sun has been such an integral part of man's life that many ancient people worshipped it as a god. One of the first

well-known believers was Akenaton, one of the Pharoahs and Tutankhamun's father-in-law, who caused considerable disquiet to the followers of the gods Isis and Osiris when he moved the Egyptian capital to worship the sun-god Aton. Although Tutankhamun died while still a young man, he was venerated by the traditional priests for returning the capital to Karnak.

The pre-colonial Americans were also sun worshippers. The Mayas, an ancient civilisation inhabiting the Yucatan peninsula, created the sun-god among several who were responsible for other benefits such as hunting and rainfall; they were followed by the Aztecs, whose god Huitzilophtli demanded sun worship and human sacrifices. The Incas had Inti as their sun-god – who ranked senior to moon- and rain-gods.

It is estimated that over its existence of nine billion years, the sun's output has been fairly constant, delivering to the earth's atmosphere the equivalent of a staggering 1.5 million horse power per square kilometre – that is, if anyone could trap it efficiently. This figure is known as the 'solar constant' but the heat varies by 2% through a combination of sunspots and faculae.

Sunspots are patches on the sun's surface which are thought to affect both climate and people, according to an average cycle of 11.23 years, but this can vary between eight and sixteen years. Each sunspot consists of the 'umbra', a relatively cool interior compared with other parts of the surface, and a warmer surround called the 'penumbra'. Although sunspots are actually cooler than the sun's surface they are accompanied by faculae, areas of higher temperature, so the overall heat delivered is positive.

The sunspot cycle stretching over the eleven or so years can be observed as a moving pattern which is visible to the naked eye. The sun is divided, like the earth, into north and south hemispheres, with an equator in between. At the beginning of the cycle, sunspots appear at thirty-five degrees north and south, then multiply and move towards the 'equator' as time progresses. The period ends with the sunspots tailing off within a few degrees of the mid-latitude before repeating itself – but this time the magnetism of the sunspots has a changed polarity to complete the 22.4-year or 'Hale Cycle'.

Quite accurate assessments of sunspots have been made by measuring the concentration of the carbon isotope C14 in tree rings (see Chapter 4). Trees absorb C14 as carbon dioxide from the air through their leaves, and the proportion of the C14 rises and falls with the amount of cosmic bombardment; low sunspots mean a high level of C14 absorbtion and vice versa in an inverse relationship.

Solar flares
In addition to sunspots, the sun emits flares which have the astonishing energy of up to 200 million hydrogen bombs over the course of a few minutes. The energy released is not just thermal; there is a dramatic increase of ultraviolet and X-rays, and the earth is bombarded by corpuscles which align themselves to the earth's magnetic field. Although the flares have been difficult to predict, they cause considerable disturbance to radio and electrical transmissions, computer functions and in telephone circuits. Landsheidt reports that they increase human creativity, citing instances of mystical experiences and flashes of inspiration.

How sunspots affect production and the birthrate
It was during the latter part of the 19th century that analysts became interested in the seeming repetition of booms and busts; Clement Juglar was one (whose work is described in Chapter 11); another was William Jevons, who noted a repetition of crashes going back to 1701, twenty years before the South Sea Bubble. Counting the number of 'unquestionable collapses' between 1721 and 1867 he obtained an average gap of 10.43 years – although he found it difficult to believe that the human mind should vary over such a strange period. Jevons' son presented a paper in 1917 suggesting his father's work could relate to the sunspot cycle.

It was during the 1930s Great Depression that two researchers, Carlos García-Mata from the staff of the Argentinian Embassy in Washington and Felix Shaffner of Harvard University, produced a paper called 'Solar and Economic Relationships'; this was first published in *The Quarterly Journal of Economics* in November 1934 and republished by the Foundation for the Study of Cycles. They thought that sunspots might affect agricultural output but little evidence could be found by the two authors; instead they found a series of astonishing correlations of the sunspot cycle with industrial and mining production, and the birth rate. It was as if the human mind moved from optimism to pessimism in tune with sunspot emissions; we seem to suffer the greatest pessimism at the end of a cycle when the light beams are pointing directly at the earth.

One of the curves García-Mata and Shaffner produced is shown in Figure 5. The upper line is the sunspot cycle generated by the Royal Astronomical Society from 1875 to 1931. The lower line is the physical output from American manufacturers over the same period but considerably smoothed to even out the peaks and troughs (mainly troughs). The charts show an amazing correspondence, the lower curve lagging by up to five years; they also show the deep troughs in output noted in later chapters: notably the depression after the American Civil War, the low point in the Kondratieff Cycle in the 1890s, the sharp depression of the 1920s, and the beginning of the 1930s Great Depression.

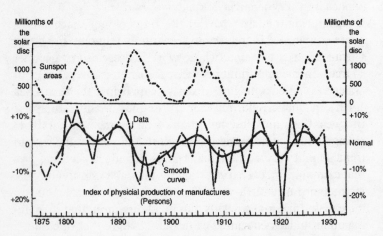

Figure 5. Relationship between the sunspot cycle and US industrial output. (From García-Mata and Shaffner's paper, 'Solar and Economic Relationships'.)

In attempting to find a reason for this relationship, the two researchers correlated the latitude of the sunspots on the sun with the years of good or poor production. They found the interesting pattern that out of twenty-nine years, twenty years of greater production occurred when the sunspot latitudes were above 12.5 degrees, and twenty years of slump happened when the sunspots were below 12.5 degrees. Noting that the sun's emissions tend to travel on straight radial lines, they concluded that on the flat plane of the ecliptic, the sunspots at low latitudes are statistically the ones most likely to affect the earth.

How people are affected by sunspots
Although García-Mata and Shaffner admitted that psychology was not their subject, they suggested two reasons:

First: Solar radiation is made up of many different waves, about 40% of which are in the visible spectrum, the rest being distributed in higher or lower frequencies or wavelengths. Although the total emission from sunspots only varies by 2.5%, those in the ultra-violet spectrum can alternate by 100% – very damaging to eyes and tissues if not absorbed by ionisation in the ozone layer. When García-Mata and Shaffner wrote their paper, it was thought that changes in the quantity of ions in the atmosphere could create agreeable or disagreeable human responses. Ultra-violet light also has an effect on bodily fats and oils, the source of some important hormones.

Second: Electro-magnetism emitted by sunspots affects the earth's magnetic field, radio reception, the skin thickness of furry animals and tree-ring thickness, which suggests that changes in sunspot magnetism could also upset human equilibrium. It is known that human beings are affected by changes that cannot be measured at present, so it is not improbable that magnetism, not ultra-violet light, could be the reason: an increase in emissions towards the end of the sunspot cycle bringing on misjudgements and pessimism.

One interesting experiment was carried out by Dr Vallot, a director of the Mont Blanc observatory, and two physicians. In a report presented to the Academy of Paris in 1922, the team showed how, over a nine-month period, sudden changes in 237 patients could be related to sunspots which were then at the minimum latitude and pointing towards the earth. Of the changes in illness observed, 51% occurred during sunspots (which were only present for nearly 23% of the nine months); of the major changes in patients' condition, 72% occurred on days with spots.

García-Mata and Shaffner held that it was not the intensity of sunspots that affected human psyche in the hospital experiment but the rate of change; it seems that we react adversely to a sudden increase in solar intensity and feel better without it. Putting these ideas to the test, they analysed movements of the New York Stock Exchange during the period leading up to the peak of buying in 1929 to the start of recovery in 1933. Sunspots, as measured by solar radiation, were considerably lower than normal from May to September 1929, reaching a minimum with stock prices as shown in Figure 6. The markets in both New York and London turned at the same time as the solar emissions increased. Figure 5 shows how the sunspot cycle continued downwards (i.e. the emissions to the earth increased) to 1932.

The reverse took place in 1932, when the sunspot cycle restarted at around forty degrees on the sun's latitude. As the bombardment reduced, the New York and London markets started to recover, had a set-back in February 1933 with a temporary increase in emissions, then continued to rally as the sunspot cycle advanced.

What the solar system is telling us

Four times in the last 1000 years our forefathers experienced conditions similar to those of today. If the sun reacts similarly to the disturbance of the barycentre passing close to its centre of mass, then we could be facing very turbulent times which, if the past is a guide, will considerably change the way we live and work, and the institutions that govern us. In addition, by 1995 sunspot emissions could place the world in a historic position similar to that in 1929 and 1930. Later chapters will describe what has happened to civilisation in previous circumstances, and the quite extraordinary possibilities for liberating the human spirit.

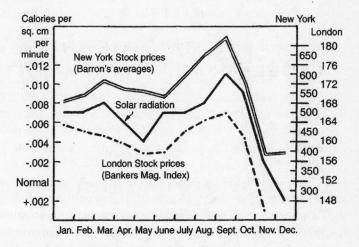

Figure 6. Relationship between solar emissions and the New York and London Stock Markets from January to December 1929. Note: the emissions are inverted – the lower the sunspots, the greater the optimism; the correlation is –.886 (–1 being a perfect inverse correlation). (From García-Mata and Shaffner's paper 'Solar and Economic Relationships', republished by the Foundation for the Study of Cycles.)

CHAPTER 3

. . . FOR MANY OF THE
PROBLEMS HERE ON EARTH

Life on earth is like being in a very large goldfish bowl sur-
rounded by huge magnets which pull the globe first one way,
then another, with quiet periods in between. Technology has
taught us much about our planet but has been remarkably
unsuccessful in anticipating, let alone countering, changes in
the environment. Instead, we blame ourselves for many of the
problems which are outside our control.

This chapter outlines some of the earthly events that are either
directly related to the solar cycles described earlier, or affect our
climate. These are not listed in any particular order but the
reader will recognise from Chapter 2 the sunspot cycle and regular rhythms when volcanic eruptions might be expected. Other
phenomena are described: the first is a strangely named wind in
the upper atmosphere called the 'Quasi Biennial Oscillation'
(QBO), which every so often causes the west coast of Europe
and the north east coast of the US and Canada to experience
particularly cool winters. There is another stratospheric wind
that could contribute to making the mid-1990s particularly dry
in the Unites States, Europe and Africa.

Another interesting phenomenon is El Niño, an event originally discovered off the coast of Peru which seriously affects
weather patterns around the world. Finally, the chapter has a

section explaining the theory of global warming – the so-called 'greenhouse effect' – which many believe will endanger life in low-lying areas by melting the polar ice caps.

How all these phenomena relate either in concert or in conflict is extremely complex, a subject for detailed computer modelling. Of all the influences, a major volcanic eruption has an immediate climatic impact – particularly if associated with diminished sunspots. El Niños are also influential when combined with volcanic action which probably occurred during the Mississippi flooding of 1844 and then again in July 1993. The disturbance to the earth's structure could mean a rising number of volcanic eruptions which would bring us to a period of global disturbance similar to the Wolf, Sporer, Maunder and Sabine eras already described.

What happens when sunspots become dim

On 20 April 1990, the combined effect of the major planets, Jupiter and Saturn, was likely to have disturbed the magnetic field of the sun which controls the sunspots – the areas on the sun's surface which move through an eleven-year cycle of multiplying, then dying away. We have since had an unusually long period of high sunspots (the highest since the 17th century) and in all probability we will suffer a period of very low sunspots in the mid to late 1990s – similar to events in other 179-year cycles.

Something of what happened in earlier times has been described by H. H. Lamb in his book *Climate, History and the Modern World*. Dr Lamb is the author of two classics on the history of climate and is now Professor Emeritus at the School of Environmental Sciences of the University of East Anglia. Assembling the evidence from earlier centuries – the 16th and 17th in particular – required delving into mainly anecdotal data from the study of glaciers, ships logs, paintings, writings and observations made at the time. In addition to contemporary work, modern climatologists have been greatly helped by the study of tree rings and ice cores.

The Maunder minimum was a time of many changes in the climate. It seems to have become rapidly cooler after the 1550s, recovering to around normal in the early 17th century, dipping to a minimum in the 1690s before again recovering somewhat in the 18th century. The world had some respite from the cold before being plunged into the cool of the Sabine minimum in the 1790s. If the future is to follow the past, something of what lies ahead has already been recorded.

It was cooler in central Europe by 1.3°C (equivalent to being some 700 miles further north) at the turn of the 16–17th centuries compared to the milder climate in more modern times. A weather diary in Switzerland showed that there was 60% more snow on the ground in the 1580s than earlier in the 16th century. Records then show that the 1690s were some of the toughest years for centuries.

The logs of ships around the north coast of Europe indicate that instead of the prevailing westerly winds it was more usual for sailors to experience air streams from the north, south and east – which is what might be expected from reading James Shirley's work. The cold weather damaged even the rye harvest – a particularly hardy crop grown in northern Europe for its resistance to frosts and droughts. In Germany the price of this grain rose to new highs in 1622, 1634, 1649, 1694 and 1699. At the turn of the 17–18th centuries, the mean temperature at farms over 2,500 feet in Switzerland was so low that snow cover persisted until 15 May, the crops suffering from a parasite, Fusarium Nivale, active under snow cover in spring. Greenland was cut off by Arctic ice, and during the summer months the Denmark Strait between Iceland and Greenland was completely blocked. In 1690 the temperature around the Faroes was some 5°C cooler than today, with no cod caught in those waters between 1675 and 1704. Although these fish thrive in cool water, their kidneys cannot cope with temperatures below 2°C, so they move further south around the northern coasts of England.

The cold caused terrible problems in Scotland through famine and poverty. Crops failed in the 1560s, 1590s and through the

17th century, compelling villages to be abandoned and many Scots to emigrate – many of them becoming mercenaries in the armies of Gustavus Adolphus of Sweden, as officers in German princedoms, or in England and America. In 1612 James Vl of Scotland, later James I of the Union, shipped around 10,000 farmers (some 10% of the population) to settle in Ulster, displacing the native Irish. It may have relieved the famine in Scotland but it has created a lasting problem in Ireland.

England did not suffer the mass migration of the Scots but it is noticeable that colonists left English and European shores, notably as the Pilgrim Fathers and the first settlers in Cape Province. There were years of poor harvests as the weather became cooler in the 1550s, 1560s, 1590s and 1690s. In 1592 it also became very dry, with the Thames unusually becoming fordable at London Bridge; the rapidly changing climate caused storms to alternate with droughts, bringing on plagues some time before the Great Plague of 1665. The countryside was also affected, with some villages reporting deaths exceeding births, a decline in fertility and women marrying later.

A reconstructed weather map of June 1588 shows how the great storm that swept the Armada up the North Sea was created from the unusual conjunction of two deep areas of low pressure to the west of England and an anti-cyclone on the Continent. Not surprisingly, there were some who took advantage of the cold. Fairs were regularly held on the frozen Thames, which for many winters was hard enough to bear the weight of coaches – speeding up communications as most towns were sited by rivers. This period was widely recorded with famous winter scenes painted by Pieter Breughel the Elder and others of the Flemish School.

The poor weather also affected the New World, with reports of the settlers at Jamestown starving in 1610, a plague in Massachusetts decimating the Mohicans, and Indians massacring colonists in 1622. Mexico was inflicted by the changeable climate with droughts in 1608 and 1613, and Mexico City was flooded in 1623 and 1645. The bitterly cold winds described by Shirley in the previous chapter were dragged south over North

America, and in New England the extreme air stream froze many in the Indian and European population to death, and drastically reduced crop yields.

Other correlations with sunspots

Climatologists have worried away at the relationship between sunspot cycles and changes in the climate in the hope of finding an explanation for the extraordinary changes that occur. Two aspects could be particularly important: the association between the Hale Cycle (the double 11.2-year sunspot cycle) and an atmospheric wind that could have an important bearing on the temperature of the poles.

Droughts seem to occur in the high plains of the United States with a regularity of around twenty years which correlates quite well with the end of the 22.4-year Hale Cycle. For example, the great Dust Bowl drought in the 1930s happened at the end of one cycle illustrated in Figure 6. There was another very dry period in 1953 in Kansas and the next cycle, a shorter one of twenty years, was due in 1973 though did not come until 1974, because of particularly high sunspots the previous year. The next low point of the Hale Cycle is due in 1995–6.

Sunspots affect US weather
During the 1950s, meteorologists noted regular easterly and westerly winds in the stratosphere (the layer outside the earth's atmosphere) that oscillated in both directions around a full cycle of some twenty-eight months. As these winds, QBOs, were around 50,000 feet above sea level, there seemed little energy left to affect climate until it was discovered that there was a marked correlation between the westerly phase of these winds and polar coolness.

It happens that when sunspots are at a maximum and the winds westerly, the upper-polar air mass is warmer by 24°C than usual (minus 54°C compared to minus 78°C) which alters the pressure distribution between northern Canada and the oceans.

Normally in winter, warm, damp winds come up the east coast of the USA from the Gulf of Mexico, but all this changes with a combination of the QBO westerly and high sunspots; then the cold air flows south down the east coast. Although the QBO-sunspot combination has not been worked out in such detail over the Eurasian land mass, it could account for varying climatic changes between Greenland and Europe. The next sunspot minimum is in 1995–6 which could bring respite from the terribly cold weather the East Coast of the US experienced in the winter of 1993–4.

More about winds that we cannot feel

Sunspots could directly affect the climate of the Unites States, Europe and Africa, according to two researchers, K. Labilske and H. Van Loon, writing in the journal *Annales Geophysicae*. It seems that there is yet another very high-altitude wind, controlled by sunspots, whose strength directly affects the westerly winds that bring essential rain to millions in three major continents.

Sunspots generate much of the deadly ultra-violet (UV) rays which are shielded from earth by the ozone layer. Paradoxically, the same UV rays that destroy life also build up the ozone layer; higher sunspots mean more shielding, lower sunspots mean less.

When high sunspots have made the ozone layer slightly thicker, that part of the stratosphere becomes somewhat warmer, generating winds at very high altitudes; these winds also seem to affect the westerly airstreams on earth with a very high statistical correlation. In addition, these high winds also appear to deflect the amount of sunlight reaching the earth. Therefore high sunspots mean high stratospheric winds and powerful rain bearing westerly winds. Conversely low sunspots mean low winds near the ozone layer and less rain carried by the westerly winds in important areas.

The existence of these winds has only been known since the 1950s and although only forty years' data is available the relationship between the winds at different levels is reported to be very close. It is also thought that when sunspots are very high, this could extend the length between the climatic affects of El Niños.

This new information could be very significant in planning for the mid-1990s. We already know that the end of the Hale Cycle in 1995–6 could be very dry. Any decline in the strength of the westerly winds could bring arid, even Dust Bowl conditions (as in the 1930s) to many important grain-growing areas in the US, and also in Eastern Europe, Russia and the Ukraine.

A problem in Peru which affects the world climate

The Peruvian economy relies on catching and processing anchovies which are normally abundant in the prolific fish-feeding grounds off the coast. Peru, along with southern California, south-west and north-west Africa, is blessed by having coastal areas that provide some of the most copious fishing areas on earth; it is said that 25% of the world's fish are caught from 0.1% of the sea area.

The fishing areas off Peru are made possible when oxygen-rich water is forced to the surface by the confluence of the Peruvian current – see Figure 7 – and the warm counter-current that flows in a westerly direction near the equator. (Note: water absorbs proportionally more oxygen when it is cold, i.e. near the poles. As the ocean flows from the poles towards the equator, some fish can live at extreme depths.) As the south-east trade winds deflect the Peru current away from the coast, the 'upwelling' – as it is called, shaded black on the diagram – provides wonderful nutrition for the plankton which themselves are ideal food for anchovies.

However, every seven years or so the south-east trade winds slacken and the warm westerly current grows stronger, replacing and cutting off the upwelling waters; the plankton then fail through lack of nutrients, the anchovy population collapses, the fishing birds leave in droves or die; Peru is thrust into penury. As the warm counter-current normally shows up around Christmas time, the event is called El Niño, the Christ child. What happens off Peru is not just a local disturbance but is part of a much larger change in ocean currents and air streams that affect the whole world.

The earth's weather systems revolve around four huge areas (gyres) of high pressure in the Atlantic and the Pacific which move within a narrow range north of the equator as the sun moves between the tropics of Cancer and Capricorn; Figure 2 in the last chapter illustrates how the earth's tilt of 23.5 degrees shows an alternating north and south face in its orbit around the sun. As the gyres move north and south, so do the trade winds, the massive, continuous transfers of air that were so essential to navigators relying on wind power to cross the oceans.

All this is dependable, except sometimes there is a slight change in the relative pressures of two locations marked in Figure 7: one is at Darwin, northern Australia, the other at Easter Island in the south-east Pacific. Normally there is a pressure difference of twelve or thirteen millibars (a measure of atmospheric pressure used by meteorologists). During an El Niño, the pressure difference between the stations is reduced by seven or eight mb which, although small, is enough to slacken the wind force of the south-east trade winds. As the pressure declines in the South Pacific, the point at which the south-east trades and the winds from the North Pacific meet moves further south than usual – so altering the weather patterns around the earth.

A similar oscillation affects air patterns to the west of Darwin to include the air over India and south-east Asia, where the areas of high and low alternate over a cycle lasting three to twenty years, called the 'Southerly Oscillation' (SO). As El Niños and Southern Oscillations are closely connected, the two have been combined into what has become known as the 'El Niño Southern Oscillation' (ENSO) – a global phenomenon bringing drought to some areas normally expecting rain and rain to places that are normally arid. This is how ENSOs affect certain parts of the world:

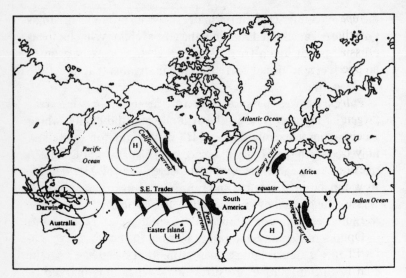

Figure 7. Diagram showing distribution of upwelling areas (in black), the associated currents, the normal position of the south-east trade winds, the normal positions of the oceanic areas of high pressure and the relative position of Darwin and Easter Island. (Courtesy Open University.)

India and South-East Asia

During an ENSO the wind patterns shift not only south but also east, denying large areas of south-east Asia and eastern Australia their normal rainfall; the rain moves further east to such places as Tahiti and Cook Island. A severe ENSO could also make the Indian monsoon fail, the cause of several famines throughout history. It is possible that the ENSO of 1972 also triggered the crop failure on the Arabian peninsula – probably a contributory reason for the explosion in oil prices the following year.

Africa

An ENSO causes droughts in south-east and central Africa which in recent years committed thousands either to starve or migrate.

Europe

Northern Europe, covering Norway, Sweden and northern Russia, can become very dry while further east, the Asian steppes become even drier than normal.

The Americas

Argentina, Mexico and California are some of the few areas to receive more rain, while the north of Latin America would probably be exceptionally dry. ENSOs generally make the Gulf of Mexico and Caribbean unusually warm, causing moist air to flow up the Mid-Western and Atlantic states. The July 1993 Mississippi flooding was a combination of warm, moist air from the south meeting the unusually cool polar air.

Opinions vary about the cause of such an important event as an El Niño. A Dutch meteorologist, Dr H. P. Berlage, believes that it occurs seven years after sunspot numbers drop below thirteen – something which happened with great regularity in the 18th and 19th centuries, but less during the 20th. Goran Windelius, whose work on the Chandler Wobble was described in the last chapter, believes the 6.2-year cycle between the earth's crust and mantle involving changing sea levels may also have a bearing. Dr Handler, a vulcanologist from Illinois State University, believes that volcanoes trigger El Niños but there is some doubt about this, as no events were reported around the time of huge eruptions, such as Tambora in 1815.

El Niños may have a direct bearing on commodity prices. In an interesting article in the *Cycles* journal of February 1990, Professor Louis Thompson, Associate Dean Emeritus of Iowa State University, shows that during El Niño years, the crop yields in the US are good from the warm, moist southerly air flows. However, Thompson also shows that a drought in the US corn belt is likely in the year *following* an El Niño. As there have been a record-breaking three such events in a row during the years 1992 to 1994, it seems that 1995 could prove a very difficult year for American farmers.

And we think that man can make big bangs or disturbances!

There is almost nothing that mankind can do to equal the force of a large volcano. In the early morning of 5 April 1815 in the Lesser Sunda Islands between Java and Sumatra, Tambora exploded with the power of about 100 × ten megaton bombs, projecting some thirty-five cubic miles of dust and over 150 million tons of sulphur dioxide into the stratosphere. The stratospheric winds – QBO – carried the debris around the equator in four to five weeks obscuring the sun for several days in the Dutch Javanese colonies and in Malaya.

The material was also carried north and south, causing a disruption of the weather in many places. Among these was the field of Waterloo on 18 June of the same year, when many of Napoleon's cannon balls disappeared into the mud. There had been an unusually heavy downpour that morning, delaying the start of the battle until around one p.m. Soldiers sleeping in the open were wet through, their tempers not mellowed by ruined pre-battle breakfasts.

Sodden breakfasts were as nothing to the damage the volcano dust cloud did to crops in the northern hemisphere, for 1816 was known as the 'year without a summer'; there were frosts, storms, strong winds and hail in the upper latitudes of the northern hemisphere. The temperature was some 2°C lower in London in 1816 (making that city feel like Newcastle), and the whole earth experienced a drop of 0.7°C on average.

There were only three or four days without rain in Merionethshire in Wales for the six months May to November 1816 – not unlike the conditions reported during the Great Famine of 1317–18. In North America there was widespread snow in Canada and New England during June 1816, and frosts every month. There was famine in parts of Wales, Ireland and Scotland, and food riots in Lancashire on 16 August 1819, when the yeomanry and hussars charged a hungry crowd in St Peter's Fields, Manchester, in what became known as the Peterloo Massacre. Travel became hazardous. Debris from Tambora caused a heavy mist to settle over parts of Europe, with delegates from Britain to the Council of Vienna complaining about crossing the Channel and travelling in France in a perpetual mist.

Earthquakes may be even more powerful locally than volcanoes and in the present century have killed many more people than atomic bombs; for example, nearly half a million people died in two Chinese earthquakes in the century to 1920; 99,000 perished in Tokyo during the devastation in 1923 and another in Peru killed nearly 70,000. Whatever the influence, be it the Chandler Wobble described in Chapter 2 or the 8.85 year lunar and solar cycle described later, the main areas affected are always the sensitive ones around the earth's tectonic plates.

One of the most comprehensive books on the history of volcanoes has been produced by the Smithsonian Institute of Washington DC, called *Volcanoes of the World*, which has records going back over 600 years when there was the first systematic attempt by European navigators to plot the world and report significant events; initially, only a small proportion of eruptions were reported which is why the record shows an exponential growth to the present day. Some two-thirds of all the world's volcanoes are in the northern hemisphere, matching the relative size of the land mass north and south of the equator.

The most northerly active volcano is apparently only 120 miles from the pole but is undersea and unnamed; the next nearest is called Beerenberg on Jan Mayen Island in the Arctic. Erebus is the southernmost active volcano, being nearly 900 miles from the pole and emits lava from time to time, producing beehive-shaped towers of ice during quiet periods. Other active volcanoes have been reported under the Antarctic ice, accounting for some noticeable melting of ice flows.

The incidence of volcanoes is explained in a highly original book called *Climate and the Affairs of Men* by Nels Winkless and Iben Browning. Dr Browning was a scientist with wide interests who became fascinated by the effects of volcanoes when working on the American nuclear programme. As the debris from an atomic explosion behaves similarly to that from a volcanic eruption the two have something in common. Browning also believed that volcanoes and earthquakes could be triggered by the same forces that drive the solar system.

During the 1920s, a German explorer and geophysicist called Alfred Wegener produced a theory on the origins of continents and oceans. He showed that continents rested on what are known as tectonic plates which move a few centimetres every year over the earth's mantle, the semi-molten mass of the globe about twenty-three miles below the land; the movement is called 'continental drift'. For example, by taking the continental shelves around the Atlantic it is possible to piece together quite convincingly the continents of the Americas, Africa and Europe; they were in fact joined together some sixty million years ago. This has been proved by the magnetism of new rock formations around the centre of the Atlantic which are very slowly pushing the continents away from each other. Figure 8 (taken from

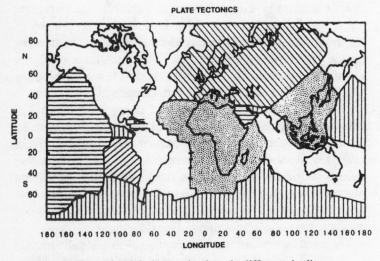

Figure 8. The main global tectonic plates in different shading showing some important interfaces. Notice the horizontal shading of the Pacific alongside North America and the diagonal shading by South America. Note also the dotted area around south-east Asia and the division of the European and African plates which pass horizontally through the Mediterranean, continuing eastwards to India.

Browning's book) shows the extent of the major tectonic plates.

The interface between the plates can be either expanding or contracting. The expanding (known as 'constructive') plate boundaries, such as the one down the centre of the Atlantic, are continually pushing the Atlantic wider by the creation of new basaltic rock in the ocean depths. Conversely at the contracting, or 'destructive', margins around much of the Pacific, the oceanic crust is actually disappearing below the land mass, causing the most tremendous tensions. It is not by chance that 65% of all the world's earthquakes and volcanoes are around the Pacific rim, called 'the ring of fire', and that the Andes and Rockies are composed of Andesite, a rock formed from volcanic eruptions. In Europe, the African plate is continually pushing northwards and is responsible for the Alps, the Pyrenees, the Caucasus and, indirectly, the Downs in southern England.

If these points of weakness are disturbed either through gravity or by additional tidal forces, then there is a considerable danger of earthquakes or volcanoes. This, then, is the basis of Browning's theory: that exceptional tidal forces with the predictable cycles explained in the last chapter provide the additional trigger, either by extra weight of water or through coastal friction, to release the pent-up energy at the plate margins.

Following the description of the cyclical times of the sun, earth and moon in Chapter 2, we would expect the points of maximum danger to occur when the three bodies are aligned and closest together – every 8.85 years. There is an even more crucial point every 18.6 years when the moon is eclipsed, the sun and moon being on different sides of the earth.

Browning illustrates his ideas by identifying the major eruptions which have occurred while the tidal forces were rising. It will be noticed that all, except for Hecla in Iceland, went off around the Pacific 'ring of fire':

> Five volcanoes with the force equivalent to a 500-kiloton bomb went off three years on either side of the high tide of 1921. These were: Tungurahua in Ecuador, Katla in Iceland, Manam in New Guinea, Puyehue in Chile and Raikike in the Kuriles.

Volcanic activity was lower around the early 1930s but Azul went off in Chile with the force of a megaton bomb and there were two smaller eruptions, Kliuchevskoi in Kamchatka and Fuego in Guatemala.

Only one smaller volcano erupted in the late 1930s; this was Rabaul in New Britain.

There was one small volcano in the late 1940s; this was Hekla in Iceland.

Volcanic activity was increasing around the peak of 1955: Bagana in the Solomon Islands, Spurr in Alaska, Nilahue in Chile and Bezymianny (a megaton equivalent) in Kamchatka.

Eruptions continued to increase in the mid-1960s: Agung in the Lesser Sunda, Sheveluch in Kamchatka, Taal in the Philippines, Kelut in Java and Fuego in Guatemala.

There was a spate of relatively small volcanic eruptions in the early 1970s; also Tiatia in the Kuriles and Fuego in Guatemala went of with the force of 500 kiloton bombs.

El Chichón in Mexico erupted equivalent to a megaton bomb in 1982 around the peak of the next tidal cycle, preceded by Mount St Helen's in the State of Washington, and by Bezymianny – again in Kamchatka.

Probably the largest eruption this century occurred between 9 and 13 June 1991 around the peak of the next tidal cycle: Mount Pinatubo in the Philippines exploded with the force of around ten megaton bombs.

One of the most interesting papers about volcanoes and their impact on the climate was delivered by Dr H. H. Lamb of the Meteorological Office in Bracknell, published in July 1970; although it does not cover the increase in vulcanism experienced since the 1970s, it contains some fascinating insights into the importance of these memorable events.

Lamb describes volcanic eruptions as being the escape of molten rock – called 'magma' – usually accompanied by steam, water vapour and other gases such as sulphur and carbon dioxide; although some of the materials come from the earth itself, the water vapour could have been trapped when the oceans were forced under the land masses – a process known as 'subduction'. The sulphur and carbon dioxides each play a part in the climate; sulphur dioxide reacts with water vapour and ozone in the stratosphere, forming sheets of sulphuric acid which shield the sun's warmth long after the volcanic dust has settled. Carbon dioxide is the main culprit in the so-called 'greenhouse effect', although a considerable proportion can be absorbed into the oceans.

Volcanoes can be of two types – 'effusive' eruptions, which emit lava flows, and 'explosive' eruptions, which discharge matter broken up into rocks or dust. Of the two, lava flows are the most immediately dangerous because they overwhelm areas around the eruption (such as Mount Pelee, described in Chapter 13); although thousands may perish, their successors could benefit from the nutrients in the lava once it has cooled, providing a fertile base for growing plants. Volcanic lava also contains other rare elements in the earth's crust, such as gold; it is no accident that the great gold discoveries have been found in volcanic areas.

Apart from lava flows, volcanoes can be very dangerous if they erupt by the sea because they can cause huge tidal waves, called 'tsunamis'. These are ocean waves with very long periods of up to a mile which travel outwards from the volcano at speeds of 500 miles per hour. The wave height may be only fifty feet in the open sea but this increases on approaching a shelving beach to produce massive heights sometimes of 120 feet; on one occasion a ship was deposited nearly two miles inland. One of the worst tragedies occurred after the volcano Krakatoa erupted in 1883 near the Java and Sumatra coasts, where it is reported that 36,000 people were overwhelmed.

The effect of explosive volcanoes can be much more dangerous in the longer term; not only can they create terrible tidal waves, as at Krakatoa, but the fall of ash can be totally disruptive. When Mount St Helen's went off on 18 May 1980, it discharged ten cubic kilometres of dust and ash, and by 9.30 a.m. the following morning the sky was black eighty-five miles downwind. Traffic and aircraft in the states of Washington, Idaho, and Montana were brought to a halt, badly disrupting the distribution of food and supplies. It was estimated that 600,000 tons of tephra were discharged covering the ground to leeward with dust up to three inches thick. The eruption of Lakigagar, which increased the violence of the French Revolution – see Chapter 7 – spread dust over some fifty square miles to a depth of fourteen inches.

But as we saw with Tambora, devastation can be created thousands of miles away by the shielding effect of the dust and droplets, known as 'aerosols', in the earth's atmosphere. Those who saw the sunsets after the massive eruption of Pinatubo will recall the vivid orange globe (like a Turner sunset, painted at the time of Tambora). After sunset there was a bright green haze above the horizon which turned to white, then pink as the eye went upwards.

Lamb also reports that the sun and moon can appear blue or green – hence presumably the term 'once in a blue moon'; and there is the memorable description by Benjamin Franklin when American Ambassador to France describing the sky during the French Revolution. After the next eruption, observers might look for the 'Bishop's Ring', a white circle round the sun tinged with pink, red or brown, reaching about twenty degrees from the sun first observed by the Reverend S.E. Bishop in Honolulu after Krakatoa.

Whatever the appearance, dust can be ejected over thirty miles into the stratosphere. Lamb reports that Vesuvius in 1631, Krakatoa in 1883 and Agung in 1963 reached this height, with others, such as Etna in 1886, Hecla in 1947 and Mt Spurr in 1953, only reaching 66,000 feet – high enough not to be quickly dissipated by wind and weather. Once in the stratosphere, at least two things happen: the ash is transported around the world and starts its slow drift towards the poles; next, it starts to fall and disperses through the thin air.

Lamb describes how dust veils screen the sunlight and diffuse incoming rays form in the stratosphere. As might be expected from the earlier description of the Quasi Biennial Oscillation, the dust and gas are quickly spread around east and west from the high-altitude winds taking three to six weeks over the equator and two to four weeks in higher latitudes. However, such were the winds at the time of Krakatoa that the dust circled the globe in a near record of two weeks. There is also a movement towards the poles but the force of this varies with latitude. Up in the Tropics of Capricorn and Cancer, the movement is outward from the equator, and from mid-latitudes there is a small drift away from the poles. Ultimately, however, much of the debris drifts polewards where it has a much greater shielding effect on the oblique sun's rays than at the equator; the net effect is that the polar regions become even cooler than usual.

The time a particle of dust or molecule of sulphuric acid stays in the upper atmosphere restricting sunlight varies according to its size and how high it was initially ejected. Some of the larger particles from smaller volcanoes take only a few weeks until they filter through before being dissipated by the weather. On the other hand, small aerosols from Krakatoa would have taken up to twelve years to disperse which probably accounts for at least some of the ten dry growing years experienced in the US during the 1880s and 1890s.

Lamb has worked out a severity yardstick for volcanic debris called the 'Dust Veil Index' (DVI) which takes into account the depletion of sunlight, the extent of the global coverage and the time since the eruption. As the DVI is related to temperature, another formula works out the cooling effect likely to be experienced from the time of the explosion. Volcanic eruptions can now be ranked, taking Krakatoa as the datum of 1000; research has shown that there were equivalent eruptions during the Wolf, Sporer, Maunder and Sabine minimums.

A volcano the size of Krakatoa went off during the Sporer minimum in the year 1500; another also in Java in 1586. It is hardly surprising that the Maunder minimum in the 17th century was a very difficult one. During the Little Ice Age there were no fewer than four volcanoes the size of Krakatoa and a large number of smaller eruptions. There was a relatively quiet period until 1766 just before the start of the Sabine minimum, when Mayon in the Philippines went off with a force over twice that of Krakatoa. Then came the combined force of Eldeyjar and Laki in Iceland in 1789. We saw earlier the impact of Tambora in 1815 which was closely followed by Beerenberg which may have been four times the DVI of Krakatoa.

The 19th century was punctuated by some large eruptions. Cosiguina in Nicaragua went off in 1835 followed by Armagura in the South Pacific – both of them spread a huge amount of dust that contributed to the next decade being known as the 'hungry forties'. Since Krakatoa itself erupted in 1883, few major volcanoes have gone off. Pinatubo, though, may be heralding a new period of high vulcanicity and low sunspots – the combination that has created the previous minima with very cool weather and disruption in the past.

Another method of reporting volcanic action, used by the author of *Volcanoes of the World*, is to produce a composite measure called the 'Vertical Explosive Index' (VEI) which couples the explosive power of an eruption with the amount of material ejected. At the lower end of the scale, a VEI of one ejects only 2750 cubic yards of debris to a height of less than 1000 feet. The scale increases rapidly in multiples of ten up to a VEI of seven – the size of Tambora – described as a colossal explosion and classified as 'ultra-plinian'!

Conversely, will we be baked in the Greenhouse?

A relatively small proportion of our atmosphere retains much of the heat radiated from the earth preventing it being lost to space and making life possible. Another planet, the same ninety-three million miles away from the sun but without the gases, would be cooler by 35 to 40°C. Three gases make this possible: oxygen and ozone reflect or absorb perhaps 5% of the radiation, particularly in the infra-red band (which is the heat we feel from the sun or from a fire); carbon dioxide reflects possibly 1% of the total, while water vapour, the substance of clouds, is responsible for well over 50% of the total.

Carbon dioxide is a gas produced from burning fossil fuels such as oil, coal and gas in power stations or petrol in cars. It is expected that the world's population will double in the next two or three decades and there is concern that the burning of fuels will rise to such an extent that the proportion of carbon dioxide in the atmosphere will trap a greater proportion of the world's heat, and global temperatures will rise. A glass greenhouse is warmer inside than out because warmth is trapped, hence the term 'greenhouse effect'. Proponents of global warming are concerned that man-made carbon dioxide gas will upset the precarious balance of the earth, causing a proportion of polar ice to melt so forcing those living in low-lying areas to move inland – overcrowding our planet even further.

The record of warming is not consistent. There was no change between 1860 and 1910, a steady rise of 0.4°C between 1910 and 1940, no change from 1940 to 1980, and a steady increase of 0.3° from 1980 to 1990. Latterly many of these changes were measured by weather stations sited at airports near towns, so some of the rise could be expected anyway – weather stations in the country showing either a negligible or very small increase.

A report in *Nature* at the end of January 1993 casts doubt on surface temperature measurements; it publishes satellite data of sensors recording not an increase in temperature since 1980 but a *decline* of 0.04°C per decade. Presumably with the environmentalists in mind, the authors of the report believe the earth must have actually *warmed* in the 1980s by 0.09°C – taking into account two cooling factors already described in this chapter, El Niños and volcanic eruptions.

What is the truth? The environmental lobby backed by governments is very strong but they may have to change tack if the work of two Danish researchers proves valid. They correlated the observed changes in surface temperatures not with the intensity of sunspot cycles but with their length. As this varies between seven and sixteen years some very interesting results could emerge if indeed we are entering a period not of global warming but *cooling* – introducing a latter-day Maunder minimum. As Iben Browning pointed out, the billions of termites in the world produce much more carbon dioxide than man will ever generate: something which puts mankind's puny efforts and concerns firmly in their place?

CHAPTER 4

A HISTORY LESSON FROM
TREES, ICE CORES –
AND THE REST

The cycles described in the last two chapters can be identified as going back to at least the 11th century AD but others, described in Chapter 6, go back to the 7th century BC. The effect of these cycles, related to historical times, can only be gleaned from scientific and anecdotal data, some of which has been mentioned earlier; tree rings, for example. The aim of this chapter is to identify the main sources of historical information quite apart from the events themselves, as they were recorded either at the time or some time later.

Several sources are described. The first is a study of tree rings to observe the intensity of sunspots and pinpoint the temperature and rainfall at a given location and year; the method confirms the 11.2- and 22.4-year sunspot cycle. A similar principle was used to extract temperature data from ice cores taken from the Arctic and Antarctic ice caps; as these are built up from consecutive snow falls they go back before the last ice age and confirm the 179-year solar cycle described in Chapter 1. A third method is to identify and measure accumulated lake and inland sea deposits for volcanic ash and other climatic events, such as prolonged and heavy rainfall, and storms.

Trees give up their ageing secrets

Most of us know that trees put on an added layer or ring every year but few have questioned how much information might be locked away, until an American scientist Andrew Douglass turned his attention to the question in the 1920s. Douglass was drawn to the study by his wish to date archaeological structures from the timber used in their construction; it was later that the research was targeted primarily to understand climate before the use of meteorological instruments. By the time Douglass died in 1962 at the age of ninety-four he had set up the Lowell Research Institute for Dentrology (as the science of reading tree rings is called) at the State University of Arizona.

Extracting past weather data from tree rings is no easy matter, because trees do not always grow symmetrically, in that the wind or ground forces one side to develop at the expense of another. Trees within a group do not always grow in the same way, so that a sample needs to be taken for a representative reading. It has been found that trees at the edge of a climatic zone provide a much better yardstick of past climate than those in the middle; considerable care must be taken in the choice of sample.

A study of dentrology does not rely on felling a tree; samples can be taken using an augur which provides the researcher with a plug for subsequent measurement; taking samples must have been hard manual work for Douglass initially but modern analysts have the advantage of mechanically powered tools. There are some trees such as the Californian and bigtree redwoods (named Sequoias, after a notable Cherokee chief) and bristlecone pines which are thousands of years old. One notable tree named after General Sherman is over 3,000 years old and stands in the Californian South National Park, 272 feet high and with a diameter of thirty feet.

But Douglass had no such continuous yardstick when he started. He had to piece together records from various samples of known age with others in a similar area whose age was indeterminate. In this way, and with the aid of an optical analyser he designed for measuring the thickness accurately, he built up a 'library' of samples enabling him to date many of the old Indian and Spanish dwellings going back several hundred years.

Later, probably in association with the work of Raymond Wheeler, Douglass became interested in the study of some of the climatic cycles covered earlier. However, the study of climate is not easy because tree-ring thickness is dependent not just on temperature but also on moisture. This makes it necessary to go back in actual measured temperature and rainfall records to calibrate the known composition and thickness of the tree rings before earlier deductions can be made. Another related problem is what constitutes a 'good' or 'bad' growing year of certain species.

Research on specific projects can provide very useful data for climatic cycles. W.J. Burroughs in his *Weather Cycles* records a study by Charles Stockton and David Mekko of Douglass' old laboratory in Arizona and Murray Mitchell of the government laboratory at Silver Springs, Maryland. Between forty and sixty-five tree-ring sites were analysed to derive a climatological history of the western two-thirds of the USA from the year 1600 to the present. The findings showed predominantly a twenty-two-year cycle relating to the Hale sunspot rhythm.

Another value in tree rings is in measuring sunspot activity from the varying proportion of the carbon isotope C14 in tree rings. (Note, the atomic weight of carbon is normally twelve, but under cosmic bombardment other atomic weights are formed, C14 being one.) Trees absorb C14 in the form of carbon dioxide from the air through their leaves in the process of photosynthesis, which turns carbon dioxide and water into nutrient sugars in the presence of sunlight. The proportion of the C14 rises and falls with the amount of cosmic bombardment associated with sunspots. It follows that if the magnetic field around the earth also intensifies with high sunspots, the field will shield the cosmic rays – hence the proportion of C14 absorption will fall. Conversely, when sunspots are low there are more cosmic rays to bombard carbon atoms and C14 rises.

In *Climate and the Affairs of Men*, Iben Browning explains how a study of tree rings and ice cores can predict the precipitation that would follow future powerful volcanic eruptions. Normally, there is a belt of high and low rainfall depending on latitude and the position of the sun in relation to the equator. It is very humid in the latitude of the rain forests, the rain tapering off between twenty and thirty degrees north and south. It then becomes much drier around the Sahara belt before becoming wetter, peaking at around fifty-five degrees before tailing off at the pole.

All this changes when the climate is cooled by either a major eruption or a period of very low sunspots. As the north pole becomes cooler, the storm track or jet stream is pushed further south than usual. This makes the upper latitudes much drier and the lower parallels at around forty degrees more humid. From this Browning deduced that if the forecast cool period comes about, many places on the northern continents will become cooler and drier while countries like the United States, China and France, which have a long north-south axis, will survive well by being able to grow crops further south than normal.

Polar ice tells a story

The poles add layers of compacted snow every year just as trees add rings, and like trees record a climatic history. But instead of measuring a carbon isotope, the ice absorbs not only normal oxygen (O16) but a slightly heavier isotope, O18, which occurs naturally. The ice, which started life by being evaporated from warmer oceans, contains slightly more O16 than O18, both absorptions being dependent upon temperature. Hence the cooler it is, the greater the ratio of O16 to O18, which can be measured by modern instruments.

The first core to be extracted was by US Army engineers in 1966 at Cape Century on Greenland, where the ice is nearly 4700 feet thick before reaching bedrock – producing a record going back 150,000 years! The cores have to be carefully preserved in freezing conditions before being analysed by a team under a Danish researcher, Willi Dansraard, at the University of

Copenhagen. The Cape Century ice cores have been used to produce the temperature variations compared with tidal forces in Chapter 7.

Although the data goes back many years, there is some difficulty interpreting it as the entrapped gas diffuses within the cores which, as the centuries go by, become impermeable. Despite these problems it is possible to detect with some accuracy warmer or cooler periods going back 800 years showing two main cycles: as one would expect, the most important cycle has a period of 181 years (equivalent to the 179-year cycle described) and another smaller rhythm of seventy-eight years.

Later work by a combined Russian and French expedition has extracted cores from Vostok over East Antarctica to depths of one-and-a-third miles. However, in addition to using the oxygen ratio as their temperature yardstick the team also measured the ratio of hydrogen (H1) and its isotope deuteriam – or heavy water – which has the symbol H2 (i.e. the atom has double the weight).They also measured the absorption of carbon dioxide. Although it may not be so immediately important for the 1990s, the team shows convincing evidence for cycles of 107,500, 45,700 and 25,300 years.

The lakes also make a contribution

Every year streams and rivers entering lakes deposit two layers: the first comes in a rush from snow or glacial melting, the second is a more gentle layer deposited from quiet water bringing down clay, mud and other particles from upstream; the presence of volcanic ash in the layers is used for dating eruptions. The Swede Baron Gethard de Geer was the first to work on *varves*, the Swedish word for layers, in 1878. Working within Scandinavia he started to build up a consecutive pattern over 10,000 years from the last ice age to the present.

Since de Geer started his work, numerous *varves* have been analysed, including some interesting results from the Caspian Sea, which must have been much lower than at present, and also from the Crimea, which show cycles from seven to seventeen years following the sunspot rhythm. The same techniques have been used to measure sand and limestone series from geological times (millions of years ago) where mudstones have built up layers similar to lakes.

Other historical measurements

Contemporary records
Until more scientific evidence was available, all dating was through contemporary records. In the West this was largely the responsibility of scholars or monks but as we shall see from Raymond Wheeler's work, in Chapter 6, a very large amount of historical evidence related to climate was collected even before he was introduced to tree-ring techniques. Among the sources Wheeler lists are C.E. Britton's chronology of Britain's weather from about the second century AD, and a study by A. Hosie, who brought together Chinese records going back to the 5th century AD – among several others.

Records are also available from such events as droughts, floods, major storms, excessive heat and cold, famines and droughts, early or late frosts affecting harvest, famines, travel through Alpine passes, the formation of bogs, weather diaries and pollen analysis of soils. Military records and battles are an excellent source of records, as are monasteries, government files and agricultural records – particularly from important events such as grape harvests. The Smithsonian record of volcanoes described in the last chapter has also used local records and local knowledge to date roughly the eruption of Changpaishan in Manchuria to 1702 to plus or minus fifty years. Others in Mexico have been related to Pueblo Indian artifacts.

Lichens
The slow but quite regular growth of lichens has been used to measure the relative ages of lava flows but the evidence seldom holds good for over a century.

Residual magnetism in rocks

Some of the evidence for the tectonic-plate movement has been gleaned from measuring the residual magnetism of the newly formed rocks on land and in the oceans. When molten rock cools it takes up the relative magnetism of the north and south poles. As the polarity changes every 10,000 years or so, the position of any rock formation is noted and the change plotted; these techniques were used to demonstrate the gradual enlargement of the Atlantic over sixty million years. The same techniques can be used for dating volcanic eruptions.

Volcanic ash deposits

If layers of tephra, or volcanic ash, can be identified and the date of one or more deposits likewise, then it may be possible to measure the source and age of the associated volcanic action. The Icelandic lava flows have been a particularly useful data source.

Radioactive dating from Carbon 14

We have met carbon (C14) dating earlier for identifying sunspot cycles; they may also be used for dating organic material caught up in a lava flow if they have not been destroyed by the heat. The radioactive carbon is no longer replaced when the organism dies and the C14 begins its decay. The half-life of the isotope, the time it takes to reduce its radioactivity by a half, is about 5568 years; so timing measurements can now be made with considerable accuracy.

CHAPTER 5

MAN IS NOT THE MASTER
OF ALL THINGS

The Victorian poet Swinburne wrote 'Glory to Man in the Highest, Man is the Master of all Things'; and looking around the world today who is to gainsay this conceit. After all, man has landed on the moon; we have made ten ears of wheat grow where our forefathers could only grow one; modern factory methods have made possible industrial productivity in hot countries unthinkable even a generation ago.

There was not the same vanity after the Second World War when men like Elsworth Huntington, Professor of Geography at Yale University, Professor Raymond Wheeler and Doctor Leo Hillmer, both at Kansas State University, and others became fascinated by the way history had been shaped by climatic changes and clearly believed any future changes could have a similar impact.

How it all started

Mankind's ability to anticipate seasonal variations developed when people left the overcrowded, warm fertile areas of the globe and moved (primarily) north where the seasons, though predictable, could be inhospitable. The ability to live away from the equator was only possible because the tilt of the earth's axis enabled man to exist in areas nearer the poles with sufficiently long growing seasons to plant and harvest crops before the next winter. To achieve this, man was forced to anticipate the seasons and to hoard food.

It all started around three billion years ago when volcanic eruptions had covered the globe with water and the atmosphere was filled with gases such as carbon dioxide, nitrogen and sulphur dioxide. Not only did these gases inhibit animal life, but they failed to filter the deadly ultra-violet light emitted by the sun that destroys most known life. Hence, the beginning of life was only possible deep in the oceans, away from the harmful rays.

It is thought that life began as a complex blue-green organism made up from a combination of at least six elements: carbon, hydrogen, oxygen, nitrogen, phosphorous and calcium. These 'prokaryotes', as the new existence is called, acted like present-day plants taking in carbon dioxide and water and, in the presence of sunlight, discharging oxygen – the process known as photosynthesis. Too much oxygen would have killed early life but luckily the gas probably combined with iron in the water to produce iron oxides which later became rock. These 'banded ironstones', can be found on the Mesalic Range, Minnesota.

Later, so much oxygen was being produced by the rapidly increasing organisms that the excess gas escaped into the atmosphere where, in the presence of UV light, it created a layer of ozone which filtered out the deadly rays. When it became safe to do so, the organisms moved into shallower water and developed oxygen-breathing lungs to make depth-keeping a possibility without continuous effort. Much later, as the land masses first emerged from the oceans, the most successful creatures developed backbones enabling them to cope with waves and currents from the coastal eddies. Our ancestors came on land when the ozone layer was thick enough to give protection.

The first land animals needed the sun's warmth to feed or breed. They were cold-blooded and warmth was essential for energy; those who misjudged sunset could be stranded on a cool evening with insufficient strength to seek refuge and survival in the warmer water. There were obvious limitations to these animals thriving in a cooler climate, so a strain of warm-blooded creatures emerged able to move on land at all times. As life diversified, a certain species developed an opposite finger – called the 'obverse thumb' – enabling them to climb trees. They also developed binocular vision – essential for judging distances and estimating the strength of branches – and of course the ability to hunt other creatures.

It is thought that our ancestors descended from the trees two to three million years ago, gradually developing the bone structure, muscles and organs to walk upright and see over long grass. Developing man also became a hunter and presumably was hunted himself. It was much later, only some 12,000 years ago, that the cultivation of wheat gave man a more settled existence enabling him and his family to live apart from the tribe.

The Naked Ape

After this extraordinary evolution, man is still affected by climate but is versatile, being able to live in most parts of the globe and adapting to a widely varied diet. For example, Eskimos live off fish, Bedouin can exist on goats' milk, and for centuries many Chinese have thrived off fish and rice. Those living in equatorial regions have adapted their skin and body shapes either to resist the sun's rays or dissipate heat; and there are some primitive tribes that can survive on a diet of raw grubs, roasted snakes and bamboo shoots!

Unlike apes, primitive people learned to live in a wide range of climates by wearing suitable clothing, and being without hair the body could regulate its temperature through sweat glands. Within a temperature range of between 63 and 70°F the body's heat losses are balanced against the internally generated warmth, creating an ideal environment for working and breeding when any excess moisture is lost from what the medical profession calls 'insensible perspiration'.

As the outside temperature rises or the body creates internally generated heat, the sweat glands increasingly discharge fluid which depletes the system's sodium supply – a deficiency that should be made up by drinking quantities of water and taking salt tablets if vigour is to be maintained. Above 105–6°F, the sweat glands cease to operate and the person is in danger of dying from heat stroke unless rapid action is taken to cool down the body and introduce fluid.

By contrast, in cool climates the blood temperature is higher, the heart beats faster, glands are more active and metabolism is higher. The blood vessels constrict to save heat and over a period fat develops to preserve body warmth. In general, cooler periods make people more alert, energetic, aggressive, stable, tolerant and intelligent. But it must not get too cold for then the body becomes numb, retarded and less stable. In some trials in America, individuals sitting exams produced better results in cooler months of the year, compared with the heat of the summer. It is no accident that shrewd salesmen visit difficult buyers in cool conditions – preferably after a storm!

Changeable or stormy weather is another factor adding to alertness which goes some way to explain the relative vigour of the Americans and Russians. Living in the middle of a large land mass like the USA with extremes of climate, temperature and storminess adds vigour. Those living in parts of Eastern Europe or Russia experience a numbing cold for much of the year, which accounts for the people's traditional passivism and fatalism.

Races living permanently in hot or cool lands have adapted to the climate. Those living near the equator have more sweat glands than usual and have developed a large skin surface area in relation to their mass to help lose heat. Eskimos, on the other hand, are generally of stocky build which helps to reduce heat loss and their eyes have adapted with a layer of fat both to stop eyeballs from freezing and as a protection against the glare.

Vulnerability to skin cancer varies with the proportion of the dark melanin pigment in the skin – those living near the equator being better protected than people with fair skins. Iben Browning reports that more British men are afflicted with skin cancer on the right side of their bodies while women suffer on their left; in America it is the other way round. Browning suggests that the position of the driving seat could be the answer as men do most of the driving and women are passengers. Hence in the UK male drivers' right sides are susceptible while Americans are prone to problems on their left.

Browning also made a study of how climatic and racial differences affect food – particularly milk. Milk contains vitamin D1 which is essential for growing bodies and although normally produced in the body those living in cooler climates need a boost; those in warmer climates normally produce all the vitamin D1 they need after childhood. Browning's theory was that the only adult creatures able to tolerate milk are cats, rats, bats, ferrets, weasels, polar bears and adult Caucasians. Browning himself could not drink milk – one of his grandfathers was a native American Indian.

However civilised we are, wearing clothes may not be a complete blessing according to some observers, who are concerned that mankind's ability to survive could be diminished when child-bearing parts of the anatomy are covered, however scantily. However, there are compensations; we can breed all the year round.

The best places to mate, live and work

In his book *Seasons of Birth*, Elsworth Huntington takes the idea a stage further by showing that in temperate climates, the optimum time for conception is in late spring, with average temperatures of between sixty to sixty-five degrees when a couple are at their physical peak. Children then are born in the first few months of the year with the parents at their mental best – at a temperature of between 39 and 45°F, some twenty degrees lower than at conception. Climate also affects the child's sex. In a rat experiment, at 90°F, the ratio is 150 females to 100 males; the ratio is reversed at fifty-five degrees –150 males to 100 females.

That temperature still plays an important part in male virility may be implicit from a study conducted by Danish spermatologists. The survey showed that since the 1940s there has been a worldwide decline in sperm production – not only in the quantity of each emission but also in quality; they found similar characteristics in wild animals. The one great exception was in Finland, a cold country, where not only do men produce four millilitres of fluid per emission (average 2.75) but the sperm count is nearly double the average. It seems that the testes work best in a cooler environment; couples wishing to start a family and produce a boy should be encouraged to take holidays not in the Bahamas but in Iceland or Alaska!

That coolness makes us more productive probably accounts for another important time for conception in the later months of the year, for birth in early autumn. Out of 12,274 entries in the American *Who's Who*, Huntington deduced that the optimum time for able people to be conceived is either in the spring or early summer or late autumn. This ensures babies are born in the cooler months. In the days before air conditioning, there was also an optimum temperature for working, with those in the higher latitudes showing the greatest energy at a midday temperature of between sixty-three to seventy degrees. In his book Huntington shows a fascinating series of charts relating climatic variations to where people live in the USA.

The diagrams show where you are most likely to be murdered, to reproduce successfully, to live a long life, to catch a deadly disease, to work with the greatest efficiency and the like. One interesting chart taken from surveys conducted during the Second World War shows that although it may be more pleasant to live in the southern states, the north-east and Mid-West provide the most invigorating climate.

As might be expected, vigour not only applies to where one lives in a country but to countries themselves. Elsworth Huntington continued his research by ranking the physical and mental energy of peoples. Countries in temperate climates such as the United States, Europe and New Zealand rated much better in agricultural and industrial production, educational standards and income per capita than those in warmer environments such as India.

Victorian and earlier researchers were in no doubt that those living in cooler climates were more vigorous, aggressive, persistent, physically stronger, larger, braver, healthier and less prone to sexual indulgence. They also found those living in upper latitudes treasure liberty, are more democratic, more tolerant, docile, more lively and trustworthy – less cunning.

By contrast, those living in warmer climates were more likely to be reflective, introverted, timid, smaller, physically weaker, less courageous, subject to tyranny and dictators but more inclined to physical pleasures. Whatever the generalities in bygone times, it is now possible to live near or on the equator and be extremely active, as the Singaporeans have amply shown.

However, the optimum temperature belts for human vigour in the northern hemisphere still run through north Europe, the UK, west to southern Canada, the northern states of the US, then west to Japan. There is some degree of latitude shift in countries with a long north-south axis; for example, some southern states in the central US become quite cool in the winter. There is a similar belt in the southern hemisphere running through Argentina, central Chile, the southern tip of Africa, and the south-east shores of Australia and New Zealand.

This distribution is borne out by the population of the world's largest cities shown in Michael Zahorchak's book *Climate: the Key to Understanding Business Cycles*. Even during the 1970s the majority of the world's major cities were distributed between the latitudes of thirty and sixty degrees from the equator with a rapid tail-off less than twenty-five and more than sixty-five degrees north and south. As the book explains, there have been no great civilisations closer to the equator than twenty-five degrees, except those living on plateaux such as the Mayas in Central America, the Khmers in Indo-China and the Tamils in Sri Lanka.

However, this pattern may be changing. A table of the twenty-five largest cities published by the *Economist* in 1993 showed that some of them such as São Paulo, Mexico City, Bombay, Rio de Janeiro, Calcutta, Jakarta, Manila, Delhi, Karachi, Lagos and Bangkok, are nearer to the equator than thirty degrees; whether this is a sign of virility or desperation is another matter.

Do people behave like rats?

The temperature effect on humans has been confirmed by experiments showing how groups of white rats behave in controlled environments. During the 1930s, Dr Leo Hillmer of the University of Kansas and a colleague of Professor Wheeler succeeded in changing sluggish rats into aggressive, alert creatures and vice versa by alternating the 'climate'. In one experiment, a number of litters was divided into three groups. One unit was put in an enclosure at a temperature of 55°F, another in a hot room at 90°F and the third was kept in temperatures which varied from 75°F in winter to 85°F in the summer.

When the rats reached the age of ten weeks, their food intake was reduced and two tests were conducted. The first tested their ability to solve a simple maze which they had to negotiate before reaching their objective; the second test was to observe their breeding habits. In the intelligence test one exceptionally bright rat in group one reached the food after thirteen trials with the average achievement of twenty-one attempts. By contrast the average rat in the second group needed fifty-six tries before the maze was solved. Finally, the third or 'control' group needed thirty-one tries on average before reaching their breakfast.

The same experiment was conducted on a second generation of rats with the result that the cool-room rats were judged to be six times as clever as their hot-room cousins. When the conditions of the first and second groups were interchanged and the rodents given time to acclimatise, the rats behaved very similarly to those in the original experiment.

The team then observed whether the rats' breeding habits went hand in glove with intelligence. The mothers in the cool room had four or five healthy litters a year with a vigorous ten to fifteen in a litter. The mothers took excellent care of their offspring, showed a lively interest in their brood and possessed ample milk. By contrast, the hot room had only two litters a year and with a smaller average number of babies between four to seven. Not only were there fewer offspring but the sexual drive was also lower. For example, when the females were on heat the males showed only sluggish interest. When the brood was born, the mother had little energy to care for her young and often killed them.

Raymond Wheeler confirms that people behave like rats

An exciting slant was given to Huntingdon's work by Professor Raymond Wheeler, who was the Departmental Head of Psychology at the State University of Kansas in the 1930s, when he became interested in the idea that history could be analysed in climatic terms. His research showed that great advances in art, science, literature, social and political behaviour moved together at certain warm times. Not only does climate affect people – and so history – but it runs in cycles. Since the earliest times people's behaviour differed when it was warm or cool, also when it was wet or dry. These alternating periods changed people's attitudes and perceptions – moving, for example, from a cool-dry period to one predominantly warm and wet.

Raymond Wheeler believed in an overall cycle of 1000 years which broke down to an intermediate half-millennium. As will be shown in the next chapter, the world's great faiths seem to work on a 500-year rhythm, as do civilisations; his work showed that it becomes very cool at the end of every half-millennium, causing people to cast out whatever had been dominant in the previous era, together with a shift in the dominant culture from East to West. The West has been paramount for the last 500 years, now it is the turn of the East.

Further down the scale, Wheeler identified a 170-year cycle but the next most important rhythm was around 100 years. Each period – which did not necessarily begin with the century – started with a warm-wet climate when good government, art and enterprise prevailed. Unfortunately, benign rulers give way to tyrants who are themselves swept away as each epoch ends with a spell of particularly cold weather; the individual becomes once more important and demands a hearing. There are four phases alternating hot and cold, wet and dry, each of which has a certain effect on people.

Cool-dry
As we have seen, people become more energetic in cool weather but when it is also dry they become discontented and demand new rights and freedoms. The 16th century Reformation was a typically cool-dry period when the perceived irregularities and distortions of the Catholic Church were overthrown, and a more pure and individual faith put in its place. Religious fads are thrown out in these times and people return to a basic faith – individual responsibility becomes more important than belonging to a benign, all-embracing institution.

Energy is infectious, which is why a cold phase is punctuated by emancipation, democratic reform, colonisation and migration. It also has a more aggressive side with likely outbreaks of civil strife, rebellion, escape from repression and religious wars. Increasing nationalism forces treaties, federations and associations that have previously worked beneficially and are no longer relevant to be cast aside – as are governments who fail to read the mood of the people.

Cold-dry periods encourage a new optimism that old problems can be solved and the associated aggression demands that power be returned to individuals, away from politicians and bureaucrats. If matters such as crime are not dealt with by the authorities, people are quite likely to take the law into their own hands; if terrorists are not dealt with summarily, individual groups could take revenge where politicians fear to act.

Art and fashion in cool-dry periods become functional, detailed and realistic, not unlike the Victorian era; colours like violet dominate, surfaces are thick and shapes angular. There is a demand for realistic portrayal of scenes, as in the Flemish School of the 17th century, with portraits showing an individual pride, and sculptures have a clean, natural appearance. Cool-dry architecture is practical, solid and is generally built on a square plan with rugs and tapestries helping to keep interiors warm.

Clothes also become practical; women revert to garments that cover the body with long skirts and high bodices.

As the coolness ends and a warm period begins, aggression is diverted into becoming more constructive .

Warm-wet

The energy from the cool-dry phase that had swept aside everything which seemed irrelevant spills over into a highly constructive warm-wet phase. Wheeler describes this as being the Golden Age, when enlightened governments reign over great achievements; it is a period of optimism, building, creativity and an increasing birth rate. In history, 90% of rulers described as 'great' or 'good', even in the time of Pericles of Athens, reigned when the weather was warm and wet. Unfortunately, many of these same monarchs upset their neighbours when exuberance turned into wars of conquest.

These are times of plenty when crops grow in the abundant rainfall, and the feeling of well-being produces great achievements. The good times herald gifted leaders, stable societies, inspired literature and music, scientific achievement, revivals of learning and economic expansion. Wheeler showed that these periods spawned the golden ages of the Italian Renaissance, the Elizabethan period in England and later the Industrial Revolution.

As individualism turns to co-operation, art during the warm-wet period is concerned with wholes, not parts. Literature can subordinate the individual to 'higher forces', painting becomes impressionistic and abstract, and shapes take on slender, flowery forms associated with spring. Sculpture takes a similar form portraying ideal or godlike subjects. Warm-wet architecture develops a curvilinear outline, such as Gothic with pointed arches, ribbed vaults and slender columns rising upwards as though to the sky; the fashion of skyscrapers which started in the 1920s stemmed from the same genesis.

The good times cannot last for ever; the climate remaining hot becomes dry.

Warm-dry

As rainfall tails off, crops are more difficult to grow, harvest and life become more difficult and depressions follow. Governments which set out as benevolent and enlightened now become tyrannical, spawning dictators and impersonal bureaucrats. The 1930s were a warm-dry time when people submitted to dictators such as Stalin, Hitler and Mussolini. Even in Britain and the United States, the influence of the government increased when people could be convinced that politicians and officialdom knew best.

As it gets warmer, people become lethargic and take less responsibility; governments assume more control, bureaucrats increase, and in the more extreme cases enforce their will with the help of secret police. Warm-dry periods bring about moral decline, the family becomes unstable, the birth rate falls (much to the chagrin of dictators like Adolf Hitler, who wanted more little Nazis) and, unlike earlier times, pessimism sets in. Authorities take repressive measures, incarcerating people in concentration camps. Wars fought at this time tend to be bloody, with a complete disregard for human life.

Rounded structures, seen in mosques and domes, symbolise warm-dry architecture with curved arches and windows. Michelangelo's marble nudes with rounded limbs are typical of this period, while artists produce introverted and imaginative painting, as in the works of Picasso and Dalí.

However, tyrants also die and life becomes better; but people are less settled.

Cool-wet

These times mark a return to good crops, but the cool and stormy weather generates aggression and people feel more vigorous. Quite suddenly there is energy to demand changes from previous despotism. The 1830s in Britain were a typical cool-wet period when railways were built, joint-stock banks created and the social upheaval culminated in the Great Reform Act of 1832, which enfranchised hundreds of thousands. The 1830s saw the end of slave ownership in British colonies following the abolition of trading in 1807.

The cool-wet climate brings a return to prosperity with increased investment, an energetic foreign trade and a drive to open up previously undeveloped areas; unfortunately the boom also brings inflation, high prices and ultimately a crash as the weather becomes drier. Great religious leaders appear in cool-wet times; Confucius lived in the 6th century; it was cool during the ministry of Jesus of Nazareth and also when the prophet Mohammed created the Muslim faith.

However, people feel a vigour in search of freedom not unlike the stimulus felt during the cool-dry period described earlier that develops into civil wars and rebellions. The climate probably had much to do with the English Civil War in the 1640s and also with the start of the Latin American wars of independence against the Spanish and Portuguese colonists. It was also cool and wet in 1848, when either kings or governments were overthrown in Austria, France and Germany.

Wheeler observed a release of vitality, enthusiasm and opportunism in art and outlook when a hot-dry spell becomes cool and wet. Literature, lyric poetry and simple rhyming verse allow people to express their feelings. There is something of the warm-wet exuberance of liberation as classical logic gives way to a Romantic period when people are more inclined to express and be ruled by their feelings. Wheeler compared the classic organ qualities of Bach's fugues written in a warm period to the more romantic chorales written when the weather became cooler.

Paintings return from the cubist and surrealist style of hot-dry climates to depict nature; simple objects such as animals, birds and landscapes become popular subjects. Women's costumes become much more ornamental and elaborately decorated, as in Elizabethan times – the same styles being reflected in baroque and rococo architecture. Wheeler describes how real people, not gods, become the subject for sculpture; and latterly the artistic use of metal and wood have provided the sharp angles similar to the cool-dry period described earlier.

Faith tracks climate

Climatic variations could also account for the distribution of the world's great religions. The more contemplative faiths are found near the equator, the more active ones in higher latitudes. Elsworth Huntington and Iben Browning, among others, have shown that reflective faiths such as Hinduism and Buddhism tend to be grouped in low latitudes where a serene and introspective religion is appropriate to the continuously warm climate.

The great monotheistic religions of Judaism and Islam flourish away from the equator but require their followers to keep a strict dietary, social and observance code in dealing with often harsh living conditions. As we shall see later, some of the greatest religious movements have been driven by a combination of the Islamic faith, a cooler climate and a tough, nomadic people. Although the other great monotheistic faith of Christianity developed directly from the Jewish religion, it has undergone its own climatic mutations.

The Latin countries around the Mediterranean and their offshoots in Latin America and elsewhere are predominantly Roman Catholic, where the papal word is regarded, next to the Scriptures, as God's message to the faithful. It was the perceived abuse of papal powers that led to the Protestant breakaway movement that thrived in even cooler climates.

Martin Luther, the founder of the Protestant churches of Christendom, stressed the right and duty of the individual to be directly responsible to his Maker without the Church as intermediary. This appealed to those increasingly individualistic people living in the higher latitudes who had to cope with stormy and often rapidly changing weather. It is probably no accident that the leading nations have progressively moved further north as the glaciers continued to retreat after the last ice age. Initially the leading people were the Egyptians, then the Greeks, the Romans and following them the Spaniards and Portuguese. After the 15th century, power moved further north to the French, the Dutch, Germans, British and the Americans.

Nomads in a cold-dry climate are dangerous

Even 800 years after his birth, the name of Genghis Khan is remembered and feared as far afield as China and Russia. In the early part of the 13th century, the Great Khan's genius united scattered Mongol tribes. He directed their natural nomadic hardiness away from the barren feeding grounds of their natural habitat and led them into the lush pastures of China, Europe and the Middle East. This was during a particularly cool-dry spell.

Elsworth Huntington shows how dangerous hard men can be when a climatic change forces them out of their normal habitat. In his book *A Basic Principle of Civilisation*, Huntington comments that although there is little racial difference between, for example, the Nomadic Arab and the Egyptian or the Mongol and a northern Chinese, their style of life is totally different. The agriculturalist may regard the nomad as a vagabond but in return he is considered a stick-in-the-mud.

Huntington, who lived with nomadic Arabs to do his research, describes their life. He portrays a curiously democratic society where the sheik lives only marginally better than the poorest Bedouin; both eat the same rice and boiled kid, both have to move when pastures are exhausted and each has to endure bitterly cold desert nights and the searing heat of the day. Moving camp is a well-tried exercise involving everyone. At dawn the women dismantle the tents and load them on to camels or horses. Many of the men will have gone ahead with the sheep, leaving the women to load their babies on camel beds, and follow on horseback; even five year olds have a job to do leading several camels.

Not only are nomads herdsmen but they are generally tough hunters able to defend their patch and to fight on their own account. The Mongols are probably the best-known fighting nomads in history; but the Masai in Kenya or the Khirghiz in Sinkiang, Central Asia, are equally striking. Huntington describes a nomadic way of life:

> His mode of life makes the Khirghiz able to endure hunger, thirst and fatigue, for these are the necessary accompaniments of long

rides in search of strayed cattle. He has no fear of raging fords or slippery passes and despises the Chanto, or Sart of the city, who shrinks from crossing a ford where his horse may lose his footing and be washed downstream. In such rough experiences, the Khirghiz learns to be self-reliant and his frequent meeting of strangers under all sorts of circumstances gives him an air of readiness and self-possession.

Contrast this to the settled dweller. Here, a flooding river like the Nile provides silt and irrigation for his crops. If he becomes rich he can surround his land with a fence to retain cattle and his house can be piled high with every luxury; he can be waited on by servants. Unlike the nomad, there is no particular need to practise hospitality because most of his needs can be bought.

When times are hard and the rains make grazing impossible, then nomads, being used to moving, will do so with little difficulty. If they meet resistance from settled communities they can generally take all they want; however, they operate best in small groups because they find difficulty in accepting a unified command. It is only under a leader like Genghis Khan or Attila the Hun that nomads can defy more organised nations.

The humbling of man

Only sixty years ago, dictators were urging couples to have more children, which was not practicable in the hot-dry climate of that decade; animals were also affected, although this probably worried the tyrants less. Only a few years earlier, in 1919, Europe was devastated by Spanish 'flu which claimed more victims in a few months than the four terrible years of war. There are now outbreaks of diseases like tuberculosis, thought to have been eradicated. These are just a few instances of nature continuing to defy man.

Man is also vulnerable to likely changes in climate in the middle 1990s if the history of drought described earlier is to be repeated. Of course many areas have been affected by drought in the past; northern China is very vulnerable to below-average rainfall if the cold polar air forces the rain belts further south than normal. India's famines have coincided with a monsoon failure generated by an El Niño Southern Oscillation. Central Sahel Africa and the south-east coast of that continent have been similarly afflicted.

Although droughts and famines are not everyday occurrences in North America and Europe these highly populated areas have been, and are still, liable to external events which could cause grave, internal dissent, bring down governments and drastically reduce the food supply.

North America
The average rainfall for the United States, taking a weighted average of all states, is about 29.1 inches per year, but this varies considerably. Ivan Tannehill's *Drought: Its Causes and Effects* explains that the wettest year from 1886 to 1944 was 1905, when 32.79 inches fell; the driest was in 1910 when only 24.63 inches

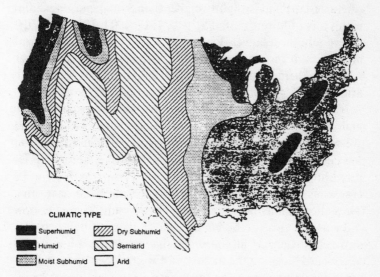

Figure 9. Climatic variations over the United States. (From Drought: Its Causes and Effects.)

were measured – a huge variation when in some states a variation of 10% would mean disaster.

Tannehill reports that in the summer of 1930 the rain deficiency was nearly 300 billion tons in seven states (Maryland,
Virginia, West Virginia, Kentucky, Ohio, Missouri and Illinois);
for each 100-acre farm this meant 60,000 tons less water over
three months – or minus 700 tons of water a day! Figure 10
shows the climatic distribution with high humidity on the West
Coast giving way to arid or semi-arid conditions on and to the
east of the Rockies. The transition from semi-arid to moist-
superhumid runs through the prime wheat-growing area of
Kansas before the humidity gradually increases to the East
Coast.

Rainfall in the US has been closely correlated with the westerly winds blowing in from the Pacific Ocean, the strength of
these currents being proportional to the difference in atmospheric pressure between San Diego in California and Portland,
Oregon. When the Pacific is relatively cool, the barometric pressure over Portland is slightly higher than San Diego, coinciding
with years of lower rainfall – 1910, 1917, 1924, 1928 and 1930.
Conversely, the relatively low pressure at Portland occurred with
high rainfall in the years 1903, 1905, 1916, 1941 and 1942.
Although there were some annual variations, it was consistently
drier when the barometric pressure was high over Portland.

In abnormally wet summer months pressure is particularly
high over the US and, as explained above, low over Portland.
Westerly winds blow from the Pacific and warm, moist air from
the Gulf of Mexico is drawn into the central states of the US
providing much of the moisture, as shown in Figure 10.
However, Figure 11 shows how the delicate balance reverses
when the continents are relatively warm and the oceans cool.
Then as the pressure builds up over Oregon, it draws cold air
down from Canada into a wedge that reaches south into New
Mexico, so blocking the warm moist westerly winds from delivering much moisture east of the Rockies.

This wedge is called a 'blocking high'; it also diverts hot, dry
wind from Mexico and Arizona into the grain-growing areas of

ACCUMULATED DEPARTURE OF STATION PRESSURE FROM NORMAL

1906 - 1915

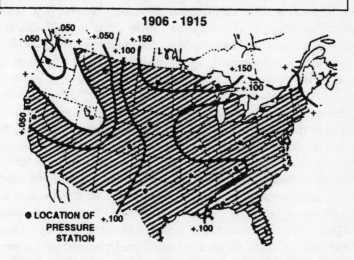

● LOCATION OF
PRESSURE
STATION

Figures 10 and 11. Comparison of wet and dry years in the United States with areas of relatively high pressure shaded. (From Drought: Its Causes and Effects.)

1930 - 1939

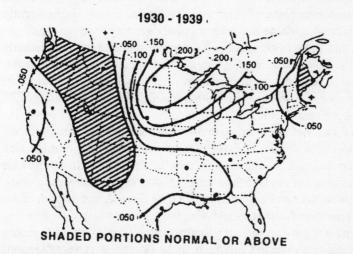

SHADED PORTIONS NORMAL OR ABOVE

the high plains which evaporates water from the soil. These dry winds in turn deflect eastwards the warm, moist air from the Gulf that normally delivers rain to the corn belt. This is the combination of events that caused the Dust Bowl conditions at the low point of the 22.4-year Hale Cycle in 1929–30, the droughts in 1954–5 and the rapid rise in grain prices in 1973–4. The next low point is in 1995–6, which will also probably coincide with a period of declining sunspots.

Europe
Unlike the US with moisture coming from several directions, the eastern side of the Atlantic relies almost totally on the westerlies which, starting from the warm seas off the Gulf of Mexico, become increasingly laden with humidity until they reach land. The next figure shows how important this air stream is to the millions of people living in this crowded part of the globe. Huntingdon in *Principles of Economic Geography* showed how the value of crops per acre reduced from Ireland to the Caspian Sea and the Ural Mountains. Although the work was originally compiled in 1940, the relative yields between the areas are likely to have changed little.

The importance of this idea lies not in the west of Europe but on the borders of what was the Soviet Union, including the Ukraine, where the relative yields are rather more than one-third those of Britain and France. Further east still, the yields in the Volga basin north-west of the Caspian Sea are well under one-third of western averages. This could be dangerous if the pattern of droughts in 1930, the mid-1950s and the early 1970s is repeated in 1995–6.

The West became so concerned about the possibility of the 1930s famine in the Soviet Union repeating itself that the CIA carried out a modelling exercise comparing the crop-growing capacity of the USSR to the USA; the results were subsequently published and updated by Evelyn Garriss, the editor of the *Browning Newsletter*. Although the air streams over the land masses are different, the analogy shows the Ukraine to have a similar climate to Canada, with the Caucasian states of Georgia and Armenia being the only areas equivalent to the prime vegetable-growing fields of southern California.

If the weather patterns change in the middle 1990s, as anticipated by the climatic cycles described in Chapter 2, then although western Europe may be cool, it will probably receive enough moisture to grow crops (the Great Famine of 1317–18 recorded in France and Britain was caused not by drought but continuous rain from May to November, which rotted the grain in the fields). The problems will come for Eastern Europe, the Ukraine and Russia where the people, suffering severe malnutrition, could move west in their hundreds of thousands, or even millions.

CHAPTER 6

THE 500-YEAR RISE AND FALL OF FAITHS AND EMPIRES

We can now start to read history with a new interest. If Elsworth Huntington, Raymond Wheeler and others were correct we can expect people not only to behave differently when it becomes warmer or cooler, but also with changes in rainfall. The early researchers believed that as we behave differently in set environments the same logic can be applied to the fortunes of nations. Wheeler went further to argue that as the course of history could be analysed in climatic terms, these same ideas could be helpful in predicting human behaviour if there was some way to forecast the climate.

Professor Wheeler found that changes in climate coincided with governments, nations and empires rising and falling in what seemed to be a predictable sequence. He was explaining these ideas to some scientists when a member of the group enquired if the fluctuations in behaviour could be compared with the work done by Charles Douglass on dating using tree-rings.

Linking historical records with continuous climatic data was to be the beginning of a major project. His research took three years from 1934, and with the help of some 200 students and post-graduates two million items of historical information relating to climate were recorded on cards from 3,000 different sources. From these, some 20,000 items were entered into an impressive 'Big Book', now at the Foundation for the Study of Cycles near Wayne, Pennsylvania. The data is analysed in columns by area from events from the earliest days on earth to 1933; when opened, the book is 8' 6" wide.

Wheeler believed business people, historians, politicians and indeed individual! could make better decisions if they had an understanding of how behaviour could be related to climate. Later the professor started a regular newsletter called the Weather Science Foundation, showing how changes in the climate explained differences in behaviour and how this might work out in the future. Although several researchers such as Michael Zahorchak, a previous director of the Cycles Foundation and of a company called Cyclomatic Engineering, sought to continue his work, little additional effort was put into extending the analysis after his death in 1961.

Not only did Wheeler alert people to the connection between climate and human behaviour but he worked out cycles varying from a few years up to 1000, which he believed explained the vagaries of history. Initially his prime sources of data were historical, archaeological and geological records which, as already explained, were later allied with the more scientific climatic records from measuring tree rings – then the most reliable and continuous sources of data on temperature and precipitation starting from the 7th century BC.

Wheeler's first real cycle started around 500 BC, although *Homo sapiens*' prehistory had preceded this by many thousands of years. Present history really began after the last ice age, when the glaciers progressively retreated enabling early man to edge further and further north. Mankind's first settlements would have been along the great waterways of the world in the lower latitudes such as the Tigris and Euphrates in Mesopotamia, the Nile in Egypt, the Indus and Ganges in India, and the Yangtse and Huang Ho in China.

Gradually village settlements united for mutual protection the storage of grain against droughts, irrigation projects and building structures. All these encouraged craft skills such as stone working, copper and bronze smelting, fashioning wood, creating and decorating earthenware pots and a system of writing to keep trading records.

Although peoples such as the Hittites, Arcadians, Sumarians, Phrygians, Medes and Persians were active in the present Middle East, the greatest advances were made by the Egyptians who had settled the Nile valley from around 7000 BC. The early people, like their talented successors, were able to cultivate their crops and breed cattle in relative peace. Egypt is singular in that any invader would be obliged to enter the country from either the Nile Delta or from the south in Nubia, any invasion from either side being arrested by the desert.

In time the two rival kingdoms formed in Upper and Lower Egypt were united by force of arms in 3100 BC. The victor Menes from the south wisely made his capital in Memphis near present-day Cairo and founded the first of a number of dynasties which lasted to the Roman invasion of 30 BC. Thus ended an epoch which considerably influenced the first of Wheeler's cycles, which would see an incredible flowering of philosophy, literature, scientific thought, democracy and military might.

Wheeler's first 500-year cycle

Every 500 years seems to track the rise and fall of empires and dynasties as one half-millennium gives way to another. Wheeler held that whatever seems applicable for one epoch is irrelevant for the next and that power alternates from East to West and back again. It is as if one group loses its will to continue and the baton passes not just to another power but to those on a different continent. On this analysis the last 500 years was dominated by the West. This is shown diagramatically in Figure 12.

Wheeler believed that his long-term cycles could be explained in terms of the climatic changes described in earlier chapters. If indeed temperature and precipitation do alternate over a cycle, then this could affect people's perception and go some way to explain why the drive and vigour which started great endeavours and conquests cannot be sustained. It could also explain why, as

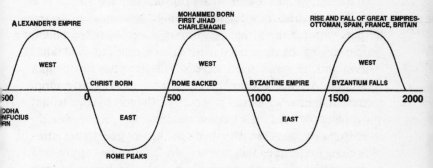

Figure 12. A diagramatic illustration of Wheeler's dominant 500-year cycle showing the 500-year switch from East to West and the most significant turning points.

the glaciers continued to retreat over the centuries, the dominant and most vigorous nations gradually moved north. An average temperature difference of 1°F may not seem much but over time those affected would feel as if they were living some 300 miles further north.

The sequence varying the temperature from cool to warmth is shown graphically in the next chart where there are two cycles: the interrupted temperature line rises more or less steadily to a peak in the middle of the phase, then drops evenly to the end. By contrast the solid moisture line completes two cycles for every rise and fall of warmth so creating four phases of cool-dry, warm-wet, warm-dry, cool-wet and then back to cool-dry. Wheeler believed that each period could be discerned in his major cycles of 1000, 500 and 100 years although, as we shall see, the shape becomes more complex.

The reaction of nations is very similar to the climatic reaction to individuals described in earlier chapters. For example, each 500 years ends with a cool-dry period when vigorous, impatient people effectively end whatever system had previously dominated them. This energy would continue to the next phase, a warm-wet period when enlightened rulers encourage a flowering of the arts, enterprise and economic well-being. The energy and rise of a collective spirit in nationalism often leads to wars of expansion.

In due course, the age of plenty finishes with the advent of a hot-dry era when the previously benign leaders give way to despots who use the earlier build-up of state power to oppress people lacking the vigour in the increased warmth to resist domination and, in some cases, slavery. Wheeler pointed out that when times are warm, people become more introspective, more interested in themselves and in security – the sort of climate that encourages the need for a welfare state.

Fortunately when weather becomes cooler and wetter, people's energy returns as they try to right the previous oppression by making laws giving more freedom – like the British passing the Great Reform Act of 1932 or the American Declaration of Independence. Eventually the rain tails off giving way to a cold-dry epoch when whatever has dominated and oppressed is itself swept away, and people become more independent and less interested in a benign state.

Each 500-year cycle also seems to begin with a remarkable event or the birth of someone whose legacy will continue many years after their own death. Wheeler believed that as empires rose and fell economic, military and cultural influence moved from the East to the West and back again. The story is told by relating events which bring out some of the influences that climate has had upon history.

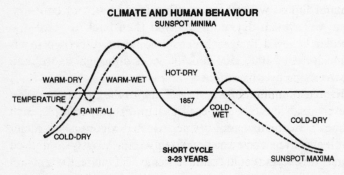

Figure 13. Wheeler's basic warm-cool, wet-dry cycle. (From *A Roadmap of Time*.)

The first 500-year cycle from the 6th century BC to the birth of Christ

Summary: Modern civilisation almost started with the birth of some most unusual men in both the east and west whose influence was to have a profound affect in later years. The cycle was to end with the birth of the most remarkable man who ever lived.

The first 500-year cycle unquestionably belonged to the West. In the 100 years until 400 BC, Greek city states rose to a peak of civilisation seldom equalled since – then collapsed, exhausted by a disastrous civil war. About the same time when Rome was starting its rise, the Macedonians from the north beat the Greeks and embarked on astonishing conquests under their charismatic leader Alexander. As the cycle ended Rome dominated not only much of Alexander's empire but also that of their colony Carthage. The Mediterranean became a Roman lake.

After a period of unity, twenty Chinese kingdoms became embroiled in a struggle later to be known as the 'Warring States' – the same cool-dry period that triggered the Peloponnesian Wars. The civil war ended when China was united under Emperor Shih Huang-ti of the Ch'in Dynasty, which shortly gave way to the Han and a period of prosperity which lasted to AD 220. India also shared the prosperity. After the invasion of Sind by Alexander, a dynasty under the Emperor Asoka was to unite the sub-continent and begin an era of prosperity at about the same time as the rise of Rome.

The West

The history of early Greece was influenced by the extraordinary hilly topography which divided and encouraged the growth of individual communities – many of which could only communicate by sea. The city states often comprised some 100,000 persons living on a coastal plain with a central town and outlying villages. The largest was Athens with a quarter of million people, much smaller than the cities of Egypt or the Persian Empire.

Although independent, the states could unite to fight a

common foe as they did when defeating the Persians at the great battles of Marathon and Salamis; they also came together to compete in the Olympic Games. In the warm-wet climate of the 100 years to 400 BC Athens was to see the building of the Parthenon under Pericles, and Greek settlements formed in Sicily, at Marseilles, at Carthage in north Africa, at Byzantium (Istanbul) and on the present-day Turkish mainland. This vigour was to see a burgeoning of artistic, dramatic and philosophic talent that has probably never been surpassed in so short a time. As we shall see, classical Greece triggered the Italian Renaissance and has continued to be the mainspring of western civilisation throughout the centuries.

Unfortunately, the prosperity of the early 500 years gave way to jealousy as the climate turned cold and dry. It turned the former allies of Athens and Sparta into bitter rivals during the twenty-seven years of the Peloponnesian Wars, which exhausted the combatants and led the way for Philip of Macedonia to beat the Greeks at the Battle of Chaeron in 338 BC; his son Alexander was to become one of the greatest conquerors of history, dominating his enemies during a hot-dry spell.

During his thirty-three years of life this strategist and leader of genius defeated the Persians in three major battles before moving south to Egypt, then east to Babylon, north to Tashkent, then south to the mouth of the Indus. It was here that his soldiers refused to go further and insisted on returning west. They eventually settled in Susa (in northern Iraq), and Alexander died shortly afterwards; the following cold-dry spell was probably a factor for his empire breaking up among squabbling generals.

There has seldom been such a bevy of talent as the dramatists, philosophers, historians and physicians that lived in classical Greece. Playwrights Aeschylus, Sophocles, Euripides and Aristophanes all lived within 150 years of each other. Philosophers Socrates, Plato and Aristotle were all active within a 100-year span, as was the historian Herodotus and the physician Hippocrates. Raymond Wheeler must have been excited to have such talent as an early example of what is possible during the warm-wet period of his first 500-year cycle.

As the great Greek era finished with the death of Alexander, so the Roman Empire was about to begin. The Republic was originally formed from a cluster of villages controlling a small area in the middle of Italy. Growth continued in the warm-wet period without much opposition from Greece which controlled the eastern Mediterranean and Carthage in the west. However, by 264 BC Rome led an Italian confederacy covering an area of 42,000 square miles with a population of nearly 300,000. With their allies, Rome was able to control nearly three million people.

It was during the hot-wet phase during the latter half of the 500-year cycle that the Romans won control of the western Mediterranean during the three Punic Wars against Carthage. In around 200 BC, Rome conquered the eastern Mediterranean when a defeat of Macedonians led to control of the Levantine coast down to Egypt over the next 100 years. By the end of the first major cycle, the Romans under Julius Caesar had conquered Gaul and, after a civil war, Caesar became its sole ruler.

The East

Early settlements have been found in China from 7000 BC on the rich loess soil around the two great river arteries, the Huang Ho (Yellow River) to the north, and the Yangtse to the south. In a spell of warm-wet weather, the so-called Sage Kings guided the agricultural settlements where people grew millet and rice; they also fashioned implements, smelted copper and bronze, and practised medicine.

The first important dynasty was the Shang, which quite soon gave way to the Chou invaders from the north; but this too collapsed leaving the country with twenty or more warring kingdoms from 328–308 BC – about the same time as the Peloponnesian Wars. Eventually a north-west border people called the Ch'in dominated and in the reign of the Emperor Hwang Ti introduced a well-organised bureaucracy which took control from the nobles and palace satraps. However, the Ch'in dynasty was not to survive Hwang Ti and there was a further period of cold-dry chaos before the Han dynasty introduced a time of plenty.

During the Chou dynasty the Chinese desire for order and control encouraged the development of a man who has dominated Chinese administrative ideas for thousands of years. Confucius was born in 550 BC in the province of Shantung. Earning himself a name as a teacher, he was appointed at the age of fifty to be the governor of a small district where his stewardship was marked by a reduction of crime and an increase in prosperity. Later he set about studying ancient texts and wrote classics on personal conduct, administration, government, the importance of filial piety and respect for wisdom.

Meanwhile, similar events were happening in India when the first people settled along the great rivers of the Indus and Ganges to the north, and the Jumna further south. Urban life started around the 4th millennium BC with copper and bronze implements appearing with the traditional stone tools. It was about then that five of the six present ethnic groups became established.

Harappa was the name given to the first of the great civilisations with stone-built towns having high citadels, solid buildings, grid-street lay-outs and complex drainage systems. The people also built granaries against the monsoon failures which have plagued the country over centuries. Other civilisations followed until the 5th century BC, when the country was united into the kingdom of Magadha with its new capital at Patna.

The peace was disturbed by Alexander's invasion of the north-west in 327 BC but this gave an excuse to Chandragupta, who seized the throne and later defeated Alexander's successor, Seleucus Nicator. It was Chandragupta's grandson, the Emperor Asoka, who conquered most of the Sub-Continent in the warm-wet phase of the cycle about the time of the Punic Wars. As with the Romans, this introduced a period of prosperity when trade flourished, roads were driven through the country and towns built. After one particular conquest Asoka became a Buddhist and renounced violence.

Like Greece and China, India had its own sage. Gautama (563–483 BC), the founder of Buddhism and the son of a king, was brought up in great luxury near Nepal. At the age of twenty-nine he renounced his wife and home to escape from the burdens of life to spend six years meditating in conditions of extreme austerity – it is said under a banyan tree, or tree of enlightenment; the word Buddha means the enlightened one. Revelation comes from four truths about pain and the Noble Eightfold Ways. The adoption of the Way leads to a state of peace – Nirvana – which exalts the contemplative and subdues the senses.

The Buddha then became a teacher, founding an order of monks and toured north India preaching Enlightenment. Buddhism spread in the Sub-Continent, in Ceylon, east to Thailand, Tibet and China. In the 12th century AD the message spread to Japan under the name of Zen, the Japanese for Enlightenment.

The second 500-year cycle, AD 1 to 500

Summary: As with the first 500 years, the second was to start with the birth of another remarkable individual, Jesus of Nazareth. The next half millennium was to see the faith He started persecuted, then become accepted, at the height of Roman imperial power. Later, the empire became dominated by bureaucrats and was so enfeebled that it succumbed to the Huns, the Goths and other tribes which invaded Europe and China in the 5th century AD. China also was to be disunited for at least 100 years at the same time and by a similar tribe.

The story is told from the birth and death of Christ whose Church was to flourish in the cool latter days of the Roman Empire, and which later helped absorb and civilise the heathen hordes from the east.

The West

The conquest of Egypt and the crowning of Octavian as Emperor Augustus was to continue the domination of Rome for at least another 200 years. The first decades were cold and dry, which stimulated reforms to the constitution, returned some power to the Senate and encouraged local autonomy. True, there were civil wars, but the 300,000-strong army and navy kept the peace and the sea lanes open for commerce and travel.

Although the exact date is disputed, the birth of Jesus of Nazareth was the turning point for the western world. His message was initially for the Jews, promising everyone who believed in Him to being reconciled and united with God. But He went further, offering the Gentiles the same gifts as the Jews provided they acknowledged Him as the Christ, the One sent from God. These claims were too much for the Jewish leaders, who condemned Him as a blasphemer and He was turned over to the Romans for judgement and subsequent crucifixion.

Christians believe that Christ's death and subsequent Resurrection were the fulfilment of the Old Testament prophesies – a message of liberation that was particularly acceptable in the cool-dry climate of the early years. Christ's message was continued in Palestine by the Apostles but it was St Paul who carried the word initially to the Jews in Asia Minor, then to the Greeks and latterly to the Romans. Christians believe that the dwelling of the Holy Spirit within them brings the reality of Christ into their lives and enlarges them as individuals in whatever they do.

The death of Jesus did not end the travails of God's ancient people, the Jews. They were a subject people after Pompey occupied their homeland in 63 BC. However, it was not until the cold-dry period around AD 66 when the whole nation rose up in revolt that the Romans destroyed the Temple. The acceptance of Christianity throughout the Roman Empire by Constantine in the early 4th century with the Edict of Milan did little for the Jews who were vilified by the Early Church; under its influence, the Jews were forced to move from their homes in the diaspora of later years.

Roman influence and power peaked about 100 years after the birth of Christ to be followed by a cool-dry period during which the central authority was questioned and the empire was ruled for a time by the 'Thirty Tyrants'. The cool climate also stimulated the movement of the Goths, a fierce nomadic people forced west and south from their home in Central Asia to challenge the might of the empire.

The Emperor Vespasian reacted by setting up a bureaucracy that divided the Roman Empire into four prefectures and twelve dioceses in a form of a military dictatorship encouraged by the warm-dry climate. Later Constantine, perceiving that Rome was under threat, set up his new capital in the ancient Greek city of Byzantium which he renamed Constantinople. It was here that Roman Law was codified under Theodosius and Justinian. The Christian Church adopted a similar organisation to the empire with bishops as the patriarchs of Alexandria, Jerusalem, Antioch (in Asia Minor), Constantinople and Rome.

Rome was finally shattered indirectly by the Huns, thought to have originated from a Chinese tribe, the Hsiung-nu. In a climate that alternated between hot-dry and cold-dry there was little to live on in the steppes and these people went south-east to China, and west. The Black Huns, as they were called, settled initially into south Russia in the 4th century, then moved to the lush pastures in the Danube basin. They also advanced west under Attila but were decisively beaten at Catalaunian Field near Orléans before retiring, when their leader died.

But it was the peoples displaced by the Huns, the Visigoths, living in present-day Romania, who eventually sacked Rome under their leader Alaric in AD 410, after failing to capture Constantinople; later they went west to settle in Spain after setting up a kingdom at Toulouse. The extreme climatic conditions triggered the Ostragoths, a tribe originating from near the Crimea, to roam the present-day Balkans. Other nomads on the move were the Vandals, who crossed the frozen Rhine, then ravaged Gaul for three years before one branch settled in northern Spain and another crossed into North Africa returning to sack Rome again in 455 from the sea under their leader Gaiseric. At about the same time England was invaded by the Jutes, Angles and Saxons.

Although Roman domination was destroyed, many of the invaders adopted imperial customs in what became a Germanic-Roman culture. This was helped by the Catholic Church which, although threatened, provided some imperial continuity in language and customs. At the end of the invasion, Italy was occupied and the Asiatic Avars drove south into Greece and part of the Balkans were occupied by another tribe, the Bulgars.

The East

As in the Roman Empire to the west, the cool-dry climate of the early years AD was to see a collapse of the Han after military adventures and reforms were undertaken briefly by the Hsin Dynasty. The Han regained control but the original prosperity could not be restored with continuous fighting with the Hsiung-nu, the same peoples that became the Huns. When the Han eventually collapsed, the country was controlled by regional warlords at about the same time that the 'Thirty Tyrants' ruled Rome. China was to remain politically fragmented until the 6th century.

The third 500-year cycle, AD 500 to 1000

Summary: It is difficult to square Wheeler's belief that the West dominated the East during the third 500 years. While Europe was reeling from one conquest after another, the Middle East and China were blossoming. The Chinese capital Ch'ang-an was laid out in a massive rectangular grid measuring nearly six miles by five, housing around one million people with a further million outside. By contrast, Charlemagne's capital at Aix-la-Chapelle was the size of a large village or small town only housing up to 3000 people.

The history of the period is a fascinating mixture of the boom times created by a warm-wet climate compared to the disintegration suffered during cold-dry spells.

The West

One of the most important Barbarian legacies was the rise of the Frankish kingdom in the latter part of the previous 500 years. In the warm-wet period, Clovis, King of the Franks, beat his rival chieftains before becoming a Christian and defending his new faith against the invading Arian Visigoths from the east; the battle of Poitiers in 507 saw the end of the war and he subsequently made Paris his capital.

Clovis' kingdom was enlarged by his sons and grandsons first by driving the Ostragoths from Provence, then establishing frontiers with the German-speaking peoples along the line of the Rhine, the old Roman boundary. The Christian king had the support of the old Gallo-Roman aristocracy but payment for support in war is expensive and the kingdom became enfeebled through loss of funds. It was Charles Martel, one of Clovis' supporters, who was to found the Carolingian Empire.

Charles Martel, called 'The Hammer', became King of France during the first part of a warm-wet period by beating the Muslim invaders at the critical Battle of Tours in AD 732. It was Martel's grandson Charlemagne who then became the first Holy Roman Emperor, crowned in Rome on Christmas Day 800 after conquering the Germans and subduing the Kingdom of Lombardy – a people menacing the papal lands.

Charlemagne made his capital at Aix-la-Chapelle, present-day Aachen, in the 790s, housing his palace, a few thousand people and a massive Romanesque church – but it was otherwise undistinguished compared to the splendours of Cordoba, Baghdad or Ch'ang-an in China. Although the empire held together in name over the next two centuries, it had already started to fragment.

Even before the Holy Roman Empire was being formed another and more durable event was occurring in Arabia. Mohammed, the founder of Islam, was born at Mecca, eastern Arabia, in 570 AD. Being an orphan and with little support he took the job of a shepherd and cattle drover until, through a successful marriage, he was able to give time to meditation and teaching, receiving his first revelation at the age of forty.

Mecca was then the shrine of the Ka'ba, a cult supported by the town's merchant aristocracy. Fearing Mohammed and his followers would pose a threat to Mecca's prosperity, the future prophet was driven out and flew to Medina where at some point he was granted asylum at the Orthodox Monastery of St Catherine – the future prophet was an honourable man and the order has been given Muslim protection ever since. The flight, or Hijira, marks the beginning of the Muslim year. Medina proved more friendly and, despite interference from Mecca, Mohammed organised his growing community to be subservient to the will of Allah, the Almighty.

Eventually Meccan hostility was overcome and he returned but this time in triumph to consecrate the Ka'ba stone as the focus for his new faith. Islam (in Arabic, the submission of the will to God) respects the Jewish and Christian scriptures but the final revelation is through the Koran. The Islamic Law is expressed through the Sharias, which not only defines personal conduct but imposes on the faithful the duty to wage a holy war, or Jihad.

The impact of a cool-dry climate on the tough Bedouin was electrifying. Only years after the Prophet's death in 632, battles had been won in Egypt, Palestine, Syria and north into present-day Turkey; they failed, however, to take Constantinople, the centre of the Byzantine Church. They then went in the Caucasus, east to Persia and on to India. The Muslim armies also went west along the coast of North Africa, across the Straits of Gibraltar to capture Spain, then into France. They were only stopped by Charles Martel between Tours and Poitiers in 732.

To the east in present-day Iraq, Muslim progress was no less astonishing. Baghdad was founded by the caliph al-Mansur in 762 when 100,000 men were employed in building a city on the Tigris with a diameter of over 1½ miles, well defended by a rampart with 360 towers. The Abbasid dynasty was descended from Mohammed's uncle Abbas, one of the most famous being Harun-al-Rashid, who sponsored a great flowering of the arts, learning, mathematics and sciences. The Abbasid Empire stretched through present-day Iran and Iraq, then north-east as far as the Aral Sea. Successors to the Abbasids were the Seljuk and Ottoman Turks, who started the Second Jihad in the 15th century.

The warm-wet period that encouraged the Carolingian Empire gave way to another cool-dry era which stimulated more attacks on the existing order. During the 9th century, the Magyars attacked Germany and Italy from present-day Hungary while the Saracens probed into Italy and southern Europe. To the north, the same cool period encouraged the Danes to invade England, France and northern Spain. Later, the Vikings attacked from the north, landing in north-east England, then down through the Irish Sea to found present-day Dublin and form settlements in southern Ireland, South Wales and France.

The East

In contrast with the West, Chinese culture and enterprise blossomed in the third 500-year cycle. After continuous strife, China was briefly united by the Sui during a warm-wet spell which saw the establishment of a central state and civil works such as a canal between Huang Ho and the Yangtse rivers. The Sui were succeeded by the T'ang Dynasty during the middle of another warm-wet phase, when the centralised empire was enormously expanded.

By 660, Chinese armies had made incursions into central Asia as far west as Afghanistan, where they were defeated by the Arabs at the Battle of Talas River in 751; the Chinese had learned the art of papermaking which prisoners then introduced to the West. It was a time of booming trade and prosperity, but the T'ang nearly fell during a cold-dry period and many of the conquests were relinquished – after that, the country became more withdrawn and inward looking. At the end of the 9th century the same difficult weather which affected Charlemagne's empire would be responsible for famines and peasant uprisings; once again the country was split into warring states.

By 960 the division of the country was clear; the Ch'ins were dominant in a fractious north of China, the Sung in the south. But even the south of a divided country was to develop riches equalling the T'ang predecessors. The southern capital Hang Chou became the grandest city on earth with booming arts, literature, philosophy, science, technology and learning. An urban middle class became very prosperous, setting up banking and credit systems, and the use of paper money. The wealth trickled down to the tenant farmers who were able to buy their plots of land. There was also the beginning of a free labour market, while most Europeans were still serfs.

The fourth 500-year cycle, AD 1000 to 1500

Summary: This 500 years spans the active life of the Byzantine Empire after its formal split from Rome to its occupation by the Ottoman caliph, Mehmed, II in 1453. The half-millennium was marked by two invasions: the first from Genghis Khan, leader of the Mongols, in the early 13th century, the next by the Ottomans 200 years later. The Mongols, a warlike tribe from north-east Asia, were to create an empire stretching from the Pacific to the Baltic, causing devastation in their path. Fortunately for Europe they went no further west than Hungary but China was ravaged. The invaders overthrew the Ch'in Dynasty in the north and destroyed the prosperous Chou to the south; in the course of some 100 years, China's population declined by 40%, a similar death toll inflicted by the Black Death in Europe.

The West
The Byzantine Empire was the only centre of Christendom not to have been overwhelmed either by the combined might of the First Muslim Jihad or the sack of Rome. Out of the five patriarchs set up by the Roman Empire, the Prophet's warriors captured Alexandria, Jerusalem and Antioch, while Rome had been sacked by the Visigoths some 200 years earlier. But in the warm-wet climate of early years, Constantinople stood fast, its formidable fortifications repelling attacks from the sea and land.

The splendour of Byzantium in the early years could possibly have rivalled the cultural and commercial wealth of the Chou Dynasty in China which happened at about the same time. In 628 the empire had stretched from the Straits of Gibraltar to the

Euphrates but 400 years later it had shrunk to an area including Anatolia, and the Balkans up to the Danube and Greece.

Constantinople, the centre of the Orthodox Church, had disputed leadership with the pope for legitimacy for several hundred years but in the cold-dry climate, the split by 1054 was officially acknowledged and Byzantium became a missionary centre for Greece, the Balkans and Russia. This zeal made them join forces with their enemy the pope in the First Crusade attempting to regain the Holy Land for Christendom.

Unfortunately, the hot-dry climate that has turned other rulers to despotism and lethargy also affected Byzantium. The initial drive which had encouraged a free people to expand and prosper turned to idleness; instead of defending their own frontiers, this duty was handed over to mercenaries often drawn from their main adversaries. Eventually weakened by the crusades and the attacks from papal-inspired Christians from the north, Byzantium fell to the Ottomans in 1453.

Meanwhile, in the warm-wet weather of the early decades, Europe was taking a shape that could almost be recognised today. England was invaded and unified by the Normans who then went on to found the present succession of British monarchs, and Germany took recognisable form when Otto I beat the Magyar invaders at the Battle of Lech. Despite attacks across the Rhine, the Franks, under the Carolingian successors, were developing Paris as the cultural centre of Europe and the Spanish were painstakingly regaining territory from the Moors. To the east, the first Russian state was forming around Kiev on the river Dneiper. But Eastern Europe was once again to be in turmoil from nomadic invaders from Mongolia.

Genghis Khan's origins are described later on. After the cold-dry spell that propelled the Mongol invasion of China, the Great Khan turned his attention west. The Khan's warriors were probably the most efficient offensive fighters the world had ever seen. The horsemen, trained as nomadic hunters, were self-contained with their own relief horses and food supplies. Apart from making brilliant use of surprise the Mongols could out-range the European archers by firing from the saddle – it is said they were the first cavalry to use stirrups for steadiness. They were also superbly led by a leader of genius.

Moving west in a warm-wet period, the Mongols over-whelmed the Muslim states in what is now Afghanistan before continuing to take Tabriz; they then moved north into the Russian principalities. The Great Khan died in 1227 and the conquests continued under his sons; but it was his grandson Batu who was to devastate Eastern Europe. The superb Mongol cavalry advanced along the frozen rivers to smash the ancient cities of Kiev and Novgorod, then west to Poland and Hungary where Batu annihilated a combined Polish-German army at Legnica; another Mogul army defeated the Hungarians at Mohi.

The death of the Khan Mongke was probably the turning point. The army that sacked Baghdad before moving west to Syria and Egypt left only a token garrison to defend the new conquests. This force was defeated then as the main armies moved east; they finally split into separate settlements not unlike the Macedonians over 1000 years earlier. The Khanate of the Golden Horde in southern Russia lasted for 200 years with Tamerlane one of the later kings. Others were the Il-Khan Empire in Persia and the Chagatai Khanate in present Pakistan.

The relative tranquillity experienced by Europe was not to last. As the climate became cooler at the end of the thirteenth century people became more fractious. While the Scots harried the English, they in turn invaded and ravaged France during the Hundred Years' War until Joan of Arc reunited the French in raising the Siege of Orleans which led to the English leaving France in the mid-15th century. The 14th century was as disastrous for Europe as the Mongol destruction of China. Around one-third of the population were to die from the Black Death – the bubonic plague carried from the East by flea-infested black rats.

But the problems were not over for Europe because another Muslim power was stirring, this time on the east of present-day Turkey, just on the borders of the Byzantine Empire. In 1281, Osman I, the ruler of a small state in east Anatolia, launched an expansionist holy war that gradually absorbed other provinces. In less than 100 years Osman's successors had crossed the Dardanelles and moved north capturing Adripole (Adirne), and went from there to defeat Bulgaria and Serbia at the Battle of Kosovo.

After a period fighting the Mongol Tamberlane the Ottomans (so-called from Osman) captured Constantinople in 1453, ending a 1000-year rule. After failing to take Belgrade the caliph Mehmed and his successors turned their attention to securing the surrounding regions of the Black Sea, then south to Syria, the Holy Land, Egypt and Arabia.

By 1500 the people of Europe felt as if they had been visited by the Four Horseman of the Apocalypse: war, famine, plague and death. But life had its compensations, with practical inventions which helped everyday life, such as new materials for house construction, canals for transport, and water conduits for drinking and irrigation. Also, Gutenburg's invention of the printing press (almost 700 years after the Chinese) made possible the Italian Renaissance, and later the Reformation.

The Ottomans had cut the overland supply route for the spices and peppers that made life bearable in mediaeval towns. The spice trade had always been highly profitable for its promoters over land and now the conventional trade routes were cut the invention of the magnetic compass revolutionised marine navigation, making possible the later voyages of exploration, and finding sea routes to India and the East.

The East

One of the most extraordinary leaders to emerge from the East was Ghenghis Khan. Born around 1167, Temujin the son of a tribal chief vowed to avenge the murder of his father by winning control of his own tribe, then defeating his father's assassins. After years of struggle, he succeeded by 1206 in uniting all the Mongol tribes and overwhelming others in north China. He penetrated the Great Wall and succeeded in destroying the Ch'in Dynasty in north China. Later, Kublai Khan, Genghis' grandson, subdued the Sung Dynasty in southern China.

The Mongol invasion reduced the Chinese population by around 50%. Countless thousands died, many more were enslaved, land went out of production, cities were reduced to rubble and trade, and industry was destroyed. It was too much for the population, which rose and finally overthrew the Mongol Dynasty in a cold-dry spell.

As in the past, a number of warlords grappled for supremacy with Chu Yuan-chang, gaining the upper hand to start the Ming Dynasty in 1368. In a benign warm-wet part of the cycle farming was revived, the north repopulated, and new crops like cotton, sorgum, sweet potatoes, corn, peanuts and tobacco were introduced. In due course canals were dug, industries revived and the capital established at Peking.

At first, the Ming were quite aggressive overseas but the adventures proved costly and the country reverted to the centralised bureaucracy that thrived under the T'ang. As the administration became more inward-looking, overseas trade was discouraged but business was still conducted along the 'silk route', kept open to the west by what remained of the Mongol Empire.

The fifth 500-year cycle, AD 1500 to the present

Summary: We have already considered the events leading to the 15th century – a momentous turning-point in history combining the collapse of Byzantium and the beginning of western domination. The cold period that has ended each 500 years was to see a remarkable drive of European expansion, prompted by a newly acquired liberation and a need to reopen the spice routes, cut by the Ottoman invasion of the Balkans and Middle East. Indian spices and peppers were essential for preserving meat through the winter and making life tolerable from urban odours. The spice trade was also highly profitable, a sure magnet for predatory monarchs.

Although changes in climate played an important part in motivating European rulers, it is probably easier to follow the years since the 15th century by describing the dynasties which rose and fell during this time. While historians should find the relationship of climate to history interesting, the general reader could find a revision of the last 500 years events absorbing. After all, those who led the Ottoman, Spanish, Portuguese, Dutch, German, French, British, American, Russian, Chinese, Indian and Japanese empires set the scene for well into the 21st century.

The Ottoman Empire

The Turkish Empire described earlier expanded the territories held by the Byzantine Empire. Under Suleiman the Magnificent and his successors, the Ottomans captured Egypt from the Mamelukes, then taking the same path as the Arabs overran the African Barbary coast to the Atlantic. Having captured the Balkans they advanced to the walls of Vienna before turning west through Moldavia around the Black Sea, then south through the Caucasus. Further to the east and south they invaded Palestine and Mesopotamia. The Venetian Republic stood almost alone against the onslaught, retaining toeholds along the Adriatic in Dalmatia, Ragusa and Corfu.

The Turks were stopped at sea when their fleet was destroyed by a combined Christian force at the Battle of Lepanto in the Gulf of Corinth. The Christian fleet under the command of Don Juan of Austria had gathered 190 galleys plus six giant Venetian galleasses which carried bow and broadside guns. The Turkish fleet under Ali Monizindade had 270 galleys rowed by Christian slaves.

The action was little different from the ramming and boarding tactics used at Actium 1500 years earlier, although Juan's sail was helped by having the wind aft of the beam. During the action, the Turkish right wing foundered on the shoals off Cape Schropha allowing Juan to defeat the centre and right. The losses were horrendous, with some 10,000 slaves and up to 20,000 Turks killed or drowned; the Christian losses were over 7,500, about the same as British casualties at the Battle of Jutland.

The Ottoman landward expansions were stopped when they failed to capture Vienna in 1683 against veteran armies led by the Pole John Sobieski. In the next century the Barbary coast was colonised by Europeans and in 1798 Egypt was captured for the French by Bonaparte, who in the process lost his fleet at Aboukir Bay. Thirty years later Greece was liberated after the Battle of Navarino when a British-led naval force beat the Turkish fleet.

Turkey made the mistake of entering the First World War on the side of Germany. Under the terms of the peace treaty, the Turks were forced to withdraw to Anatolia, although keeping a toehold in Europe at Istanbul; they also lost their source of oil at Kirkuk which became part of Iraq, a British protectorate. The last caliph resigned in 1924 when Mustafa Kemal, the victor of the Dardanelles campaign, became the first president of Turkey, so ending an empire that had lasted nearly 600 years.

Spain

The first of the European empires was launched by winning freedom from the occupying Moors. The Iberian Peninsula had been part of the Roman Empire and converted to Christianity by their patron saint St James, one of the Apostles. The Romans provided a period of peace which was shattered by the Visigoth invasion but, as elsewhere, the invaders became integrated and in turn were also converted to Christianity. As described earlier, the First Jihad swept through the Peninsula in 711 to be stopped by Charles Martel twenty-one years later near Tours.

Spain's modern history began after King Ferdinand V of Aragon married his cousin Isabella, Queen of Castile, to unite the two great Christian states on the Iberian Peninsula. The Spanish war against the occupiers had been spasmodic and brutal, any attempts by the natives in the hills to occupy the fertile plains being met by the Moorish cavalry; the campaign was also inconsistent, the Spaniards fighting as much amongst themselves as against the invader. However, by the mid-fifteenth century, the Moors had been pushed back to their southern stronghold at Granada and the Spanish were united under Ferdinand.

When Ferdinand and Isabella came to the throne they could only muster 500 horse but two months later had assembled a force of 40,000 with the initial aim of defeating their neighbours, the Portuguese. Wishing to cut off supplies to Granada Ferdinand moved on to Malaga where, hemmed in by the Aragon fleet, the city capitulated and two-thirds of the defenders were either sold as slaves or bought themselves freedom. Other cities fell on similar terms and Granada was isolated. After a long siege the city finally capitulated in January 1492, so completing Charles Martel's victory some seven and half centuries later.

However, the royal couple's first act was not so propitious, with the Christian world showing an intolerance quite different from the Muslims in their First Jihad. Prior to expelling the Moors from Spain the Jews – the commercial and cultural elite of the country, and the mainspring of Spanish commerce – had been forced to leave. Then followed the Inquisition, a device introduced by Isabella's confessor, Tomás de Torquemada, ostensibly for rooting out heretical beliefs but used by the unscrupulous to pay off old scores. Instituted by the queen, the trials of suspected heretics were conducted in secret using torture to extract confessions. The penalties ranged from flogging, fines and penances to burning for those who obstinately refused to repent and become Catholics.

Rather more constructively, Isabella gave the Genoese explorer Christopher Columbus financial encouragement to find a spice route to the Indies going west, not east around Africa; this was a perilous venture, as the given wisdom believed that the far horizon ended in a gigantic waterfall. On his first voyage, Columbus discovered Cuba and Haiti; on the next, the explorer discovered other islands in the Caribbean and sighted South America for the first time. His flagship, the *Santa María*, was rediscovered in 1968 having sunk off *Hispaniolia*, in the Dominican Republic, on Christmas Day 1492. Columbus himself died impoverished in Spain.

The discovery of the American continent unleashed a succession of explorers, plunderers, missionaries and later settlers. One of the first was Hernando Cortés, a remarkable soldier and diplomat who, with a small force of several hundred men, landed in Mexico in 1519 to be welcomed by the natives as a deliverer from the ruling Aztecs, a people who had invaded Mexico from the north. The Aztecs, builders of massive stepped temples, palaces and roads had, under their elected King Montezuma, conquered most of central and southern Mexico. The people greeted the Spanish as gods, with superior military skills which probably explains why such a vigorous people put up so little resistance to the invaders.

Another reason is that the Conquistadors carried the small-pox virus which later became known as the 'red plague' because it can devastate people particularly in a warm climate who have no immunity. Henry Hobhouse describes how the virus produces a fever which raises the temperature to 104–5°F, a rapid pulse and a pock-like rash covering the body and extremities; there is restlessness, delirium and a coma often leading to death. The red plague devastated the Aztecs and when it reached Mexico City it diminished the population by 90% within a decade.

However, the Aztecs were not the first to create a civilisation on the North American continent. Before them were the Mayas whose roots have been discovered in the Yucatan Peninsula going back to 2600 BC. In their 'classic period', when Europe was in its Dark Ages, the Mayas created remarkable buildings and pyramids without the aid of metal tools; they were also skilled in agriculture, pottery, weaving, mathematics and astronomy.

Further south, the Incas in Peru had built up a formidable civilisation on the west coast of Latin America 200 miles wide and 2000 miles long. The warrior Kings, Pachacuti and Popa, built empires of great splendour with a hierarchy of nobles and rulers creating an administration even down to village level. Like the Mayas, the Incas had built road communications, granaries against unpredictable harvests and beautifully shaped buildings.

Like Cortés in the north, Francisco Pizzaro, with a small force crossed the Panamanian isthmus, sailed down the west coast of Peru to conquer a well-organised people – almost certainly aided by the red plague of smallpox that had allowed Cortés to overwhelm the Aztecs. Spanish conquests also extended east and south in the Mediterranean. To the west the Neapolitan Empire controlled Sardinia, Sicily and southern Italy, while to the south there were Spanish colonies along the north coast of Africa and parts of Morocco.

The Spanish Empire lasted 300 years before British forces occupying Buenos Aires showed that the colonial powers could be defeated. In the north and west, Simón Bolívar, with British support, won the independence of Venezuela, Colombia, Ecuador and Peru by 1825; at about the same time San Martín beat the Spaniards to gain independence for Chile. Mexico fell under insurrections instigated by priests, and the Spanish Emperor was eventually forced off the throne by a group including Santa Anna, the victor of the Alamo, and the man who lost Texas to the American settlers.

Portugal

Like Spain, Portugal had conducted its own campaign against the Moors and, as we have seen, one of Ferdinand's priorities was to dominate the country through marriage links with the House of Castile – leaving Portugal a virtual province of their neighbour. But the country gained its independence through John, grand master of Avis, who conquered the Castilians at the Battle of Aljubarrota in 1385, supported by a force of English archers. The king then married John of Gaunt's daughter Philippa, so creating one of the most durable relationships in European history.

It was John and Philippa's third son, Prince Henry the Navigator, who brought together skilled geographers, astronomers and navigators to fit out and equip a series of expeditions that propelled Portuguese interests around the world. One of the first places to be colonised was Madeira, where sugar, grown by slaves, gave the island considerable economic importance; next to be visited was the Gold Coast, the known source of gold in Africa and slaves to work the sugar plantations. After Henry's death, John's successor sponsored Bartholomeu Diaz to sail round the Cape of Good Hope and reach the East African coast.

In the age of grand designs the pope divided the non-European world between Spain and Portugal, concluded by the treaty of Tordesillas. It was agreed that Spain claimed the Americas west of the Cape Verde islands, while Portugal had the right to what is now Brazil, and to explore Africa and the seaway to India. For a time the Portuguese had it their own way, with explorers like Vasco da Gama sailing for India to return with tribute and exotic products. Fortunately for da Gama a formidable competitor, the Chinese admiral Cheng Ho, had died leaving the coast clear for the Europeans.

The Portuguese created trading posts and colonies on the east coast of Africa, on the Indian sub-continent, at Colombo in Ceylon, then east through the Malacca Straits up to Macao on the Chinese coast. But the drive to colonise was not to last. When the Portuguese king died without heir, the Spanish king, Philip II, took over the throne and the Portuguese became more preoccupied with removing foreign control than further expansion. Eventually during the cool period of the 17th century, when the English executed their king and the Chinese overthrew the Ming Dynasty, the House of Braganza claimed the Portuguese throne with the help of France.

The Portuguese Empire lasted rather longer than the Spanish. The royal family fled to Brazil during the Napoleonic wars but the liberating movement was strong and helped by the British admiral Cochrane, the colonists were defeated and Dom Pedro became the first emperor. In the east, almost all Portuguese possessions were taken by the Dutch or English, all except for Angola, and Goa in India – both being lost within two decades of the Second World War. By 1994 Macao is the only remaining colony due for ceding to China in 1997.

Russia

It took the Russians 200 years to recover from the Mongol invasion, the lead being taken by Moscow, a city largely untouched by the Golden Horde. The first stirrings were in the 15th century when Ivan III forcibly annexed the city republic of Novgorod and declared the region independent of the Tartars. It was the start of greater Russia. The Orthodox Church was separated from Constantinople, and there was a drive westwards to share in the growing prosperity and cultural development in Europe.

As with almost all liberated countries the new vigour was channelled into expansion and some westward advance into the Baltic states provided an ice-free port for fur and timber exports. The lucrative fur trade also lured enterprising Russians deeper east but it was not until the middle of the 17th century that explorers reached the Pacific coast. In 1613 the first of the Romanovs was elected Tsar Michael and the first moves were made to push the Russian frontiers west, south and east.

During the reigns of subsequent tsars Peter I and the two Catherines, Russia expanded south to the Black Sea, disputing the conquests of the Ottoman Turks, and Odessa was created to trade with the Mediterranean. The tsars' drive west wrested Latvia and Estonia from Sweden; they acquired the port of Riga and founded the city of St Petersburg. To the east, an industrial base was started in the Urals, an area abundant in iron and copper ores with forests to provide the charcoal for smelting.

The Russians found a new vigour after driving out Napoleon and concluding European peace at the Congress of Vienna in 1815. They then marched south towards the Balkans where the tsar had a twofold interest. First, he felt a special responsibility for protecting his co-Orthodox Christians, the Serbs, against Turkish repression; second, he wanted a guaranteed outlet to the Mediterranean through control of the Dardanelles. This southwards ambition was challenged by Britain and France in the Crimea War when, despite the allies' poor campaign, Russia was defeated and disallowed to operate warships out of the Black Sea.

Undeterred by the Crimean reverse, Russia forged eastwards, consolidating what the trappers and explorers had already discovered. Vladivostok was founded on the east coast in 1860 with China conceding a connection through to the Trans-Siberian railway. Russia also occupied the territory north of Korea in 1897 but this clashed with Japanese ambitions and in the short war of 1905, Russia was forced to concede the disputed territory and southern Sakhilin. The eastwards advance took the Russians to Alaska but this was sold to the United States in 1867, just after the American Civil War.

But it was at home that the real trouble was brewing, because unlike other western nations serfdom was still legal, only to be abolished in the cool weather of the 1860s. Unfortunately, there was too little time for a property-owning yeoman to become established before the first attempted revolution in 1905, which was brutally repressed; this triggered a mass movement to the towns, where workers were needed for the growing industrialisation.

The move to a modern nation never had time to consolidate until the First World War when, once again, Russia came to the support of the Serbs. Despite overwhelming numbers the Russians were soundly defeated by the brilliant generalship of Hindenberg and Ludendorf; but the war continued and the ensuing despair fatally weakened the tsar's authority, made worse by crop failures and famines.

The second revolution in 1917 by Lenin's Bolsheviks finally 'kicked in the rotten door', to declare the era of universal socialism. But this was not an easy passage, because just as the French Revolution was challenged by monarchists, Soviet legitimacy was disputed by anti-socialist forces from dissident Russians and western powers. The attacks were uncoordinated and came from all directions but the Bolsheviks, directed by the military genius of Trotsky, brilliantly countered each attack in turn, using railways to fight on internal lines.

The next invasion might have been successful but for the terrible cold of the early 1940s and the astonishing steadiness of Russia against the German invaders. After 1945 the paranoia of another invasion from the West and the memory of the millions who died decided the Russian leaders to subordinate civilian needs to those of the armed forces. It was a fatal mistake. Industries capable of mass-producing tanks, fighting aircraft and warships are seldom adaptable to producing consumer goods; the empire crumbled in 1990.

One after another the Eastern European satellites broke away.

The power of the military complex started to disintegrate and money was pumped into firms to avoid mass lay-offs. The resulting inflation and internal chaos reminded historians of similar collapses that followed the French Revolution and in Germany in the early 1920s; both led to fascist dictatorships.

Holland

The states making up Holland and Belgium were independent republics in the Middle Ages, with the towns becoming prosperous weaving and trading centres controlled by a group of senior merchants. However, the ownership lay elsewhere and in the 15th century the states passed to the Dukes of Burgundy, through to the Austrian Habsburgs and then by marriage to Spain. Thus the fate of an independent and largely Protestant people fell in the hands of a repressive Catholic power. It was not a happy period.

Determined to crush heresy, Philip II of Spain instituted a harsh regime of taxation on the wealthy cities, and introduced the Inquisition and executions to root out the non-Catholics. This was too much for a proud and intelligent people. Led by the Prince of Orange and other nobles, a rebellion succeeded in clearing Spanish troops from the northern states and forcing out Cardinal Granfella, held to be the Inquisition's leader.

Philip responded by appointing the hard-line General Alva to control the provinces, eliminate heresy and restore Spanish control. But this did not stop the rebels, who acting as privateers made Flushing their base to harry the Spaniards. The guerilla tactics worked and tiring of warfare the Spanish agreed to split the Protestant north under William of Orange from the Catholic south only nine years before the Armada sailed in 1588.

The uneasy relationship continued between the north and south of the Netherlands but Spanish power was ebbing and finally ended with the conclusion of the Thirty Years' War. As with other liberations it was a golden age for Holland under the Prince of Orange. While neighbouring states in Germany were being laid waste, the Dutch reached dazzling heights of literature, learning, painting architecture and navigation.

During this cool period, Dutch seamen founded colonies on
the Cape of Good Hope, then east to Batavia on Java where the
Dutch East India Trading Company became the most formidable in Europe, forcing the Portuguese from many of their
settlements. They also settled the Dutch Antilles in South
America. Like all empires, weakness at home and growing
unrest abroad forced independence on the Dutch colonies after
the Second World War. In particular, the Dutch East Indies
became Indonesia but this did not end the role of international
companies like Unilever and Shell, which had their beginnings
during Holland's time as a great trading nation.

France

After the Hundred Years' War with England, France had
become a united monarchy, but power lay with chief ministers
such as Cardinal Richelieu, the architect of Austrian defeat in
the Thirty Years' War. It was towards the end of that conflict
that Louis XIV reached his majority and decided, against tradition, to become his own first minister. The reign of the 'Sun
King', although glorious at the time, was to create havoc in
Europe – and lead eventually to the collapse of the monarchy.

However, Louis' reign was a golden era for France, with a
flowering of the arts, literature and science. France also became
a major military power through Jean-Baptiste Colbert, who created the financial, economic and military strength for his
country, founding overseas colonies in Louisiana, Canada,
India, the Caribbean and Madagascar.

Encouraged by the French war minister Louvois, Louis
invaded Holland in an increasingly warm period, only to be
repulsed by William of Orange. Holland also fought on the
allied side with England in the War of the Spanish Succession
when Louis, through his wife, accepted the throne of Spain for
his grandson. The French lost and the Treaty of Utrecht ended
French supremacy in Europe – that is, until the rise of Napoleon
Bonaparte a century later.

The French Revolution (described in more detail in Chapter 7)
followed a time of great privation for France, with crop failures in

the 1780s and public finances in tatters after support for the American colonists in their War of Independence. Out of the revolutionary chaos emerged Napoleon Bonaparte who, in the space of two decades, conquered and lost a continent, causing death and untold misery to millions.

France was still a colonial power until the end of the Second World War, with overseas possessions stretching from Indo-China through Syria into Africa and Algeria. By 1994, little is left except for client African states.

England

It was the Tudor Dynasty, described in more detail in the next chapter, that was the foundation for England's, then Britain's, domination of much of the next 500 years. Henry Tudor came to the English throne in 1485 after the Battle of Bosworth when the House of Lancaster defeated the House of York. His son Henry Vlll split from Rome when the pope refused to grant a divorce and he was obliged to build a navy to counter retaliation from the papal allies. Investment in this navy proved its worth when England defeated the Armada during Henry Tudor's grand-daughter's reign – so initiating the decline of the Spanish Empire and the expansion of Britains overseas influence.

The first overseas colony was established by the Pilgrim Fathers at Plymouth, Massachusetts seventeen years after Elizabeth's death. Others were founded in the Carolinas, Maryland, Delaware, Virginia, Pennsylvania and up the north-east coast of North America. Britain also added to her overseas possessions through the Treaty of Utrecht.

British seafarer Captain Cook followed other great explorers, such as the Portuguese Ferdinand Magellan who had discovered the eponymous straits north of Cape Horn and sailed across the Pacific to discover the Philippines; another was Genoese John Cabot who, sponsored by Henry Vll of England, set sail from Bristol and discovered Newfoundland, after the original sighting by the Norsemen. In an effort to discover a north-west passage around America Henry Hudson sailed into a bay that was later named after him, believing he had reached the Pacific

Ocean. The last great area to be explored and colonised was Australasia and the South Pacific – primarily by a government-sponsored expedition commanded by Cook in HMS *Discovery*.

It was in Elizabeth's time that the East India Company was granted the monopoly to trade between England and the East. The company threw up some remarkable men, such as Robert Clive, who joined the East India Company as a clerk but turned soldier. He captured Madras and Calcutta, then beat a vastly superior combined Indian and French army at the Battle of Plassey, allowing the company to claim Bengal. Clive was followed by another able man, Warren Hastings; Hastings also started as a clerk and rose in the ranks of 'Johnnie Company' under the sponsorship of Clive to become Governor of Bengal – then Governor General of India.

What were known as the East Indies also became of interest to the British – particularly the Straits of Malacca, the channel between Sumatra and Malaya. The area had first been colonised by the Portuguese Alfonso de Albuquerque who set up fortified trading posts on the Malayan peninsula, but most of these were later captured by the Dutch based in Java. The area was disputed by the British when Stamford Raffles became Governor General of Java. In what proved to be an astonishingly far-sighted move, he bought a swampy island jungle called Singapore from the Sultan of Jahore which became one of the world's greatest trading ports. The dispute with the Dutch ended by drawing a dividing line through the straits of Malacca, the British gaining the land to the north, the Dutch Java and Sumatra to the south.

Australia and New Zealand had already been sighted by the Dutch and Spanish before New South Wales was discovered by Cook and claimed for Britain. Originally a convict settlement, other coastal areas were to be colonised by the British, and local governments set up in the newly created states. New Zealand was also discovered by Cook but, through a dispute with the Maoris, settlers did not arrive until well into the 19th century.

The strain of the Second World War and the debilitating advance of socialism were to strike at the heart of Britain's ability to maintain an empire. Canada, Australia and New Zealand were already self-governing, and India soon gained its independence. Other countries in Asia, the West Indies and Africa followed with varying degrees of success. Almost without exception countries that were once part of the empire are now in a loose association as the Commonwealth.

United States of America

The North American continent had been settled by three nations. The French and British had created colonies in what is now Canada, there were a number of British colonies on the East Coast, the French had occupied lands around the Mississippi and the Spanish had a toehold in Florida. To the south, the Mexicans occupied what is now Texas, New Mexico, Arizona and southern California.

The drive for independence came from the British-dominated thirteen eastern states, which resented the imposition of taxes and British laws. The colonists numbered one-third of the British population and not unreasonably were unwilling to be governed by statutes without parliamentary representation.

The revolutionary flame was lit after a row over dumping tea in Boston harbour which led to the redcoats opening fire on the local militia at Lexington. After declaring their independence, the thirteen states embarked on a revolutionary war which, with French help, was won by the colonists who then declared freedom for the new republic. In 1783, the US had an area of 300,000 square miles much of it rich agricultural land. Twenty years later, the area was more than doubled by the Louisiana Purchase, bought for £3 million from Napoleon who needed the cash to fight wars. West and east Florida was annexed from the Spaniards in 1820 to create a huge continental nation with incredible natural resources and human talent. Next to be absorbed were the southern states.

Texas had initially been settled by the Spaniards in the 17th century but had become independent of Spain as part of Mexico. The state attracted American immigrants who banded together to seek independence; this lead to dissent from the

Mexicans and the massacre of the Alamo garrison by Santa Anna. Later, the Mexicans were defeated by Sam Houston at the Battle of San Jacinto and Texas became independent as the lone-star state, with Houston as the first governor. California was also settled by the Spaniards but this too was ceded to the US with New Mexico and Arizona in 1850.

The American Civil War, or War between the States, although ostensibly about slavery was really over whether the southern cotton growing states had the right to run their own economies and trade without interference from Washington. Conversely, the northern states, not needing slaves, wished to develop their own industries which initially were not competitive with those in England. In the terrible conflict that followed more Americans died than in all the nation's other wars combined. The result was a defeat for the South, and a considerably increased power for the federal government.

The growth of the United States under the free-enterprise system was phenomenal. The republic had an abundance of natural resources, a growing home market and a huge pool of motivated immigrants – primarily from Europe. The Americans were not colonisers in the European sense, although they created spheres of influence in Central and South America, and bought Alaska from Russia. Under President Theodore Roosevelt, the US pushed the Spanish out of Cuba, the Dominican Republic, the Philippines and other strategic islands in the Pacific. They also leased the Panamanian isthmus to build the Panama Canal, making a sea route between the East and West Coasts.

The US assumed world leadership after the European powers had been fatally weakened by the First World War, with the dollar replacing the pound sterling as the world currency. The 1920s were a boom time for America, giving way to self-doubt after the Crash of 1929 and the 1930s Great Depression. However, the Second World War made the US the greatest power on earth, able to restore the battered nations in Europe and Asia after the conflict. The US was then able to provide a bulwark against the predatory advance of the Soviet Union through a series of military alliances both east and west.

By the mid-1990s it must be questioned whether the political institutions of the Unites States have the capacity to pull the nation through the very difficult conditions likely to lie ahead or whether, like Europe, it has to consolidate, while power and influence move to the East.

Germany

The Thirty Years' War had left the country divided into 300 principalities, with the countryside wasted from perpetual plundering and fighting. It was not until after the Napoleonic Wars that a more definitive pattern was to emerge with Prussia to the north and east, Austria to the south and the Confereration of the Rhine to the west. These later formed into a tax union but without any formal political integration.

Germany industrialised later than Britain but used many of the same inventions, such as blast furnaces, steam engines and railways. The industrial centres grew in the major ports and cities using the tremendous resource of the guild, or *Handwerk*, system for many of the new skills; one of the most successful entrepreneurs was Alfred Krupp of Essen, who developed a highly successful iron and coal business in the Ruhr. Unfortunately Germany, unlike Britain, had no developing capital market which in the 19th century forced the government of Continental states to invest in railways and other industries to encourage industrialisation.

The first Industrial Revolution, originated in Britain, was concerned with iron, steel and textiles. The second, spearheaded by Germany, was to invent diesel engines, automobiles, electric generation and electric traction. Perhaps of greatest significance to Germany was the development of her chemical industries, replacing products made from vegetable and natural oils with such products as synthetic dyes, ammonia, drugs, insecticides made from coal and phosphates.

The 1848 revolutions in France, Germany and Italy shattered the calm of a developing Europe during the cool period of the 1840s, and triggered a drive for unity under the right leadership. The man of the hour was Prince Otto von Bismarck of

Prussia, a career diplomat and statesman who finally achieved German unification in a series of brilliant political and military strokes that included war and alliances with Denmark, Austria and France. As with most new states, the First Reich, established in 1871, overshadowed any European country in the development of industry and the arts, and provided one of the first attempts to introduce a form of social insurance.

It was after Bismarck was dismissed by the Kaiser that the vigour that had gone into industrialisation was channelled into a formidable war machine for expansion in Europe; encouraged by Admiral von Tirpitz, Germany also created a navy aimed at challenging Britain's domination overseas. In the course of thirty years, this vigorous, talented, artistic and aggressive nation started two world wars, the second of which created a new empire that expanded and died all within the space of six years, with the loss of millions of lives.

India

Babur set up the Mughal empire in Delhi early in the 16th century. A descendant of Tamerlane, the Mongol conqueror of Persia, Armenia and Georgia, the new ruler entered India through Afghanistan – a similar route taken by other conquerors. The attempt to overrun the rest of the Sub-Continent continued through Babur's grandson Akbar, who extended Delhi's rule from Kashmir in the north to Bengal in the east and about the latitude of Bombay in the south. At about the same time as the Elizabethan age in England, this was a golden time for Indian culture, with the court's patronage of music and arts winning Akbar the title of 'Guardian of Mankind'. Akbar's grandson Shahjajan built the Taj Mahal.

The years of Mughal prosperity attracted merchants to India and as we have seen earlier, trading posts were set up by the Portuguese, Dutch, French and English. Like most dynasties, the Mughal power waned, to be succeeded once again by Afghan invaders from the north-west. The early 18th century was not an easy time for India because the French and British war in Europe spilled over into the Sub-Continent as a war for supremecy along the Carnatic coast in the south-east of India. As we have seen, this was settled by Clive at the Battle of Plassey.

Still managed by the East India Company, 'Johnnie Company' won effective control over more of India through the generalship of Arthur Wellesley, brother of the then Governor General, who defeated Tippu Sultan at the Battle of Seringapatam. Further expeditions gained larger areas of India until, in 1805, the Mughul emperor placed himself under the Governor General's protection.

British rule in India lasted for nearly 150 years but it was not all plain sailing. In 1857, nearly a decade after Europe had experienced revolution, the Indian Mutiny was to challenge the whole basis of the British administration. There had been unrest in the largely Indian-manned and British-officered army, which was brought to a head when the Minie rifle was introduced, whose grease-coated cartridge had to be bitten before loading. The grease was taken from the cow, an animal holy to the Hindu, and pigs, which are unclean to the Muslim. This act of incredible stupidity triggered the conflict.

The mutiny was conducted with great violence, atrocities being committed by both sides. After severe fighting around the capital Delhi, Cawnpore, Lucknow and Jhansi, only a few thousand British troops, with the support of loyal Indian regiments, were able to quell the mutiny and restore peace. The British, however, had learned their lesson; the government of India was removed from the East India Company and transferred to the India Office in London, with a viceroy in India.

India gained its independence after the Second World War – although as two countries, not one. The predominantly Muslim north-east and west opted to become a separate nation called Pakistan, while India itself was a mixed Hindu and Muslim state. The division was achieved with much bloodshed, and the continuing conflict between the religions, avoided in the years of British India, still rankles in the 1990s.

China

The Mongol invasion and the terrible flooding of the Yangtse happened at about the same time as Europe experienced the famine and black death early in the 14th century; both were to reduce populations by up to 50% and neither recovered for 200 years. The Mongol Dynasty under Kublai Khan achieved its own splendour but the people were still destitute and rebellion was once again triggered by massive flooding on the Yangtse, which caused yet further famine. The uprising which swept aside the Mongols left a vacuum that was filled by another group of warlords; one in particular, Chu Yuang-chang, gained the upper hand to become the first of the Ming emperors.

There was much to be done. The emperor's first priorities were to revive agriculture by restoring the irrigation and draining works, plant trees and repopulate the devastated areas of the north; he also boosted output by breaking up some of the large estates, encouraging the peasants to own and work their own land – a move completed by Chairman Mao seven centuries later.

China thrived under the Ming in the 16th century. While not putting the same emphasis on external trade as earlier dynasties, agriculture thrived and new crops, such as cotton, sorghum, sweet potatoes, corn, peanuts, Irish potatoes and cotton, were introduced. Industry also boomed, and the great cities such as Nanking, Suchou and Hang-chou became major industrial centres. But China still suffered from bureaucratic centralisation and inertia, and by abolishing the post of chief minister, the emperor kept all the major decisions to himself.

The Ming were initially aggressive abroad but costly reverses, and the emperor's capture in an abortive invasion of Mongolia in the middle of the 15th century, reduced their appetite for conquest and the dynasty became more protective against increasing Japanese raids. Like all empires before it, the quality of leadership declined and power passed to the court eunuchs who, with their own army and secret police, terrorised officials into raising even more taxes. It could not continue. The same cool period that fermented the English Civil War and Thirty Years' War triggered riots which swept the Ming from power five years before Charles I was executed.

The next dynasty were northerners, from Manchuria. The Ch'ings emerged victorious from the rebellions that swept the

Ming from power, so creating more than a century of peace under able rulers. As happens often in the administration of such a large country, insurrections had to be quelled and there was drive territorially to provide room for the booming population. By the early 19th century China was the world's largest empire, with the greatest population, controlling territories north to Manchuria and Outer Mongolia, west to Eastern Turkestan and Nepal, and south to Burma and Siam.

China had remained in many ways superior to the West until the 17th century but this changed with the West's rapid industrialisation. Like Japan at the same period, China was a self-contained country not prepared to trade products like porcelain, silks and tea with the West for anything except payment in silver; the authorities showed their disdain by offering the foreigners only a few storage godowns on the Canton river. This was unacceptable to thrusting Victorian traders who, pandering to Chinese fondness of opium, smuggled the drug into the country in exchange for merchandise.

The trade infuriated the Chinese, whose warships attempted to stop the opium being landed but it was an unequal struggle. Armed junks were no match against western warships and the Chinese were forced to admit defeat at the end of the so-called Opium Wars of 1842. It was a terrible humiliation for a race who despised foreigners. China was forced to concede Hong Kong to Britain and trading concessions were granted in five treaty ports: Canton, Amoy, Foochow, Ningpo and Shanghai. The Chinese never came to terms with western power and the authority of the regime crumbled.

Beset by enemies on all sides, a revolutionary group tried to force through reforms in the late 19th century but these were rejected by the reactionary Manchus. The final defeat of the dynasty came after the hated foreigners defeated a group of fanatical Chinese who detested anything not Chinese – the Boxer rebellion was so called because the warriors believed they could deflect bullets with their fists. The Manchu Dynasty ended with the revolution of the 10 October 1910 when Sun Yat Sen declared a republic.

It was too late; parts of the country were already in rebellion against foreigners and the weakness of their own government. Sun died in 1925 to be replaced by a young general called Chiang Kai-Shek who became leader of the Kuomintang (nationalist) party. Initially, Chiang led a programme of reunification in combination with the nascent communist party but the aggression was soon turned against his former allies. Unable to match Kuomintang's military strength, the communists conducted the celebrated Long March to create a soviet homeland in the hills of north-west China.

But the immediate danger to China were the Japanese who, having created an industrialised puppet state in Manchuria, marched south occupying the major cities and lines of communication. Resistance was minimal and the nationalists retreated to the mountainous south-west. The Japanese occupation during the Second World War was brutal. The Japanese disdained the Chinese, and the country was used simply as a base to supply food and armaments.

The nationalists returned to Nanking after the Japanese were expelled after the Second World War, but the regime was corrupt and widely discredited, leaving a vacuum to be filled by Mao's communists.

Armed by the Russians, the communists occupied the north; then civil war broke out as they fought Chiang's troops using tactics perfected by Sun Tsu, who commanded a warlord's army over two millennia earlier. Mao's victory in the civil war ended the industrial destruction of China but the new regime made exactly the same mistake as Stalin a decade earlier; in its anger, it eliminated many of the middle-class and professional people who could have led their country's revival.

By the mid-1990s the old guard are joining their ancestors. Will history repeat itself, as has happened so many times before, and thrust China into the melting pot of a civil war – with the break-up of the communist regime? Or will the present dynasty reform itself into a recognisable social democratic party, perhaps with a north-south divide, just as with the Chin and Sung nearly nine centuries earlier? Unfortunately, the future is not propitious, if we remember the history of fragmentation after other strong regimes that have fallen into disrepute.

Japan

Unification after chaos came sooner in Japan than in China, with the Tokugawa defeating his rivals to become the Shogun; he then ran the country through some 250 feudal lords under the authority of the government. Outside influences were not tolerated in the 1630s as thousands of Christians were brutally crucified and foreign traders were excluded, except for a small Dutch mission based at Nagasaki. Despite the restrictions, the country was very prosperous with increasing trade and a high standard of education. It was much better equipped than China to withstand the future western onslaught.

About ten years after the Opium Wars, Japan was itself given an ultimatum by Admiral Perry of the US Navy to open the country for trade – but this time the result was different. Perry sailed his 'black' warships into Tokyo Bay during 1853 to demand trading concessions. Unable to match this strength, the Japanese were forced to agree to Perry's demands, but the national disgrace overthrew the Tokugawa and the Meiji emperor assumed direct rule. In the latter part of the 19th century, Japan introduced the ideas of a modern industrial western state with a bicameral form of government, a legal and education system, and encouragement for industry.

The results were astonishing. Japanese scientists, engineers, businessmen and bankers applied themselves to creating new industries and institutions, and in less than seven years after Perry's landing the Japanese produced and manned a modern ship that crossed the Pacific. A few years later they had built a navy with Britain's help and, in 1905, Admiral Togo astounded the world by defeating a Russian fleet at the famous Battle of Tsushima, the straits between Japan and Korea.

Like Germany after 1870, Japan turned to territorial expansion after a period of rapid industrialisation and a liberation from past constraints. First to be annexed was Taiwan from the Chinese and the volcanic Ryukyu islands to the south. After

Tsushima the Japanese felt strong enough to annex Korea and went further to win victories in Manchuria, Port Arthur and Mukden on the mainland. After the First World War, when they fought on the side of the Allies, the Japanese gained control of southern Manchuria and the previous German concession in Shantung. It was then that Japan decided to be the leading Asian power.

As we have seen, Japan occupied the major Chinese cities in the 1930s, which created an ideal launch pad for controlling the essential raw materials necessary for Japan; these included basic foods in China, rubber in Malaya, and oil in Java and Borneo. Their opening advance in the Second World War staggered the world with the sinking of American battleships at Pearl Harbor, and the defeat of American, British and Dutch land and sea forces. At their peak the Japanese controlled an empire stretching west to India, south to New Guinea and east to the Gilbert Islands.

It did not last. American-led forces from the east and British-commanded armies from the west caused a series of rolling defeats against stubborn defence which culminated with the dropping of atomic bombs in August 1945. Japan was devastated but under the reforms instituted by Douglas MacArthur and American aid, this talented and resilient people worked their way to regain a position of leadership in world finance and industry.

CHAPTER 7

THE 179-YEAR EPIC
OF CULTURES
AND CONFLICTS

After the 500-year cycle identified by Raymond Wheeler, the next is a 179-year rhythm created by the conjunctions of the sun, earth, and the planets Jupiter and Saturn. This cycle described in an earlier chapter found a practical meaning in a paper co-authored by Dr Iben Browning, Dr Robert Harrington and others, which appeared in *Nature* magazine on 12 September 1975. Its purpose was to find a relationship between 179-year tidal forces within the solar system and temperature, and measured, not through tree rings, but through the analysis of ice cores described in Chapter 4. It will be recalled that more oxygen is absorbed as water becomes cooler – hence the proportion of the isotope O18 in the polar waters gives an excellent measure of temperature. The readings were taken from Cape Century on the ice cover over Greenland.

The paper examines Browning's proposal (described in Chapter 3) that the earth's temperature is largely caused by volcanic action – itself triggered by the long-term tidal forces moving from one hemisphere to another. Browning argues that when the tidal forces increase, the additional weight and friction of water is likely to set off earthquakes and volcanoes on the sensitive coastal margins – particularly those around the Pacific.

The tidal forces reach their maxima just at the times when, historically, sunspots are at their minimum. So the northern hemisphere is caught by the 'double whammy' of high volcanic action and low sunspots – both of which have a decided cooling effect on the earth.

The results are shown in Figure 14, which plots what the paper calls the 'tidal stress envelope' measured by the rate of additional units of water pressure against the changing percentages of the oxygen isotope absorbed. The results, although not perfect, are really quite striking, particularly as other considerations such as sunspots were not taken into consideration. The major discrepancies occur during the time of the Maunder minimum – otherwise known as the Little Ice Age.

It should now be possible to put Wheeler's climate-related hypothesis to the test outside his own work of historical data related to tree rings. Although there is no measure of rainfall, the human reaction to increasing warmth or coolness should work

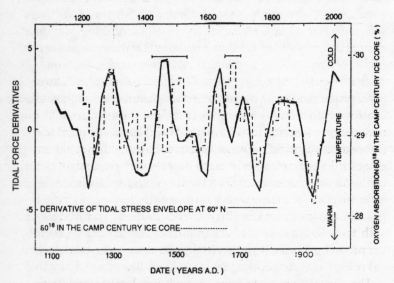

Figure 14. Long-term tidal forces plotted against changes in temperature from the years 1150 to 2000 AD. (*Nature* magazine, 12 September 1975.)

just as well, providing an equally fascinating insight into history as Wheeler's own cycles.

For example, when the temperature became warmer following a cool period, one could expect an era of energy, creativity, prosperity, a flowering of arts and commerce, sound government and probably wars of conquest. By contrast, moving into a cool period should be a time for throwing off oppressive regimes with an increase of personal freedom and democracy. In this way one should be able to relate what happened in the past to make reasonable calculations about what would happen in similar conditions in the future.

Although the cycle has been in existence for as long as the solar system, the year 1210 is a convenient starting-point to mark the origin of the modern world. Like the Renaissance some 180 years later, the change from a cool to a warm climate diverted energies from the land when there was less of a struggle to grow crops. In the 12th century, this allowed man's energy to build cathedrals and castles which are still the glory of Europe.

The glory of European Gothic in the early 13th century

It seems extraordinary that the Goths, the scourge of Roman Europe, could have given their name to such grandeur as Gothic architecture. Despite this, they originated a style that, in the right hands at the right time, was to prove the first step in liberating the human spirit in the warm-wet climate in the early part of the 13th century; the skills that created the earlier buildings were switched to create wonders of light and space. Although primarily inspired by the Church, these wonderful structures, with their elaborately carved ornaments and sculptures, were the product of masons and skilled men emerging from the gradual release of feudal bondage.

The clergy, architects and craftsmen were vital to the design and construction but they also needed labourers who could be released from the land by the good weather – something not possible 100 years later, as we shall see. In combination, the teams built simple and beautiful churches with high, decorated vaults, large stained-glass windows and pointed arches, doors and windows. In their effort to introduce the maximum light and create space, new devices such as flying buttresses, gables and vaulting ribs gave added structural strength allowing slender supporting columns or piers which directed the eye upwards.

Gothic architecture in France

The earliest form of Gothic is the great abbey church of St Denis started in 1140. Abbot Sugar attempted to create the most beautiful church in France by assembling the greatest painters, sculptors, metal workers and builders. Other contemporary cathedrals were in Sens, Senlis and Noyen, followed by Notre Dame in Paris, begun in 1163. These early cathedrals showed the advance over previous designs with each pier, arch, vault, buttress and rib created for a particular purpose. The nave height of 110 feet at Notre Dame, for example, was made possible by the use of flying buttresses and as time went on, the skills of designers and masons and better materials were to make slimmer structures which added to the sense of height and aspiration.

The first cathedrals were followed by others such as those at Chartres and Rouen as architects vied with each other to produce higher vaults on slimmer piers or columns, but some of these went badly wrong. In Beauvais, for example, the vault rose to 154 feet only to fall and to collapse once again after being rebuilt. Eventually by doubling the number of bays, the vault has remained stable but at the expense of width. It was during this phase that the great Rayonnant windows were created reaching the greatest perfection of tracery and light.

Unfortunately, little remains of the third phase, the flamboyant style, a stage similar to the decorated period in England, with structural simplicity but elaborate ornamentation. The early 14th century was a particularly difficult time for France with foreign occupation at the start of the Hundred Years' War, famines and the Black Death.

Gothic architecture in England

The English were some forty years behind France when the first Gothic cathedral was started at Canterbury in 1175 by the Frenchman, William of Sens. Others were Lincoln (1192–1250), Peterborough (started in 1200), Wells (1220) and Worcester (1222). One of the most interesting buildings is Salisbury Cathedral, built in the remarkably quick time of thirty-eight years. The chapter at that time comprised some remarkable names including the treasurer, St Edmund of Abingdon, later to become Archbishop of Canterbury, and Master Elias of Dereham, who supervised the building.

The original plan was to build the cathedral high on the site of the royal castle at Sarum but guards were not prepared to give access, so a more sheltered and accessible position in the Avon Valley was chosen. After receiving permission from the king and pope, the first foundations were laid on the 28 April 1220 in the water meadows not far from the bishop's house.

By 1225, the east end had progressed far enough for three altars to be consecrated by Archbishop Langton who preached to the people; the church was subsequently visited by Henry III and other dignitaries. The whole church was consecrated in 1258 and the roof finished eight years later at the same time as the great belfry west of the cathedral; at the close of the century the tower was raised and the spire added. The cloisters and chapter house were finished in the early 1280s to complete perhaps the most beautiful cathedral close in the world.

Unlike the Hundred Years' War, which ravaged France, the impetus to build continued in England, despite the famine of 1317–18 and the Black Death thirty years later. The new style was decorated, which meant there were more sculptures, the mouldings were more elaborate and decorative figures were much in evidence. Examples are Lincoln Cathedral, the great west window of York Minster (1338) and Exeter Cathedral (built between 1290–1367).

Finally, a new style called perpendicular appeared in the late 14th century, just as the climate was once again becoming warm and wet. True to the climatic influence, curvilinear lines give way to vertical forms directing the eye upwards. The first such cathedral was built in Gloucester in 1337 and others include St Mary Redcliffe in Bristol and Lavenham church in Suffolk. The climax of fan vaulting was reached in Kings College Chapel at Cambridge.

Gothic architecture in Europe

The same conditions that stimulated the French and English seem also to have encouraged the Spanish, with the Gothic cathedral at Leon started in 1204, the foundations of Burgos began in 1221 and Toledo was started in 1227. Spanish churches tend to have small windows, high columns and lavish ornamentation. German styles of Gothic churches came later with Strasbourg Cathedral started in 1298, Regensburg in 1275 and Erfurt in 1349. Although the Italians did not build in the style of northern Gothic, the churches created in the early part of the 14th century, such as the cathedral at Siena were richly decorated with marble and the work continued throughout the terrible years of the Black Death.

The four horsemen of the Apocalypse at the beginning of the 14th century during the Wolf minimum

From the late 13th century it started to become cold and dry in northern Europe with some brief warm spells in between. The weather made it particularly difficult to harvest crops, culminating in the Great Famine of 1317–18. At the same time the textile manufacture in Flemish and Italian cities declined; trade fell sharply and banks failed. The first such was Buonsignori of Siena in 1298 culminating in the collapse of great Florentine houses in the 1340s.

The appalling weather continued with the coldest winter ever known in 1323–4 when the Baltic froze over totally. It was hardly surprising that the plague, when it came, destroyed on average one-third to half of the population whose condition was weakened by malnutrition. The Black Death, or bubonic plague, is a severe, infectious disease which attacks the buboes or lymphatic glands. Unless treated with modern antibiotics, death comes within a week – in the majority of cases after a feverish state like drunkenness.

The disease was most common in the tropics, China and India from where it spread to Europe arriving, it is thought, from ships unloading at Naples. The plague spread rapidly through Italy in 1347, then to France and Germany in 1348 and over to England the same year, and to the remoter parts of Scotland and Ireland in 1350. The plague continued intermittently for another three centuries – only ending, it is believed, after the Great Fire of London in 1666. Another view holds that the plague ended with the appearance of brown rats who did mankind a favour by exterminating the rats' black cousins.

In many countries, 1348 was a terrible year. In England it rained solidly from July to December with great floods ruining the harvest which could not be collected anyway with the death of so many labourers; the crops rotted in the fields and cattle roamed unattended. In the Baltic it was reported that Hanseatic and Venetian ships just drifted on when their crews perished. With the labour shortage serfs left their masters to look for work.

The shortage of serfs ultimately forced a breakdown in the feudal system, although the Peasants' Revolt led by Wat Tyler and John Ball was inconclusive. The rebels, demanding an end to serfdom, occupied London and forced concessions from Richard II but after the murder of Tyler, the peasants were obliged to withdraw and the concessions were revoked.

The cool climate energised the Scots to make forays into England, which Edward I countered by invading the country in 1296. Edward's army advanced up to Elgin before returning south after a number of encounters. It was the king's successor, Edward II, who was to suffer a disastrous defeat at Bannockburn in 1314. However, by 1334, areas of southern Scotland were occupied by the English. Uprisings were not confined to the Scots; there were Flemish revolts in 1302 under

Matins of Bruges leading to the Battle of Courtrai.

The cool weather encouraged the nobles in England to ask for more freedom than had been given by the Magna Carta in 1215. To divert their attention, Edward III invaded France believing he was the rightful heir to that throne through his mother. The Hundred Years' War went England's way at first with victories at the naval battle of Sluys, and the two great actions of Crécy and Poitiers; but by Edward's death in 1377, only Calais, Bordeaux and Bayonne were in English hands. The action swung England's way when Henry V won at Agincourt in 1415 but after his death, Joan of Arc raised the siege of Orléans forcing the English to retreat and leaving them occupying only Calais.

The Quattrocento

The warm period in the late 14th and early 15th century, shown in Figure 16, witnessed a revival of the human spirit probably not seen since classical Greece. The Black Death meant many fewer mouths to feed and agriculture was concentrated only on the better land, thus increasing productivity and reducing the fatality of potential disasters. Despite the setback in England of abolishing serfdom after the Peasants' Revolt, freedom was only a matter of time as a practical expedient. It was pointless trying to hold on to a system when the market encouraged its abolition.

As with the Gothic period nearly 200 years earlier, the new thinking was demonstrated not only in buildings but also in literature, painting, science and thought. There is a debate how the Renaissance started. Some believed it was a totally new creation whose time had come; others thought it was a revival of classical glories. Whatever its origins, it released a tremendous amount of creative energy.

It is thought that three writers were primarily responsible for launching the Renaissance, each of them experiencing the very difficult times of the early 14th century. The first was Dante, whose love for Beatrice and the work of the Roman writer Virgil inspired his greatest poem, *The Divine Comedy*, written from

1300–1321; the imaginary journey through Hell to Paradise under the guidance of reason and faith encouraged others to think outside the reigning theological orthodoxy.

The second notable writer was Giovanni Boccaccio, who also survived the Black Death to write the *Decameron*, a tale about young people seeking refuge from the plague. His journey to Constantinople to rescue ancient scripts from the city before its fall in 1453 preserved priceless documents that might otherwise have been lost. The third person, Francesco Petrarch, wrote about the greatness of Rome, and the discovery of man and the world; he was to trigger a revival of learning, perceiving man to have dignity, to be a rational individual born to use and enjoy the earth.

The texts provided by Boccaccio and others encouraged an explosion of interest in the classical world made widely available through a Venetian printer. Scholars initially published their research and scholarship in the original Greek texts, then later in their Latin translations; the scope was tremendous, including biographies, grammars, commentaries, encyclopaedias and dictionaries. One city, Florence, was fortunate to have the Medici family, whose founder Giovanni acquired a fortune in commerce and banking early in the 15th century; this was continued by his great grandson, Lorenzo the Magnificent. The Medicis were great patrons of the arts, literature and scholarship, and under their guidance Florence became one of the centres of European culture.

The skills were not confined to literature and scholarship. The architect Brunelleschi designed and built the great Duomo of Florence with a conically supported dome that became the pattern for St Peter's in Rome and St Paul's in London. The sacristy doors were designed and cast by the goldsmith and sculptor Ghiberti, one of the greatest bronze castings ever produced.

The vigour continued well into the 15th century with the remarkable 'double dip' in the temperature line shown in Figure 16. One of the greatest men of this period was Leonardo da Vinci who began work as a painter under the patronage of

Lorenzo Medici. He then moved to Milan where he was employed as the state engineer, court painter and director of court festivities; it was there that he painted *The Last Supper*. Da Vinci later returned to Florence where he was Cesare Borgia's architect and chief engineer. His last years were spent in France, where he lived at the invitation of the French king.

Not surprisingly the Renaissance gave a huge impetus to learning. The universities of Bologna, Padua and Salerno had been famous in the Middle Ages for the study of law, physics and medicine but the 15th century gave pride of place to the classics, their language, history and philosophy; as we have seen, learning was helped by Gutenberg's invention of the printing press in 1448. Boarding academies were started which serve as models to this day. Students were instructed in the classics, philosophy and mathematics, and in their recreation hours they were taught physical exercises, fencing, riding and gymnastics.

Typically, the weather at the tail end of an exceptionally long warm period became dry, bringing out corrupt men like Cesare Borgia. Borgia was made a cardinal at the age of seventeen by his father Pope Alexander Vl but resigned to become captain-general to the papacy to lead a number of successful campaigns against city states. Accused of wanting to set up his own kingdom, he was exiled to Spain and then to Navarre. Lucrezia Borgia, Cesare's half-sister, was first married at the age of twelve, again at thirteen and yet again at eighteen. After the previous unions were annulled by her father the pope, she finally married Alfonso of Este, who later became Duke of Ferrara.

The Reformation and other discontinuities in the early 16th century during the Sporer minimum

The Reformation pursued the logic of the Renaissance by returning once again to fundamentals but this time to the Bible, not the classics. It happened during the cold period shown in Figure 16 which was delayed by the unusual 'double dip' in the temperature chart which, as we saw, prolonged the Renaissance. The Reformation was to be a very remarkable era, completing the liberation of the individual started in the quattrocento.

One of the first cool-era people to challenge the established order was the friar Girolamo Savonarola who was elected prior of St Mark's Convent in Florence in 1491. In three years his denunciation of the worldliness of the Medici and his prophetic utterances earned him such a following that he was able to overthrow Lorenzo and bring in a more democratic form of government. The pope was not beyond his criticism but the monk went too far and should have known better. Excommunicated, Savonarola was arrested, tortured, hanged and burned for heresy.

Objections to the papacy did not end in Italy. In Germany there was indignation that Pope Leo X was raising money to build the present St Peter's through the sale of indulgences, a sort of pass reducing the time a soul spent in purgatory. The Vatican marketing department made the offer not only to the living but also for the dead, so putting the onus on the faithful to look after their deceased relatives. Such procedures were not uncommon in the Church of those days and, for a further source of funds, it was common for the pope to sell benefices to bishops. The German banking house Fuggers would be happy to finance the deal on security of the prelates' living.

Into this imbroglio and with brilliant timing, in a cool period, came an Augustinian monk Martin Luther. Born the son of a miner in 1483, Luther studied at the University of Erfurt before becoming a novice at the Augustinian monastery, much to the unhappiness of his father who wanted him to become a lawyer. After three years he was ordained priest and shortly afterwards transferred to the University of Wittenberg where he practised as a professor of theology. During this time he visited Rome in an effort to receive personal redemption but was appalled at the venality and worldliness of the Holy City.

It was when Luther was writing a commentary on St Paul's Letter to the Romans that he read the words 'now we are justified by faith, let us have peace with God through our Lord Jesus

Christ'. This meant that man could seek personal redemption through faith without the intervention of the Roman Church, which up to then had been the sole means of redemption. In addition he argued that the selling of indulgences was both hypocritical and deceitful. Denouncing the Dominican monk Tetzel, a papal seller of indulgences, he nailed his famous ninety-five theses on the church door of the castle at Wittenberg, setting out his own scriptural interpretation.

So began a long period of examination by Cardinal Cajetan, John Eck and others, encouraging Luther to retract his papal criticism. But the rift only widened. The monk's popularity had grown through the new medium of printing – people hailing him as a German nationalist in their dislike of foreigners. Eventually Luther was summoned to Worms in an effort to force his final retraction. His reply were the famous words: 'I cannot and I will not recant anything, for to go against conscience is neither right nor safe. Here I stand, I cannot do otherwise. God help me, Amen'.

A heretic would normally have been burned at the stake but such was Luther's popularity that he was spirited away by the Elector of Saxony to the Wartburg fortress for his own security, where he proceeded to translate the Bible into German and ceased to be a monk. On returning to Wittenberg, and under the protection of its ruler Frederick the Wise, Luther attracted his own followers by preaching from the Bible and returning to Christian principles.

Luther's response to the Roman Church was typical of a cool-dry period. He did away with bishops, and returned church life and authority to the local community, abolishing convents and monasteries, and rewriting prayer and hymn books in German instead of Latin. At the age of forty-three, Luther married an ex-nun, Catherina von Bora, who bore him many children; having been a monk for so long, he was said to have found it strange waking up in the morning to see pigtails on the next pillow.

Luther attracted many who were similarly concerned by the state of the Church. Probably the most famous was the Dutch priest Erasmus, who published widely but never left the Roman

Church. It was John Calvin who was to have a great influence on future events. Calvin, a Frenchman, was forced to leave Paris after publishing papers supporting Luther's ideas. Invited to Geneva in 1537, he established a type of theocracy where the citizens were required to conform to strict moral and religious principles. Their code, however, did not stop them becoming prosperous – many believing that Calvin inspired the original disciplines of capitalism.

It was not only the Spanish expulsion of the Jews that benefited England but also the Religious Wars in France, where the Protestant Huguenots were repressed by the French monarch. In over ten years of fighting, thousands of Protestants were either butchered or fled across the Channel bringing their skills with them. The war ended with the St Bartholomew's Eve massacre, where thousands of Protestants were lured to Paris for consultations, then slaughtered.

The Tudor Revival in England

The House of Tudor has been traced back to Ednyfed Vychan of Tregaranedd in Anglesea who was the steward to Llewellyn, prince of North Wales. The family continued in the service of the crown until Owen Tudor, then a squire, appeared at the court of the infant king Henry VI; a good-looking man, he attracted the attention of the Queen Mother, and from around 1428 they lived as man and wife.

Some twelve years later, the dowager queen died and her five children, including sons Edmund and Jasper, were taken away and their father, after some time in Newgate jail, escaped and returned to his native Wales. Edmund was duly knighted and later became Earl of Richmond after his birth had been declared legitimate. It was Edmund's son who was to become the future Henry Tudor and his brother Jasper Tudor survived Edmund to become Earl of Pembroke. Jasper took the infant Richmond to Brittany, to return together in 1485 with an army of 3000 before Richmond won the Battle of Bosworth and claimed the throne of England.

The then king Richard III became protector to his nephew Edward V on the death of his brother, Edward IV. Claiming that the infant king and his brother were illegitimate, Richard had himself crowned and the two young princes suffocated in the tower to confirm his legitimacy. The Tudors, helped by William Shakespeare vilified Richard as a monster but modern scholars have cast him in a rather better light.

The issue between Richmond and the king was settled at Bosworth, a small village in Leicestershire, on 22 August 1485. Henry Tudor landed at Milford Haven in Pembrokeshire and gathered forces as he advanced east and north towards the king who had suffered desertions, although his forces still outnumbered those of Henry. The battle raged and although Richard had superiority, the enthusiasm of Henry's troops was greater. The climax occurred when the king, a brave man, charged Henry with a posse of knights and nearly succeeded in his mission but he was overwhelmed and died fighting.

The Tudor dynasty heralded a golden era for England but it was not to be easy, because the new king, Henry VII, had to deal with numerous uprisings typical of the cool period which had brought him to the throne. The problems continued for his heir Henry VIII who defeated a Scottish army at the Battle of Flodden Field in 1513.

But Henry had no male heir and, being disallowed by the pope from divorcing his wife Catherine, sought legitimacy from the English Primate, Thomas Cranmer. This caused a rift with Rome only seventeen years after Luther's ninety-five theses were nailed on the church door at Wittenberg. After six marriages Henry succeeded in producing only a sickly male heir and two daughters: Henry's eldest daughter Mary married Philip II of Spain but, being childless, she was succeeded by Elizabeth. Philip's claim to the English throne indirectly triggered the English Renaissance and the decline of Spain.

Henry's break with Rome encouraged the French, and later the Spanish, to reclaim England for the papacy. There was little his enemies could do militarily, but after several abortive landings the king decided to build a navy and erect coast defences against other attacks. Perhaps the greatest innovation was the design of a cannon specifically for seaboard use where, on discharge, the recoil was taken up by a trolley controlled by tackles. This not only allowed the weapon to be reloaded from inboard the hull and run out for the next broadside but allowed a battery to be mounted on each side of the ship. The gun carriage also permitted a barrel of twenty calibres in length (times the bore), enough to hurl a cannon ball up to some 600 yards.

The navy played a decisive part in the defeat of the Spanish Armada which Philip sent to claim the throne of England for himself and Catholicism, the sort of conquest that quite often accompanies warm-wet spells. Spain had also developed a navy but their tactics relied totally on boarding their foe and attacking with soldiers – little had been done to develop naval gunnery. Although outnumbered, the manoeuvrable English ships could stand off from the opposition firing at will. It is reported that many of the Spanish ships eventually returning to Cadiz still had most of their complement of powder and shot.

This difference was decisive in a number of small engagements in the English Channel. After the English sent in fireships the Spanish commander ordered anchor cables to be cut, leaving many ships of their great fleet to drift at night; most were then finally destroyed by unprecedented storms during August and September 1588. Out of 130 ships that sailed, sixty-three were known to be lost, fifteen were sunk or captured and the fate of thirty-three is still unknown.

The Elizabethan age encouraged some remarkable men, even before the Armada. Francis Drake, a Devonian, was already an experienced seafarer owning a coastal vessel before he left to accompany his cousin Sir John Hawkins on a voyage to the Guinea coast. Drake then set out to pillage Spanish treasure ships before starting on a round-the-world cruise through the Straits of Magellan, round Cape Horn, and sailing home via the Cape of Good Hope after pillaging Spanish ships off South America and as far north as California.

After serving as Mayor of Plymouth and in Parliament, he was recalled to lead an expedition to Cadiz, where he burned

10,000 tons of shipping the year before the Armada. He later served as a vice-admiral against the Spanish under the command of Lord Howard of Effingham. Drake's voyages to America later encouraged the first English colonies on the East Coast.

Another notable man was Sir Thomas Gresham, the son of Sir Richard Gresham of an old Norfolk family. After acting for Henry VIII he was called upon by the English government to manage their money. This was a shrewd appointment, for Gresham's manipulation of the pound sterling on the Antwerp exchange considerably reduced the debts of the new king Edward VI. Returning to London he built the Royal Exchange at his own expense after the aldermen of London had bought the site. He was also a benefactor in other directions and, as master of the Mercers' Company, set up a college to teach astronomy, geometry, physics, law, divinity and music. He is also credited with announcing Gresham's law that bad money drives out good.

Another was Francis Bacon, a politician, philosopher and relative of Sir William Cecil; after becoming a lawyer he applied unsuccessfully for a place in the court. Entering Parliament he became a confidential adviser to the Earl of Essex, the queen's then favourite – ostensibly a good move but Essex, a schemer, was thrown into prison and later executed. On Elizabeth's death Bacon, through the services of the king's favourite, became Lord Keeper and later Lord Chancellor. Accused of bribery he was to have been fined and imprisoned but was pardoned by the king and never again held public office – retiring as Lord Verulam. Bacon is probably best known as a historian, writer, philosopher and thinker, developing ideas which were to become the foundation of modern science.

Perhaps the greatest contributor to the English Renaissance was William Shakespeare, the son of a prosperous wool-dealer. He became established after joining a company of players in London where he wrote his earliest plays, *Titus Andronicus*, and the comedies, *The Comedy of Errors* and *The Taming of the Shrew*. Later he became a member of the king's company of players, where he had no serious rival as a dramatist and was sufficiently prosperous to buy a coat of arms. His last years were spent in Stratford-upon-Avon where he died aged fifty-two having made the greatest contribution to the English language after the King James Bible.

The English Civil War during the Maunder minimum

While the 16th century cool period created a revolution against the existing clerical order, its successor in the 17th century generated bloody wars in Europe and overthrew the Ming Dynasty in China. As earlier chapters explained, the displacement in the temperature curve in Figure 16 away from the tidal force envelope was almost certainly due to the very low sunspots experienced in the 16th and 17th centuries.

The Thirty Years' War
The series of wars that raged in Europe between 1618 and 1648 were the bloodiest conflicts since the Mongols invaded four centuries earlier. The prime contestants were the Catholic Habsburgs of Austria who wanted to control Germany on one hand and the Protestant countries of Denmark, Sweden, and the German principalities with the support of Catholic France on the other. The conflicts devastated Germany, leaving it destitute, divided and ravaged by the opposing armies; but the conflict was not confined to Germany – it also spread into France, Spain, Italy and the Netherlands.

The contention between religious tolerance and Austrian domination started in Bohemia, where Jan Hus, a reforming cleric, had attacked ecclesiastical abuses a century before Luther and paid for it at the stake in 1415. The rebellions continued until after some initial successes the emperor, Maximilian of Austria, was obliged to bring in reinforcements from Austria and Spanish troops from Flanders to beat the rebels, sack Prague and depose Frederick, the Bohemian king.

The defeat of Bohemia stimulated the formation of a Protestant union to include Holland and the German principalities but this was also soundly defeated by the Austrian general Tilly – a reverse that encouraged France to enter the struggle in support of the Protestants. The years of 1627–8 were terrible for Germany; the harvest failed, and mercenary armies roamed the countryside looting and destroying; disease was also widespread and the plague returned.

After the unsuccessful entry of Denmark into the war, the Protestant Gustavus Adolphus from Sweden joined the war landing at Usedom with a small modern army of 13,000 men. Adolphus had created groups of rapidly deployable units, including quick-firing cannon led by skilled and experienced men. In two memorable battles, Breitenfeld and Lutzen, the wedge-shaped battle formations beat the serried ranks of pikeman and musketeers, and the imperial generals Tilly and Wallenstein were defeated, although Adolphus himself was killed in a cavalry engagement. After the Swedes were themselves defeated, France entered the conflict inflicting setbacks on Maximilian's allies.

The terrible war ended in the Treaty of Westphalia which ceded south Alsace and most of Lorraine to France, and Sweden gained provinces on the Baltic. Spain, which had been defeated by England at sea, ended their military presence north of the Pyrenees after the Thirty Years' War.

The English Civil War

Just as the Thirty Years' War was about to finish in Germany, the same cool period contributed to conflict in England between the king and Parliament. Among other issues, Charles I wanted to support the Spanish against the Dutch in the Thirty Years' War but the problem was money. The king had already dissolved the predominantly Puritan Parliament for failing to raise funds for other ventures, and support for England's old enemy was bound to be unpopular.

Consequently, Charles set about levying an ancient tax called Ship Money, which was bitterly resented by the Puritans in

Parliament; one dissenter was William Prynne, who was fined, had his ears cut off, was pilloried and sent to prison for criticising the royal family. One of the king's supporters was William Laud, the Archbishop of Canterbury, who infuriated the Presbyterian Scots by attempting to force on them the English prayer book; enraged, the Scots invaded England and the king needed even more funds to repel them.

Even a Scottish invasion failed to move Parliament unless its list of grievances was met and the king encouraged one of his advisers, the Earl of Strafford, to visit Ireland and raise an army – ostensibly to quell a rebellion (the population of Ireland being then little different from that of England). Believing the leaders of the Commons to be responsible for blocking his wishes, Charles sent the Attorney-General to arrest the Puritan ringleaders: Holles, Hazelrig, Pym, Hampden and Strode. The five were not found when the envoy arrived.

The Civil War, like the American Civil War two centuries later, started slowly, both sides needing time to gain support. The king was backed by most of the nobility, the gentlemen and their tenants – these being drawn primarily from the north and west of England. Puritan squires and farmers were the backbone of the Parliamentary cause supported by the trading classes of the towns, including London; the men and funds came mainly from the south and east of the country.

The prime difference was in the quality of the cavalry; as Oliver Cromwell, a Puritan farmer, said: 'it would never do to trust a set of poor tapsters and town apprentices to fight against men of honour'. And so it proved at the first battle at Edgehill, where the Royalist cavalry charge carried all before it.

Cromwell then set about creating the Ironsides, the most famous and competent cavalry ever produced by England, and under his leadership they were decisive at two subsequent battles, Marston Moor and Naseby. Defeated, the king gave himself up to Scottish allies of Parliament, who turned him over to the English for imprisonment at Carisbroke Castle on the Isle of Wight. Not wishing to depose the monarch Cromwell started negotiations hoping that the king would agree to rule through

Parliament as a constitutional monarch. The war was not over, however. The Duke of Hamilton led a Scottish army south to be soundly defeated at the battles of Preston and Worcester.

Parliament still hoped that the king would accept its terms but it was not to be. Discovering that the king was secretly encouraging the Irish to invade England and restore him to the throne, Parliament brought the king to trial and duly committed him to death as a tyrant, traitor, murderer and public enemy to the people. He was executed on a very cold morning on 30 January 1649 and Oliver Cromwell then ruled as Lord Protector, not via Parliament, but through twelve military districts in England and Wales each governed by a major general.

The amazing 1770s

Apart possibly from the time of classical Greece or the Italian Renaissance, almost nothing could compare to the extraordinary events of the warm-wet latter quarter of the 18th century. For Britain it was the dawn of the Industrial Revolution and for the Americans the beginning of independence. It was also a golden age for music and the arts.

The Industrial Revolution in Britain
As with all revolutions, the seeds were sown some time before with the invention of the blast furnace to produce iron. Until then iron had always been produced by heating iron ore with charcoal; the carbon combined with oxygen which then bubbled off as carbon dioxide leaving the molten metal behind. Most iron had been made in the wooded areas of Sussex and Gloucestershire but there was grave concern whether this could continue as the forests were becoming exhausted. Abraham Darby solved the problem in 1709 with his blast furnace, substituting coke for charcoal. Two generations later, the furnaces of Abraham Darby III produced the sections for the Iron Bridge over the Severn.

It was a remarkable period of inventions: Richard Arkwright, a barber by trade, designed a spinning frame operated by water power – so enabling good quality yarn to be produced with a fraction of the labour needed earlier. Later it was possible to substitute steam for water power when James Watt invented the reciprocating steam engine and condenser system for returning water to the boiler. In a typically idiosyncratic way Dr Edmund Cartwright, rector of Goadby Marwood in Leicestershire, invented a power loom without ever having seen a weaver working; it is said he substantially improved his design when he saw a weaver in action.

Another genius was James Brindley who, sponsored by the Duke of Bridgewater, designed the Bridgewater Canal. Later Brindley built the Grand Trunk Canal with Josiah Wedgewood of pottery fame and constructed a flint mill for his partner at Leek. Jesse Ramsden invented the screw-cutting lathe when it was recognised that machine tools were essential for production. Others, such as Henry Ball, invented the copper cylinder for calico printing, while Andrew Meilke produced a threshing machine.

None of this could have happened but for the resources of capital, favourable political institutions, a history of commercial dealing, the common law and a legacy of free trade. All this was helped by Adam Smith's *The Wealth of Nations* – perhaps the most important treatise on practical economics and principles ever written. The vast increase in wealth encouraged an enormous growth in the arts, with the founding of the Royal Academy in 1768 by George III with Sir Joshua Reynolds as its first president. The theatre also flourished, with actors such as David Garrick making famous the roles of Richard III and King Lear. From overseas, composers such as Joseph Haydn visited England to write masses and symphonies for the general public.

American Independence

Unusually for a revolutionary conflict, the American War of Independence happened in a warm period although it was also dry – a situation, as we have seen, which normally encourages tyrannical rule. In this case, the American colonists were reacting against British laws passed by a parliament in which they had no representation.

At least one of the contentious issues were the Navigation Acts, a measure going back to 1381, forbidding imports to England or her colonies except either in British ships or those of the producing country. Adding to the insults London imposed a stamp tax on the American colonies to be followed by a tea tax that precipitated the famous Boston Tea Party.

This action inflamed the governor of Massachusetts who sent 700 men to seize arms and ammunition gathered at Concord. Forewarned by the celebrated ride of Paul Revere, the colonists were ready and the first shots were fired at Lexington on 19 April 1775. Shortly after that Colonel George Washington was appointed to command the colonial forces and the thirteen rebel states declared their independence on 4 July 1776.

The first pitched battle was outside Boston at Bunker Hill where, although technically a British victory, the Americans fought bravely against regular troops and acquitted themselves well. However, actions at Saratoga, Brandywine and German-town failed to settle the war, and Washington found it difficult to keep his army together during the winter at Valley Forge outside Philadelphia. Further actions were planned by the British, who hoped to conduct amphibious operations using their naval strength. But in the summer of 1778, France and Spain entered the war on the American side making naval operations more difficult.

After suffering reverses in the north, General Cornwallis planned to invade from the south where loyalists were more numerous. At first the action succeeded but attempts at coercion alienated the colonists and the drive north bogged down at Yorktown, Virginia; besieged on land by Washington and the French general, Lafayette, and at sea by the French admiral, de Grasse, Cornwallis laid down his arms and was shipped back to England.

War between Britain and America did not finally end until the cool period in the early half of the 19th century. Irritated by Canadian attempts to stir up Indian aggression on their northern border, the United States invaded Canada in 1812 and the

British responded by blockading the east coast and raiding the mainland; it was on one such incursion that the new capital at Washington was burned.

The final action was at New Orleans, when a force under General Pemberton attempted to capture the mouth of the Mississippi in an effort to control the waterway. He was met and defeated by General Andrew Jackson who later became president. The war decided nothing – the US did not again attack Canada and the British laid off naval operations.

The rise and fall of Napoleon Bonaparte during the Sabine minimum

It is in the nature of cycles that great men are thrown up from chaos and despair. In the previous cool period it was Cromwell in England, Gustavus Adolphus of Sweden, and Cardinal Richelieu of France. In the cool period of the early 19th century, the man was Napoleon Bonaparte. As with Cromwell's assuming the title of Lord Protector, Bonaparte, on appointing himself emperor, is said to have exclaimed, 'I found the crown in a gutter and put it on my head'.

Born in Corsica of noble parents who had opted to become French, the young Bonaparte studied at the cadet school in Brienne before completing his artillery and officer training at the Ecole Militaire in Paris. On subsequent training he studied the work of Jean-Jacques Rousseau, who had provided the French Revolution with many of its democratic and temporal values.

It was during the wars following the French Revolution that Colonel Bonaparte was first called upon to help clear a British and Spanish raid from Toulon. Although promoted to a general of the artillery, he fell out of favour with the Directorate until he saved them from a royalist rising by mowing down the insurgents on the steps of Saint-Roche Church. For this exploit he was awarded the hand of Josephine, the widow of an aristocrat guillotined during the Terror, and also the command of the army of Italy.

It is said that Bonaparte was no great military innovator in the sense of introducing new weapons, he just was extraordinarily good at adapting ideas to his own purpose. Usually fighting with fewer numbers than the enemy, he would combine rapid movement and deception to pass around the enemy's flanks to reach their lines of communication which he would attack to his advantage. In the Italian campaign he took his ragged army through the St Bernard Pass into the rich plains of Lombardy, where he won famous battles.

Realising that the true enemy of the Revolution was Britain, he persuaded the Directorate to send an expedition to Egypt to interrupt Britain's communication with India. Although the invasion succeeded, his fleet was destroyed by Nelson, and Napoleon was forced to return to France where he was acclaimed a hero of the Revolution. It was then that his political career was launched. Elected the Premier Consul, Bonaparte was to introduce reforms dividing France into *départements* and *préfectures* which have survived with only some alteration until today. To unite the monarchists with the republicans he proclaimed himself emperor in the tradition of Charlemagne.

But Britain still remained the enemy. Failing to invade the island after his fleet's defeat at Trafalgar in 1805, Napoleon set about denying Britain Continental allies by conducting campaigns against Austria, Prussia and Spain. He invaded Russia in the ill-fated 1812 expedition in what was one of the coldest winters for decades which decimated the Grande Armée. It was the beginning of the end. Spurred on by the cool climate, one defeated nation after another rose up against the tyrant forcing his abdication on 11 April 1814 and exile in Alba. In a whirlwind 100 days, he escaped from exile and regrouped the Grande Armée, only to be finally defeated at Waterloo. Napoleon ended his days as a prisoner at St Helena aged fifty-two.

Like Adolf Hitler whose career followed closely that of Napoleon, the man who rescued a nation from the chaos of economic and political collapse was to lead his nation's rise and fall. Both men created a superb fighting machine, both achieved dazzling victories but then failed in the almost impossible venture of invading Russia in the winter – something only achieved by Genghis Khan.

The collapse of Napoleon's empire in the cool climate of 1815 was only the first of several liberation movements. In the rising tide of nationalism, Greece was liberated from the Ottoman Turks and by 1825 Simón Bolívar had freed Venezuela, Colombia, Ecuador and Peru from the Spanish. San Martín helped to free Peru and liberated Chile, Brazil declared independence from Portugal in 1821 and Mexico declared itself free from Spain the same year that Florida was ceded to the United States. Some twenty years later Texas and the south-west states of the US were freed from Mexico.

The hottest period since the 1770s, the Great War and the 'Roaring Twenties'

The First World War was the climax of German imperialism, the almost inevitable result of the industrialisation, self-confidence and vigour that followed unification. Germany was not alone in being aggressive; each of the empires described in the earlier chapter followed either unification or liberation from another imperial power. Like Napoleon before him, the Kaiser destroyed not only other nations but his own regime.

Wheeler said that wars of aggression occur during warm times and those who wrote about 1914 remember a perfect summer in England of village cricket matches, and strawberries and cream. A young officer volunteering for service believed it would be like another corps camp. It was a highly insular view of a nation which had not been involved in a national conflict for nearly a century. The French, who had fought the Germans in 1870, knew otherwise, how dangerous a war could be.

Ostensibly the war started when a Serbian national shot the Archduke Ferdinand of Austria in Sarajevo on 28 June 1914. Then, as now, the Balkans were an explosive area with the Russians backing their Serbian co-religionists and Germany backing Austria who, for centuries, had been the bulwark between Europe and the Ottoman Empire.

The Imperial German staff had prepared for the eventuality of war on two fronts first by crushing Russia's ally France in the west, then dealing with Russia in the east. The plan did not work. The Schlieffen Plan to encircle Paris failed at the Battle of the Marne and the trench warfare that followed created a stalemate which destroyed millions of men. With troops held up in the west, the German High Command could not defeat Russia and faced a two-front war.

The United States became a world power during the First World War. Although reluctant to become a belligerent, American industry was happy to supply arms to the allies in their own ships but American lives were lost when these vessels were torpedoed and sunk by U-boats. Ultimately, the US declared war on 6 April 1917 and an expeditionary force was sent to France. Although relatively few in number, this injection of fresh troops into the front line proved a tonic during the critical days of the German offensive of March 1918; they encouraged the Allies and dismayed the Germans.

The resulting peace treated countries differently. For the defeated Germans and Austrians peace was a disaster; both countries lost their possessions, suffered raging inflation, civil disorder and a collapsing currency – in Germany this led directly to the rise of the National Socialism under Adolf Hitler. Both France and Britain had suffered terribly during the war but France recovered more quickly and, through a devaluation in 1928, boomed for a time while most other countries suffered the 1930s Depression.

The US assumed world leadership from Britain in what must be one of the most effortless transfers of power ever. While Britain mistakenly returned to the gold standard in 1926 and experienced the General Strike, America boomed and the dollar replaced the pound as the world's leading gold-backed currency.

The transformation during this warm period was unlike any other described in this chapter. True, the war encouraged innovations such as the car, tracked vehicles and aircraft, but the real benefit was the emancipation of women and the introduction of another world power quite separate from the squabbling Europeans. It is a tragedy that the peace was not to last in the next hot-dry period, which saw the rise of the aggressive dictators Mussolini, Hitler, Stalin and Togo.

CHAPTER 8

THE 100-YEAR CYCLE OF WEATHER AND NATIONS

It seems almost too neat to have a temperature and rainfall cycle lasting 100 years but this has been identified not only by Raymond Wheeler, whose work has been described earlier, but also by a more modern researcher, George Modelski. Modelski, in particular, has related a 100-year rhythm to the rise and fall of dominant world powers since 1500 and the discernible features of any new empire that might emerge in the next century.

Wheeler brings together cycles of 100, 180 and 500 years

The 500- and 180-year cycles described in earlier chapters were brought into sharper focus by Professor Raymond Wheeler when describing his basic 100-year rhythm. All these coincide in Wheeler's famous 'Drought Clock' which rather neatly brings together the themes of this and the two previous chapters in Figure 15.

The clock starts at the cataclysmic period around the sack of Rome in 410, then traces three cycles: one of 510 years, one of 170 years and the shortest of 100 years; the first two are slightly different lengths from those described elsewhere in his work but the basis is similar. Starting at AD 410, three cycles of 510 years brings

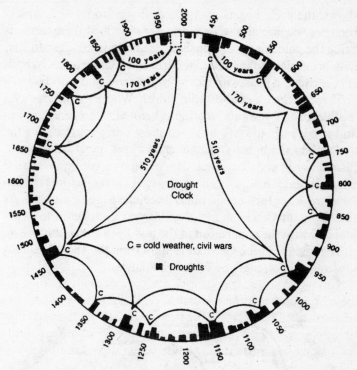

Figure 15. Dr Raymond Wheeler's 'Drought Clock' combining three cycles of around 100,180 and 500 years. (Courtesy of the Foundation for the Study of Cycles.)

us to 1980, nine rhythms of 170 years also ends up at 1980. Finally, the last 100-year cycle ends in 1975. As these predictions were made in 1950 it is remarkable that these differ by only 2% over a span of 1500 years compared to more recent measurements.

Wheeler's 100-year cycle of temperature and rainfall

The basic 100-year cycle is similar in form to that described earlier in Chapter 6, but instead of two wet cycles superimposed on a single temperature, the two move in unison. As the next chart shows, the cycle begins with a cool-dry period which rapidly becomes warmer and wetter; Wheeler described these times as being the golden ages of Renaissance and industrial expansion, with benevolent rulers and high birth rates. Unfortunately, both curves rise to a peak with federal movements and world wars.

There is then a cold-dry dip, which Wheeler describes as a 'saddle' of civil wars and rebellions before the temperature rises and it becomes drier. This is the most dangerous part of the cycle when the hot-dry climate encourages dictators, communism, fascism and decadence. There follows a cool-rainy period which Wheeler believed encourages civil unrest, before the temperature drops further and rainfall declines as the cycle ends. As the 'Drought Clock' shows, the 100-year cycle tends to begin and end with the cool period in the middle of the century.

The history of the German Empire from the 1848 rebellions illustrates the strength of Wheeler's analysis.

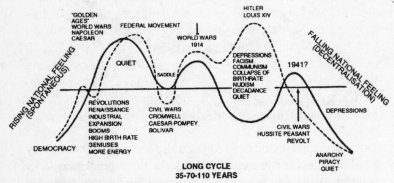

Figure 16. Raymond Wheeler's longer term climatic cycle showing the typical events that occur at each phase. (Courtesy of the Foundation for the Study of Cycles.)

Increasing warmth and rainfall
Germany industrialised after Britain but instead of using foreign firms to erect plants, the country employed the intrinsic skills of the *Handwerk* or craft guilds, using British blueprints. Krupp of Essen discovered iron ore and coal in the Ruhr, where he built a formidable iron and steel industry. Prussia was the leader of a

loose federation governed by Prince Otto von Bismarck, the diplomat and statesman who was to become the architect of a united Germany.

First warmth and rainfall peak

In a series of brilliant diplomatic and military moves Bismarck defeated Austria, Denmark, then France in the 1870 Franco-Prussian War which united Germany, and separated Alsace and Lorraine from France. The same drive also encouraged overseas expansion into German East Africa and Shantung in China. During a cold spell, the chancellor was in conflict with the Catholic Church and there was a dispute with Kaiser Wilhelm II which led to Bismarck's dismissal in 1890. The caption of the famous *Punch* cartoon likens the event to a ship 'dropping the pilot'.

Second warmth and rainfall peak

Without the constraints of Bismarck, Wilhelm II was now able to indulge his imperial ambitions of rebuilding the army and challenging Britain at sea. Through an unwise alliance with Austria and Turkey he precipitated the First World War in which eight million combatants died and in which conditions were created in Russia that triggered the Russian Revolution. The war also created a vacuum in Europe which encouraged dictators like Mussolini and Hitler, while Stalin imposed himself on Russia.

Warm-dry peak

The despotic Axis powers, primarily Germany and Japan, terrified the world during the Second World War with a series of devastating victories which created new empires in only a couple of years. They had bargained without the strength of the US, Britain and its allies which deployed huge forces that not only destroyed the Axis homelands but liberated the millions who had been enslaved.

Cool-dry trough

The war left the vanquished destitute and swept aside the old regimes, leaving the survivors to create new democratic systems.

More evidence for a 100-year cycle

Quite independently of Raymond Wheeler, George Modelski, Professor of Political Science at the University of Washington, has proposed a 100-year cycle of the rise and fall of dominant nation states which corresponds quite well to the cold periods identified by Wheeler several decades earlier. Modelski has identified five long cycles where four nations in turn have dominated and influenced others in providing a continuum from 1500 to the present day. These are Portugal, Holland, Britain and the United States; their history over the last 500 years has been described earlier but Modelski throws a new light on our understanding of the events.

Portugal from 1450 to 1550

As we saw earlier the turning point for Portugal was when John, the grand master of Avis, beat the Castilians at the Battle of Aljubarrota in 1385 just when the climate was turning cool. As with each of the four examples, a successful battle of liberation gives that country a new dynamism. This time it was in overseas expansion during the warm 1400s through John and Philippa's third son, Henry the Navigator. By a stroke of genius, he brought together the greatest seafaring specialists of the age to equip a series of expeditions that propelled Portuguese interests around the world.

Madeira was first, developed as a sugar producer. The next settlement was the Gold Coast on the west of Africa which not only provided slaves for the sugar plantations but gold to finance further expansion. After the death of Prince Henry, the king's successor sponsored Bartholomeu Diaz to sail round the Cape of Good Hope and reach the East African coast where he set up fortified trading posts.

Portugal also advanced west after Columbus reached the Caribbean, leading to the treaty of Tordesillas when the pope, with breath-taking effrontery, apportioned the new discoveries between Spain and Portugal. This gave Portugal the present-day Brazil and the right to explore Africa and the seaway to India. Later, another Portuguese, Vasco da Gama opened the

Cape route to India discovering Natal and crossing the Indian Ocean to form a trading base at Calicut.

Da Gama was followed by another formidable explorer in Alfonso de Albuquerque. Known as the father of naval strategy, as Viceroy of the Portuguese he conquered Goa and Ceylon, continuing east to form trading posts at Malacca and Ormuz. The Portuguese were also the first to set up a trading post in Macao in China, and in Japan.

Portuguese seafaring domination was not to last and territorial ambitions were finally ended in a misconceived venture against the Moors in Morocco, at the Battle of the Three Kings at Alcazarquivir in 1578. When the King of Portugal died without heir, the throne was seized in 1580 by Philip II of Spain who brought with him Spanish possessions in the Netherlands, the Americas and in Italy.

Modelski identifies Portugal as the first of the modern European states. After removing the Moors and achieving freedom from Spain, she set up a trading empire through sea power using talented seamen and explorers. The country, like Holland, was never destined to be a great manufacturing nation but in their time the Portuguese were unsurpassed in vigour, innovation and in pioneering modern overseas trade. In a very few years, this small country spread its prestige throughout the East, a model for the Dutch and English who were to follow.

Holland from 1550 to 1650

If Philip II of Spain was to end Portuguese domination he was the unwilling instrument in the creation of the next nation to dominate the seas. As with all possessions, Spain's ambition in Holland was to tax the available wealth and root out heretics through the Inquisition. This was too much for the recently converted Protestants who, as we saw in an earlier chapter, rebelled and eventually gained their independence from the Catholic south only nine years before the Armada sailed in 1588.

During the Spanish occupation, the Dutch had set up a guerrilla force at Flushing to harry Spanish shipping; the local force was deadly in its own low terrain – the dykes, rivers and marshes known to them but not to the Spaniards. Fortunately, the Dutch also had the opportunity to start a vigorous trade in the Baltic. When eventually the northern provinces became independent Holland celebrated with a golden age of art and architecture, and an expansion in commerce. Following the Portuguese lead, Dutch seafarers created an overseas empire stretching from the Cape of Good Hope through to Java and Sumatra where the East Indies Company became the greatest trading organisation ever known. The Dutch almost totally eclipsed the Portuguese who were left only with trading posts in Goa and Macao.

Dutch power started to decline when fighting the English for control of the eastern trade routes. In three Anglo-Dutch wars lasting twenty-five years from 1652, the Dutch were taking on a nation that had beaten the Spanish Armada and had developed considerable military skills during the Civil War. Although the Dutch admirals, the two Tromps and de Ruyter, were fine seamen, they did not have the same skill in gunnery and handling large formations in line ahead as did the English admiral, Monck, de Ruyter, in particular, conducted daring and successful raids up the Thames and Medway. The wars ended with the Treaty of Breda which acknowledged the English capture of New Amsterdam (renamed New York). A further blow to Dutch overseas expansion were the wars with France which, although allied to Britain, sapped Holland's strength as a great power.

Britain – Phase I from 1650 to 1760

Although not acknowledged at the time, Britain should also thank Philip II for her launch as a sea power; it was Philip's claim to the English throne after the death of his wife, Queen Mary, that precipitated the Armada. As described earlier, England had learned the art of ship-borne gunnery which gave English vessels an advantage over the Spanish and Dutch, who relied on boarding to quell another ship. Fighting the Armada had produced a set of battle instructions which were a distinct advantage, as signalling during a mêlée was almost impossible.

Although the Dutch wars had given Britain supremacy at sea, the enemy was now the France of Louis XIV – a formidable foe with a population of nineteen million, nearly three times that of Britain. The French king assumed direct rule working through able ministers such as Colbert and Louvois. Within a few years France's finances were strong enough to emulate the Portuguese and Dutch through an aggressive foreign policy.

In an effort to prevent further Spanish advances north of the Pyrenees, France first attacked the Netherlands but was frustrated by an alliance between Holland, England and Sweden. After persuading Charles II of England not to intervene, Louis invaded again, which was too much for the Dutch; after taking several cities Louis was stopped at Amsterdam by William of Orange, who cut the dykes and flooded the countryside. By now, alarmed by French aggression, William created alliances with the Protestant states in Germany and Emperor Leopold of Austria.

The French continued fighting on land but this time the conflict was over the successor to the Spanish throne. Charles of Spain, the last of the Habsburgs, was childless, the crown being contested between Louis XIV for his grandson and Leopold of Austria for his son. The War of Spanish Succession was fought by Prince Eugene of Austria with the Duke of Marlborough for the Grand Alliance opposing the combined forces of France and Bavaria. The action spread from the Netherlands, through France, Spain, Germany, Italy to Austria where one of the greatest battles was fought beside the Danube at Blenheim. The Treaty of Utrecht in 1713 concluded the war, ending French domination until Napoleon.

Modelski suggests the British first phase ended in 1760, consolidating a trading empire that benefited from the Treaty of Utrecht and from contesting Portuguese and Dutch possessions. The wars with France had spread to India where Robert Clive's generalship at Plassey in south-east India effectively left Britain's claim on the Sub-Continent uncontested.

British domination as a trading empire could have ended here, as it had done with the Dutch and Portuguese, but the island was changing from being primarily a trader to a manufacturing power house based on the mass production of iron and cotton driven by steam engines.

Britain – Phase II from 1760 to 1860

The American colonies gained their independence during this next phase, a loss that might have severely damaged any other nation. But in the same year, 1776, James Watt invented the steam engine and Adam Smith wrote *The Wealth of Nations*. In an astonishing blossoming of enterprise, Britain was able to set up power-driven machines that could weave fine muslin more competitively than the hand looms in India.

There were also innovations in sea warfare. Naval guns could now be trained round on their trolleys so it was not essential for a ship to be parallel to the enemy; in addition, the time to fire could be judged more accurately by a flintlock that fired a spark directly into the touch-hole charge. Commanding ships of the line had also become more flexible with a code of flag signals and the more innovative admirals like Nelson had perfected techniques of dividing the opponent's line, thus causing confusion among the enemy where superior gunnery would count.

The combination of a weak king and an empty treasure chest from helping the American colonists gain independence from Britain triggered the next major contest with France in the Napoleonic wars that followed the French Revolution. It is said that Bonaparte was never a great technical innovator but his ability to handle armies rapidly overwhelmed first the Italians, then the Austrians, Prussians, Spanish and Russians to create a Continental empire in an astonishingly short time.

Napoleon had never studied sea power, not realising that a quite different technique was necessary to manoeuvre and fight ships. The Royal Navy did not help him by keeping a year-round blockade of the French harbours which disallowed the opposing fleet going to sea except on rare occasions. It was a French attempt to lure the British fleet away from the Channel to allow an invasion that gave Nelson his great chance. Catching the French and Spanish fleets off Cape Trafalgar, Nelson's two columns penetrated the enemy's line destroying much of the combined force and any further chance of an invasion.

British ascendency was ensured after Napoleon's defeat at Waterloo in 1815 for at least the next seventy-five years, although

Modelski argues that it ended about the time of the American Civil War in the 1860s. Certainly Britain retained supremacy at sea with the introduction of the dreadnaught battleship in 1906 and Europe provided many of the inventions which shaped the early 20th century, such as chemical derivatives from coal, the diesel engine, radio telegraphy, the motor car and tyre.

Whatever the date of Britain's decline, it bequeathed a uniform trading, legal and banking system in many parts of the free world which, coupled with the English language, enabled the post-Second World War recovery to proceed as smoothly as it did. As the pound sterling was replaced as the reserve currency by the dollar, the free world also gained a new protector.

The United States of America from 1870 to 1980

As suggested earlier, Modelski may not be correct in starting the US hegemony from 1870 although both he and Wheeler would agree that the century began and ended with a cool period. Certainly, by the end of the Civil War, US manufacturing industry was growing fast with a considerable degree of sophistication, particularly in arms and railroads. At about that time, Samuel Morse had invented the electro-magnetic telegraph, Graham Bell the telephone, Thomas Edison the electric bulb and Henry Ford was to build his first car. In the early 1900s Orville and Wilbur Wright built and flew the first powered aircraft at Kitty Hawk, North Carolina, on 17 December 1903.

During the First World War, the US assumed world financial and then technical leadership when Britain first went off the gold standard in 1914. Although the American Expeditionary Force (AEF) was armed with mainly British and French weapons (for example, Captain Harry Truman of Battery D fought with French 75mm field guns), US industry was tooling up techniques using the ideas of F.W. Taylor, the American high priest of work study and mass production. During the 1920s large-scale manufacturing brought cars, kitchen appliances and homes within the price range of working people.

However, during the Second World War, American industry and banking led the West with the US at one time producing

50% of the free world's output. With a huge internal market, the US dominated aircraft and electronic design and production, and assumed world leadership in the design and competence of arms manufacture. By the mid-1990s America still retains world leadership but its percentage of output has declined as Japanese production techniques are being applied to low-cost countries, putting considerable pressure on American and European manufacturers.

Modelski may be right in suggesting that the US era is coming to an end but there appears no alternative in the looming Asian and European chaos of the 1990s. In the conclusion of his book, *Explaining Long-Term Cycles*, Modelski suggests that following the end of the American cycle, the world should be shaping up for another war which will launch the next world leader. He believes that the continuum from Portugal through to Holland, Britain and the US will make it necessary for the next leader to be a maritime power, just like its predecessors.

Modelski's criterion for the next leader

In *Explaining Long-Term Cycles*, Modelski lists four important factors: 1. A secure geographical location; 2. A cohesive, open society; 3. A sound, preferably leading economy; 4. A well thought-out global plan.

Secure location

All four examples come within this category, although Portugal and Holland were invaded several times before expanding; in both cases, it was vigour following liberation that created the drive. There are other examples: the Nile valley could only be approached from the north giving most of the ancient Egyptians a high degree of security. Vigorous islands are secure which explains much of Britain's history and perhaps that of Japan also. Each of the examples were, or became, a maritime power.

Open society

There should be a stable, open society with good communications and a middle class which has the opportunity of expressing itself and becoming prosperous. Modelski cites Portugal and Holland after removing the Spanish. His other examples are England at the time of the Armada, the Puritan revolution in the mid-17th century, creating capitalism in England, and the thirteen colonies in the US at the time of becoming independent. The countries should also accept refugees. It is likely that Portugal accepted refugees from the Spanish Inquisition (as they did during the Spanish Civil War) and Holland was glad to accept migrants from Spanish-occupied territory. England benefited from Jews fleeing the Inquisition, the Huguenots from France, weavers from the Low Countries and Jews from Nazi Germany. The US gained talented people first from Europe, then from Asia.

Sound economy

A country should be sufficiently well endowed to pay for expansion or defence – something common to all the four nations. Although Portugal, Holland and England during Phase I were not strong economies in their own right, their prosperity came from trading the products of their overseas territories. Britain during Phase II became industrialised, which gave it the second wind to fight and win another major war and continue its strong position after Waterloo. America was emerging as a sound economy when it assumed world leadership in the latter part of the 19th century.

Global reach

This is what Modelski defines as the naval clout to secure and hold an overseas trading group. The Portuguese had it when they devised a system of fortified trading stations and the naval strategy to secure the trade routes, an arrangement the Dutch copied and expanded. Britain learnt her naval gunnery and tactics the hard way, having to defend the island first after the Reformation and then against the Armada; these skills became particularly useful when following the Dutch to create an overseas empire. This lead was consolidated by the Industrial Revolution which gave Britain the capacity to be a leading player in the defeat of Napoleon, then to benefit from absorbing the ex-French colonies. The Americans established unquestioned naval superiority after their defeat at Pearl Harbor when they were able to crush the Japanese with overwhelming power.

Why these countries and not other nations?

None of these countries at the time of their victory and hegemony was among the most powerful countries but Modelski argues that others are ruled out by one of the four factors.

Spain made a bid for global leadership and created impressive overseas conquests but the country lost many of its best people through intolerance and internal division; it was also open to invasion across the Pyrenees.

France, another powerful nation, could not absorb their dissenting Huguenots and seldom found the vigour for expansion, except through dictators like Louis XIV and Napoleon; like Spain it was open to invasion.

Germany could have been a prime example for leadership with a powerful and industrious people, but it was a battlefield for much of its history; and even when the Germans did achieve economic and military power they found adversaries who were, in the end, more powerful.

Russia might have had the capacity for global domination but it was never an open or free society; the country was also open to invasion – although all aggressors failed, except the Mongols. Neither the tsars nor Soviets were able to create a strong enough home base for overseas expansion and their huge country, like China, has been exceptionally difficult to keep together for any length of time.

China also has the capacity for being a global power but the country's history has shown how difficult it is to control people in so vast a land mass.

CHAPTER 9

IS THERE ANYTHING IN THE KONDRATIEFF CYCLE?

It was a requirement amongst the ancient Jewish people that every fifty years the Chief Rabbi blew on a ram's horn to signal a jubilee. Although Leviticus Chapter XXV describes this as being a holy year, when fields were left fallow, the grapes unharvested and all returned to their home, it also had a very important commercial function. A jubilee was the signal for debts to be forgiven, those sold into bondage released and prices to be adjusted according to the number of good or poor harvests. In short it was a year for unwinding the pent-up debt, misunderstandings or sharp practices that had built up over the previous fifty years. *Would that we had the same today.*

Instead, in our sophisticated world of instant communications, politicians and central bankers have the means to manipulate currencies and markets; this implies we have no means, short of bankruptcy or a currency collapse, to unwind all the built-up tensions of earlier years. Yet we have due warning that a latter-day version of the jubilee is powerfully at work. As we shall see, it is part climatic and part man-made.

The first to spot a cycle of between forty-five and sixty years was a little-known Dutch Marxist called Van Gelderen, who noted in 1913 a long wave of around fifty–sixty years; in particular he noted that production, prices and economic activity increased from 1850 to 1873, then declined to a low point in the 1890s. Whether the Russian economist Nicolai Kondratieff, who worked at the Agricultural Academy and the Business Research Institute in Moscow during the 1920s, was influenced by Van Gelderen is not known.

Kondratieff was given the job of analysing capitalist economies – no doubt to prove their inevitable decay, according to communist dogma. The results first published outside Russia as '*Die langen Wellen der Konjunktur*' – or, as they appeared in English, as 'The Long Waves in Economic Life' – astonished Kondratieff. Instead of forecasting failure, he predicted that although capitalism would suffer a decline in the 1930s, it would recover once again in yet another cycle. This was most unwelcome news to his Bolshevik bosses, who condemned him to a solitary death in Siberia.

The analysis of cycles was not new for Van Gelderen or Kondratieff. Clement Juglar, a French economist in the 1860s, worked with commodity prices and interest rates to suggest an eight–eleven-year cycle described in a later chapter. Seventy years later, Kondratieff had available much more data, including wholesale prices and interest rates in England and France from 1789, English agricultural and cotton manufacturing wages, and French trade; he also analysed the production and consumption of coal, pig iron and lead. From this, Kondratieff calculated three waves which each had two components: an upswing with rising prosperity amidst some periods of recession, followed by a downwave with generally declining economic activity.

The first started in 1789, called K1, rose to a peak in 1814, then declined to a low point in 1849. K2, the second, started in 1849, reached a high in 1873, then took a fall to 1896. K3 started in 1896, reaching a peak in 1920 – Kondratieff was removed before he could complete the cycle which probably had its low point between 1937 and 1939.

K1, the upwave from 1789 to 1814
The first K-wave did not start well either in Europe or the newly formed United States. In France, the combination of a bankrupt

national treasury, an ineffectual ruling house and bread riots in the streets of Paris exploded in a revolution causing much bloodshed and the break-up of the *ancien régime* of Louis XIV and his successors. Rulers then, as now, failed to learn from history; if anyone on the king's council had read the history of the English Civil War the outcome might have been very different. But history is seldom a strong point with rulers and the tsar never learned from the mistakes of Louis XVI, or indeed of Charles I; both perished in the resulting conflagration.

Probably the most serious event for France was the collapse of the currency. Bread prices had rocketed through a series of crop failures in the 1780s so that by 1789, the poorest were spending 80% of their income on food. In an effort to relieve some of the pressure, a paper currency called the '*Assignat*' was issued, unbacked by any collateral. Initially the notes were printed to pay for Church lands bought by the state but soon these came into general use and rapidly lost their value. Unfortunately, the National Assembly had other obligations, so the printing presses were kept working and by 1797 the *Assignat* was worthless; not for the first time, politicians had defrauded people relying on their government's integrity.

As night follows day, a collapsing currency leads to a dictatorship. Fearing for their future, the Directorate elected a resourceful Corsican general called Napoleon Bonaparte, who rapidly became the premier consul and then emperor. In what otherwise should have been an upswing in the economy for the benefit of the nation as a whole, most of the industrial output was switched to war production not only in France but in many other European countries as well. Only in Britain did the pace of industrial output quicken, particularly in cotton production and improved communication through digging canals.

Meanwhile across the Atlantic the new republic, whose war for independence had bankrupted France, itself nearly became insolvent. The general euphoria after Cornwallis' defeat at Yorktown released a pent-up demand for European merchandise, and easy bank credit encouraged speculators. As always this led to raging inflation and as people became more cautious, the momentum lost steam, speculators became bankrupt, banks failed, and the government's revenue fell dramatically. Fearful of the future, holders of cash and gold transferred their investments elsewhere.

The Americans handled the problem much better than the French. At around the time when George Washington was elected president, the government passed a debt moratorium, the old Articles of Confederation were replaced by the Constitution and the newly formed First Bank of the United States issued a new currency backed by gold. There was a justified rebellion by the farmers over tax obligations; but these were duly forgiven when the government realised they were guilty of an injustice.

The United States experienced a typical upwave; the country was at peace, crops were plentiful, interest rates were low and inflation remain subdued. Europe was at war and for the first time American exports were shipped to the combatants with gold flowing back into the country. The country also attracted immigrants, with the Ohio valley and Great Lakes areas gaining settlers in unprecedented numbers. Between 1800 and 1805, the population of Cincinnati and Chicago rose by over 25% and land speculation was becoming a danger. The expanded demand forced the price of cotton to rise 60% in the four years to 1818 and the price of slaves doubled.

The year 1812 was a watermark for America and Europe. Blockading British warships had disallowed US cargo ships from entering Continental ports, and the price of grain rose – as did shipping and insurance rates. Investment in agriculture increased in Britain, with the first general use of fertiliser, as did the rapid growth of railways. In France, Bonaparte's loss of a third of the Grande Armée in the Russian campaign was the beginning of his decline.

The year 1812 was not a good time for relations between Britain and America. That year's war, fought at sea and in the northern states and Canada, ruined American finances when banks were able to issue paper notes without gold backing, prices exploded, and there was wild speculation in dubious ventures and real estate. The bubble burst and unfortunately some of the loans raised by the US government were not repaid.

K1, the downwave from 1814 to 1849

While an upwave has several setbacks during a rising trend of prosperity, a downwave has the reverse, there are spurts of activity during a downward trend. As we saw in Chapter 7, this downturn coincided with a particularly cool period which saw considerable social unrest, particularly in Latin America where many countries gained their independence. In Europe, the Congress of Vienna had settled the boundaries of a number of countries, including the Netherlands which lost the states that are now Belgium. It was an uneasy relationship and a revolt by the largely French-speaking southern states led to the independence of Belgium in 1839. There was also a revolution in France at about the time when the autocratic Charles X was disposed in favour of his cousin Louis-Philippe. The end of the downwave was punctuated by a series of revolutions in France, Germany and Austria.

Britain did not escape the unrest despite a steady rise in output of 3.5% annually from 1815 to 1840 during a mania of railway building. The political dispute arose from the uneven distribution of parliamentary seats, some of the older constituencies, called 'rotten boroughs', having two members representing a few hundred persons while some of the new industrial towns were unrepresented. Amidst considerable unrest politicians, mindful of rebellions in France and Belgium, passed the 1832 Reform Act, the first of a number to create a wider and fairer franchise.

The downwave was not a happy time either for America. The previous boom had left many states and individuals heavily indebted with no means of repaying their obligations. After Michigan reneged on its debts, President Andrew Jackson took on some state liabilities with the result that a few creditors were forced to accept only a few cents for their dollar loans. Most foreign loans to the US were repudiated and the prices of railroad stocks dropped 80% by 1843 – there being no market for US stocks. Conditions were made worse by excessive rains in 1844 spoiling many of the crops in the Mississippi basin and causing food riots in several parts of the country.

K2, the upswing from 1849 to 1873

The boom passed from Britain to Germany and the United States in the K2 upwave. As described in an earlier chapter, Germany had already started to industrialise in the middle of the 19th century, using its extensive guild system to make the best use of British and other inventions. One of the most important of these was steel making; another was the manufacture of sulphuric acid using a lead-chamber process which was invented the same year as the blast furnace but did not come on line until much later.

Perhaps the most important event for Europe was the unification of Germany in 1870, when Bismarck made a dazzling series of treaties and acts of war, which ended with the fall of Paris. The creation of the most powerful state in Europe added impetus to the Industrial Revolution and lead indirectly to the First World War.

The 1846 war with Mexico ceded huge areas of additional territory to the United States, including the states of Texas, New Mexico, Arizona and California. Two years later there was an additional bonus of the first gold strike giving the US an extra tranche of credit and foreign-currency reserves. In a financially conservative regime of low interest rates, a booming economy and a gold-backed currency, industry and agriculture blossomed, helped by railways extended to the Mid-West and then to the coast. Apart from the domestic market, grain farmers found useful additional overseas markets once Britain repealed the Corn Laws (restricting the import of grain to keep up prices for British growers). Another group to benefit were the cotton growers who, with the invention of the gin, were able to grow, process and bale cotton for shipment to Britain.

Expanding US internal and foreign markets demanded extensive communications which were partly answered by river and canal traffic but also through building railways. They also initiated their own inventions. Goodyear was the first to produce commercial vulcanised rubber, the rotary printing press came out in 1846 and the Singer Sewing Machine Co went into production in 1851. The federal government was becoming more active, state colleges and universities were introduced through the Morrill Act of 1862 and the Homestead Act gave free land to western immigrants. Public works were also undertaken to build harbours, lighthouses, wharves and canals.

The four-year civil war from 1860 ended the boom for the South and initiated a huge industrialisation programme for the North. However, wars are expensive and over $450 million of new notes were issued without gold backing; in the latter two years of the war the price of most commodities almost tripled. The end of the upswing saw a collapse in land prices, many war-related activities became insolvent and easy credit disappeared as banks called in loans. Interest rates rose to 10% for three months in Britain in response to America's inflation.

K2, the downwave from 1873 to 1896

As often happens, concessions given easily in boom years become problems in a recession. This time American farmers, industrialists and labour unions won congressional approval for tariff protection. As raw material prices declined, so the clamour increased and by the end of the Civil War a prohibitive tariff of 47% was imposed but this did not stop the price of steel rails falling by 80% in the US. As in the 1930s many industrial nations retaliated and other countries in Africa and South America faced disaster. By the beginning of the downwave, international trade had reduced to a trickle and ocean freight rates halved.

Although this was to be one of the deepest recessions for years, it did not stop innovations on either side of the Atlantic. Graham Bell came out with the telephone in 1877, Thomas Edison the lamp bulb three years later, and Clarke Chapman of Britain produced the first commercial turbine in 1884. By 1896, Americans and Europeans were producing such inventions as electric power, electric railways, the four-stroke engine, bicycles, motor cars, portable cameras, the pneumatic tyre, motion pictures and the diesel engine. New agricultural lands were being opened up in Canada, Australia and Russia. Argentina benefited from the American demand for grain in the 1890s when the US suffered a succession of dry years (see below). Output increased as pampas were cleared and fenced, and immigrants were attracted into the country.

This depression upset the civil peace in many countries. In the USA the collapse of commodity prices, loan defaults and the insolvency of railways and other firms caused strikes and marches in Chicago and Pittsburgh. Andrew Carnegie and others who could see what was coming sold all their peripheral business and remained solvent; as the debt default reached a climax of 50%, unemployment rocketed. In Europe, maritime rivalries over African colonies between Britain, Germany and France caused an arms race and the rising power of Germany caused nations to consider protective alliances, such as the pact between France and Russia. None of this increased confidence, and there were falls on the Vienna and London Stock Markets which closed the Austrian *bourse* for several years.

It was to be the longest-rolling recession anyone could remember. No one was prepared to lend money and none was required; such was the deflation that British Consols (consolidated annuities – irredeemably fixed-interest British Government stock) rose to 114, only six points short from the level in the 1930s Great Depression. It was also one of the first times the Bank of England intervened to save a failing bank. Barings, a highly respected City firm, had loaned heavily to Argentina at the height of the boom but in the appalling conditions of collapsing commodity prices interest payments were suspended and the bank could have been forced to close with incalculable repercussions. Barings was only saved by the Bank guaranteeing certain deposits which gave others the confidence not to remove their own loans.

However, help was at hand. Gold was discovered in the South African Rand, in south-east Australia and in the American Klondike to inject much-needed credit into the world's financial system and by 1896 the worst was over.

K3, the upwave from 1896 to 1920

As George Modelski pointed out, the 20th century belonged to America, with its tremendous expansion of power, wealth and might. It was a time for all the inventions that were perfected during the downwave of K2 to come into production on both sides of the Atlantic, supplemented by others such as the first powered flight at Kitty Hawk on 17 December 1903. Three years later at Portsmouth in England, the Dreadnought, which made all previous designs obsolete, was launched; it was powered by steam turbines, the guns could be controlled centrally and its armour was superior to any ship afloat. The new warship could, similarly, deliver twice the weight of shells in a broadside to any competitor.

While ominous tensions were increasing in Europe, the United States under President Theodore Roosevelt was forging a new overseas presence. As Assistant Secretary to the Navy in 1898, he had commanded a volunteer force of 'Rough Riders' to expel the Spanish from Cuba and the same Spanish American War ceded the Philippines to the USA. President McKinley was assassinated in 1901, to be succeeded by Roosevelt who conducted a vigorous foreign policy in South America and took over the cutting of the Panama Canal from a collapsed French company.

The presidential vigour encouraged a surging pride in the US, a nation confident that anything could be achieved with enough energy and determination. It was a wonderful start to the century. Food was plentiful and cheap, a new generation of entrepreneurs took over from those made insolvent by the last recession, taxes were negligible, credit was available and the unions quiescent. As confidence increased, the government continued its public works with road and harbour building, and encouraged communications with the opening West. These were heady days and the Americans took every advantage of them.

The First World War was almost the inevitable result of inter-European rivalry that swept up nearly every nation in a bloody four-year grind that exhausted the combatants; only the US benefited, first by supplying arms, then by armed intervention on the side of the Allies. As with the peak of K2 during the American Civil War, there was a raging inflation of commodities and foodstuffs in 1919–20 at the summit of K3 that was slowly to decline until the low point in the cycle near to 1939.

K3, the downwave from 1920 to 1939

The beginning of the downswing was marked by a year of high interest rates and collapsing bond prices as the authorities attempted to quell rocketing inflation. Not surprisingly, stock and bond markets collapsed, wiping out many wartime speculators. Luckily, it was not to last long, the 'Roaring Twenties' sparking off the biggest speculative boom ever, before the 1930s collapse.

Nobody had seen anything like the 1920s in America. Ordinary families dreamed of owning their own home, as easy credit allowed mortgage purchases; the mass-production techniques pioneered by Henry Ford and F. W. Taylor provided a dazzling range of products, including labour-saving devices such as electric washing machines, refrigerators for preserving food, family cars and radios for entertainment. The easy credit fostered Stock Market speculation where, to the delight of 'punters', more purchases could be made for the same investment by putting down only 10% of a buying order which could be easily paid back as the stocks climbed. The speculation spread to housing where in Florida a spiralling market allowed plots of land to change hands almost as fast as shares on the Stock Exchange.

The 1920s were very similar to the 1980s and the speculation could not last. As price inflation took hold, bond prices started to fall and credit became more difficult; almost overnight credit managers took over from salesmen, the Stock Market crashed and purchasing power boiled over. By mid-1930, the USA was starting the deepest depression the world had encountered; it also encouraged some of the most interesting public-works and job-creation programmes ever seen.

After the war European recovery was patchy, most countries being over-indebted and exhausted by the loss of life. Britain attempted to return to the gold standard at too high a parity and suffered a debilitating financial squeeze, which depressed wages and caused the 1926 General Strike. France, although still on a gold standard, devalued in 1928 and was able to find markets when other countries were entering the Depression. Germany's fate was the saddest. The nation had funded its world war largely on debt, which became so onerous that the government's only course seemed to be in money creation which it pursued with vigour. By 1924, the entire money stock was being doubled in a few weeks, inflation was rampant and the mark worthless. As with the collapse of the *Assignat* at the start of K1, inflation led to dictatorship.

K3 ended almost in despair for most democracies, except Britain, which had the least to lose from the 1920s excesses. A wise budget in 1931 had balanced government expenditure with income, and the low interest rates and stable currency attracted investment into the same mass-produced products that the US had on offer a decade earlier. The investment climate also stimulated a building boom, many houses being built in the distinctive Art Deco style. The free world was only driven out of depression by rearming against an aggressive Germany and Japan bent on launching the next world conflict.

K4, the upswing from 1939 to 1971
The Second World War left the United States the most powerful, productive, wealthy and militarily strong nation on earth with a currency supported by 60% of the world's gold reserves. Its only possible rival was the Soviet Union which had gained a huge armed presence after defeating Nazi Germany. The US was to provide the umbrella of the free world against Soviet expansion and, through the Marshall Plan, the credit needed for rebuilding not only its allies but also its enemies. Winston Churchill described this as the 'the most selfless act ever performed by a government'. Also, to avoid the debt problems that slowed recovery from the First World War, the US largely forgave $30 billion of loans the Allies had built up buying American war equipment through a series of lend-lease programmes.

Just as in former K cycles, the recovery was encouraged by easy credit and low debt which attracted entrepreneurs who first cleared the debris left by the conflict, then turned their hand to providing the consumer goods that few countries had been able to afford during the war. It was also decided that the dollar should be the yardstick of value now that few countries could afford a return to the gold standard. The Bretton Woods agreement set out various parities against the dollar, which itself was anchored to gold at $35 per Troy ounce.

Despite the amount of credit available, many countries had a slower rate of growth at the beginning of K4 than earlier in K3. The war had encouraged corporatism, and union power favoured a socialistic state authority which inhibited private enterprise, and increased central spending and debt rose. Fortunately, the US dollar was still the bedrock of financial conservatism, until John Kennedy was elected in 1960; in three years he radically increased the money supply of the central bank by 50% relative to the conservatism of the Truman and Eisenhower presidencies of the 1950s.

The ensuing boom in America coupled with tax cuts lasted until 1970; it sucked in imports, ran down the gold reserves, increased government debt and created deficits. The problem was worsened by two events both of which were within the control of the administration. The first was the Vietnam War, when arms expenditure, for the first time since the Second World War, rose above 10% of the gross national product. The second was President Johnson's 'Great Society', a welfare programme that added billions to national expenditure. Lyndon Johnson was succeeded by Richard Nixon who, after engineering a mild recession, opened the money spigots once more with the result that inflation rocketed.

By late 1967, governments were opting to hold gold at the convertible value of $35 per ounce rather than a dollar that declined against other currencies. These losses rapidly ran down the US gold reserves, forcing President Nixon to remove the right to convert in August 1971 which allowed the dollar to float freely against other currencies.

This was the peak of K4, replicating the same action in earlier cycles: Britain went off the gold standard during K1, the US printed 'greenbacks' during the Civil War at the height of K2, and Britain again left the gold standard after the upswing of K3. In all previous cases the reserve currency has always returned to the gold standard during the downswing – but it has not happened yet.

K4, the downswing from 1971 to 1997?

The western world was shocked by the price increase of the oil-producing countries in 1973. As the next chapter will show, the Kuznets' Cycle, which peaked in 1974, is primarily a climatic not a real-estate cycle, and the hike in crude prices was the direct result of higher food and commodity prices. In two years, the prices of a basket of twenty-one traded commodities more than doubled; the rise in inflation led to a collapse in the bond market; then, as governments were forced to increase interest rates, stock markets also plummeted.

The decline in real-estate and housing markets was the worst since the collapse of land speculation in the late 1920s in America; the rise in property prices had attracted many fringe banks which failed with the falling of collateral values. Weak political leadership on both sides of the Atlantic made the late 1970s a period best forgotten but all this changed with the emergence of two remarkable people. One was Margaret Thatcher, the first woman Prime Minister of Britain, and the other, Ronald Reagan, the President of America.

As in the early 1920s, the 1980s started with a massive price rise in oil and other commodities which increased by 50% over eighteen months to peak in 1980. Western governments took remedial action to stop inflation and very quickly were plunged into recession, the second in eight years. However, also as in the early 1920s, there was a swift recovery with easy credit stimulating consumer and capital expenditure which fed through to stock markets. Those who could remember the 'Roaring Twenties' were struck by similarities of the new entrepreneurs building financial empires using highly priced share values to acquire other more lowly rated companies. Many people thought this would continue forever – just as they did in the 1920s.

Of course, all students of previous cycles knew it had to end with rising inflation which forced an increase in interest rates in Britain and elsewhere. Those highly leveraged businesses which suffered a rapid decline in sales failed quickly, some spectacularly, just as they did in the early 1930s. Real-estate and housing prices fell steeply and many who had mortgaged themselves heavily became doubly squeezed from falling incomes and 'negative equity' from house prices that had declined faster than the ability of the householder to repay the mortgage. It did not help when economists described this as a 'credit vortex', a condition when asset prices fall faster than the collateral loans.

By early 1994 many countries in the European Union and elsewhere are in deep recession but no nation, except possibly New Zealand, has taken sensible remedial measures. Britain was one of the few countries that expanded in the 1930s, almost entirely due to the budget presented by Neville Chamberlain in 1931; as chancellor he had the courage and foresight to balance expenditure to income and so allowed the economy to recover without a crippling increase either in government borrowing or in taxation. The bottom of K4 should be in the latter part of the 1990s but whether this will end similarly to other cycles remains to be seen. Perhaps our politicians and bankers really have found the secret of emerging unscathed from suffocating debt and budget deficits – but it would be unwise to depend on it.

What is likely to happen and when

The timings and events described earlier can now be put into graphic form to show how the cycles have varied in length and what events could be expected at each phase.

Wars and rebellions: International wars are likely to happen at the cyclical peaks and rebellions at the troughs. This holds quite well with the Napoleonic, Franco-German, First World and Vietnam Wars at the peak, and the French Revolution, the 1848 rebellions and Boer Wars at the trough. The exception is

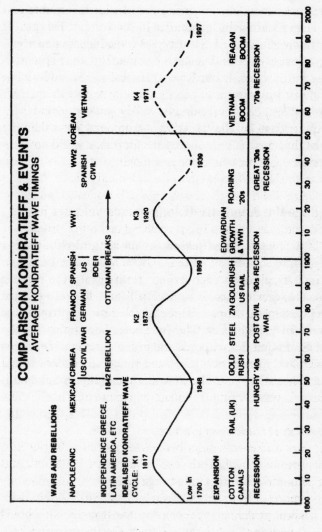

Figure 17. Kondratieff mean timings from 1789 to 1920 with estimate to the present.

the Second World War, which can be reasonably described as a continuation of the First World War.

Expansions and recessions: As might be expected there is a drive for investment in consumer goods during the upwave and longer term government spending in the downwave. This profile was certainly true of the US during K3 when spending on appliances, houses, cars and leisure boomed up to 1930, then collapsed; this was only partly compensated for by government spending in programmes such as the Public Works Administration (PWA) and the Tennessee Valley Authority (TVA) for hydroelectricity. In the 1990s, governments are so highly indebted that there is little spare cash for public works to compensate for declining consumer spending.

Why does the Kondratieff long-wave cycle work?

There is no one accepted reason for the long wave, although many eminent economists since the 1930s have suggested them. The Great Depression encouraged research into the reasons because few, except Nicolai Kondratieff himself, ever expected the Depression to happen. Three of the main arguments are rehearsed in this chapter: The first is the innovation theory argued by Joseph Schumpeter, the noted Austrian economist who migrated to America. The second is a suggestion by the economic historian W. W. Rostow that the timing is due to differences in consumer or infrastructure investment. Finally, there is an intriguing climatic theory proposed by Iben Browning, whose work was described in Chapters 2 and 3.

Schumpeter's innovation theory
Schumpeter proposed that long-range cycles were controlled by the emergence of innovators capable of taking business risks. When conditions were poor, only a few innovators could succeed during recessions and only the best would be attracted. However, when the economic climate eased and credit became more plentiful, this attracted what Schumpeter would call a

'swarm' of entrepreneurs; as we saw earlier, these were bunched at the beginning of K1 in Britain, K2 in Germany and K3 in the United States. In certain cases one innovation encouraged others; for example, the ability to roll steel rails had a beneficial effect on another industry like the railways – which would in turn stimulate other industrialists needing transport.

As we have seen each cycle starts with a recovery which inevitably turns into a boom and rising inflation. At some point the authorities are forced to raise interest rates, which dampens activity and discourages further risk takers. The decline then turns into a slump which does not end until all the bad credits have been removed from the system. Only then can the cycle bottom out and start once again.

The process of innovation

It is important to distinguish between an invention (or scientific discovery) and the later stage, when the theoretical design or experiment becomes a commercial product or process. There are three basic phases: the first is the experiment or idea that is shown to work in a laboratory or workshop; next, there is a development process when a small-scale version is made to test and smooth out mainly practical details. Finally, there is the commercial decision to produce for the market.

For example, Abraham Darby invented the blast furnace for making iron from coke instead of charcoal early in the 18th century; it then went through a period of development but the process did not come regularly into production until the Industrial Revolution some fifty years later when his grandson built the Iron Bridge at Coalbrookdale. Van Duijn, in his book *The Long Wave of Economic Life*, lists the time differences between invention and innovation of 160 significant inventions in the 19th and 20th centuries.

A sample shows it took seventy-nine years between the invention of the lead battery to its innovation by Plante in France; it took some forty years from the invention of the elevator before it was produced by Otis Elevator of America. The span between invention and innovation becomes shorter as competition compresses the time scale, forcing greater commitment. From the 1950s onward, the time between invention and innovation is an average of twenty-three years, considerably skewed by the seventy-three years it took to produce the fuel cell.

Schumpeter believed that innovations did not just apply to products but to other changes. These could be new production methods, such as Darby's substitution of coke for charcoal or the availability of a new market – the opening market for US goods in Mexico after signing the North American Free Trade Area (NAFTA) in November 1993 could be one example. It could also be a new source of raw materials, such as a gold or silver strike, or a new production organisation, as with F. W. Taylor's ideas of mass production taken up by Henry Ford.

Other researchers have difficulty with Schumpeter's ideas, arguing with some force, for example, that the invention of the railways was unlikely to have encouraged the production of a drug such as quinine, an antidote to malaria. An economist, G. Mensch, proposed a way out of Schumpeter's 'swarming' difficulty by proposing that recessions made the production of older products so unprofitable that innovation was essential to solvency.

One interesting example was General Motor's response to the Great Depression. In the classic book, *My Years in General Motors*, by Alfred P. Sloan, the author describes the growth of the Chevrolet marque at the expense of dearer models and how necessary it was to give customers choice at the lowest end of the market. GM also scored a coup by buying a diesel-engine and locomotive manufacturer at rock-bottom prices, then bringing out a new range of diesel electric-powered engines which were cheaper and more economic to run than those driven by steam.

The long-wave investment cycle
A further explanation could be the timing of investments: it is normal for there to be an investment cycle of around fifty years for long-term projects, such as power generation, and a much shorter product cycle of nearer ten years for consumer goods.

The Kondratieff Cycle had mainly been argued over by economists and statisticians until the early 1990s. Then, George

Modelski, whose 100-year cycles were described earlier, suggested that the Portuguese, Dutch, British and American eras could be bound up with long-term developments over their century domination. Each of the 100 years is divided into two Kondratieff Cycles. For example:

The Portuguese first fifty-year investment was in Madeira, followed by only a small overlap with a further fifty years in Asian shipping.

The Dutch first fifty-year investment was in Baltic shipping, the next in Asian exploration and trading .

The British first-century development was concerned with trading to the Americas and Asia.

The next British century saw two K waves: the first was up to the peak of K1, with investment in coal, iron, steam and cotton production transported through an infrastructure of canals and new ports. The investment turned to railways and associated engineering in the latter half of K1 to the early part of K2.

The American 100-year cycle is divided first into the fifty years when railroads were built to transport the rapid investment in crops and cotton growing. The next wave was after the First World War with huge investment in car production and the road system to carry them; during the 1930s there was also massive public investment in docks, harbours and hydro-electric programmes. The investment during K4 has been in interstate highways and air transport.

Another researcher is Jay Forrester, a professor at the MIT Sloan School of Management, who believes the explanation for the K waves lies in infrastructure development, where capital is invested in such projects as canals, railways, steel or electricity-generating plants and oil refineries during the upswing. As the economy peaks then slows down, the plant becomes progressively worn out and underused until it becomes only fit for scrap, being financially written off at the end of the cycle.

Iben Browning's climatic explanation
Chapters 2 and 3 described how alignments in the solar system and differences in the sun's radiation affected life on earth in

regular cycles; the most regular are the tidal forces which can be calculated with great accuracy years ahead from knowledge of the moon's movements around the earth. Browning describes how the alignment of the sun, moon and earth cause additional ocean water to pile up on the edges of the sensitive tectonic plates dividing the seas and continents, so triggering the forces that cause earthquakes and volcanoes. As we saw earlier, sizeable volcanoes cause a shielding dust veil to form over the poles, so further reducing the amount of sunlight absorbed on earth. Sunspots have their own rhythm of increasing or reducing radiation.

Wishing to combine the two major cooling forces, Browning calculated the likelihood of a volcanic eruption from the 8.85-year tidal-force cycle at the latitude of thirty degrees north going back in time to the 18th century. He then modified the impact of possible volcanic action by adding the sunspot cycle in such a way that the two are additive or subtractive (technically, he produced a non-dimensional index by dividing the 8.85-year tidal-force cycle by the 22.44-year sunspot rhythm) and the result is shown on the lower graph of Figure 18.

The resulting tidal force and sunspot envelope bears an uncanny timing relationship to the average Kondratieff waves described earlier, which could explain the varying length of the K cycles; in fact, Browning calculated there was a chance of 68,000 to 1 that the similarities were random. Iben Browning backed up his proposal with empirical evidence that a major volcano had gone off a short time before the low points of each Kondratieff Cycles.

As we saw earlier, volcanic eruptions disrupt the weather patterns, some areas becoming drier, others wetter. If food production is disrupted and becomes more expensive, then people will be forced to provide a higher proportion of their income – already depressed by the recession – for basic living, leaving less for other spending, which only steepens the decline.

Chapter 3 covers the subject of volcanic eruptions but a summary of Browning's empirical evidence may be worth repeating:

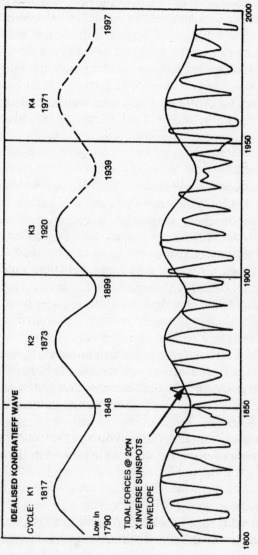

Figure 18. Comparison of the idealised Kondratieff cycle with the envelope of tidal forces times inverse sunspots at a latitude of thirty degrees north.

The beginning of K1

Icelandic volcano Lakagigar erupted in 1783 and 1784, both times with the equivalent force of a one-megaton bomb. Each time around one cubic kilometre of dust and gas was propelled into the stratosphere before drifting south. Benjamin Franklin, then the US Ambassador to France, described the effects of the 'dust veil' as a dull, white, leaden sky with the sun only appearing over twenty degrees above the horizon as a bright, copper-coloured disk. There were grape and crop failures several years during the 1780s and food prices rose to 80% of their income at the time of the Paris bread riots in the 1790s.

The beginning of K2

The Central American volcano Cosiguina erupted during January 1835, causing a dust cloud to move north and around the world cooling the polar air masses. The volcano occurred at the same time as an El Niño (see Chapter 3) – together causing terrible flooding in the Mississippi basin during 1844, food shortages and, in some places, riots in the USA and Canada. The volcano was probably also responsible for the terrible Irish potato famine and food shortages elsewhere in Europe.

The beginning of K3

One of the mightiest volcanoes in modern times was Krakatoa which went off with the force of a 100-megaton bomb on 26 August 1883 near the Sunda Straits between Java and Sumatra. The immense tidal wave overwhelmed 96,000 people living in the area and the dust cloud drifted north, reducing the sunlight by 30% in the northern latitudes. The volcano caused ten dry and cool years adding to the depression in 1884–5 and in the mid-1890s.

The beginning of K4

Five relatively small volcanoes went off between 1929 and 1937 which, coinciding with the end of the sunspot cycle, were probably responsible, with the westerly wind failure described in Chapter 5, for the extremely dry conditions creating terrible dust bowls in the Mid-West states of the US. Although global food prices were dropping, the conditions were so bad in 1937 that the US was obliged to import corn – so contributing to the panic of that year.

Is the Kondratieff Wave real?

There have been a number of criticisms from economists that Kondratieff used dubious statistical methods to prove the existence of his long waves and suggesting that the number of cycles analysed were too few to be reliable. They also argued that the series of commodity prices, interest rates, wages and finished-goods prices did not show a consistent pattern, thus invalidating the whole existence of long waves.

Time will tell whether these criticisms are justified, but as the 1980s showed remarkable similarities to the 1920s, the 1990s are showing major parallels to the 1890s and 1930s. After all, Kondratieff *was* one of the very few people who predicted the Great Depression of the 1930s!

CHAPTER 10

A CLUSTER OF CLIMATIC CYCLES

By now we have collected several cycles around twenty years. The first from Chapter 2 is a lunar cycle of 18.6 years in duration when the moon precesses around its earthly orbit with an inclination of five degrees to the equator. The second is the Hale, or double-sunspot cycle, when every 22.4 years the magnetic polarity of sunspots has completed its second round of 11.2 years and the weather becomes very dry. The third is a real-estate pattern in America of from fifteen to twenty-five years, when a cyclical rise and fall of commercial property and housing has been identified going back to around 1800. As the sunspot cycle has been well rehearsed in Chapters 2 and 3, it is proposed to confine this chapter to the other two, the lunar and real-estate cycles.

The lunar 18.6-year cycle

As was explained earlier, the moon completes its orbit around the earth crossing the ecliptic (the path of the earth around the sun) twice in a lunar month, its path ending a bit further west each time. Each end position is called a node and a line joining these points takes 18.6 years before reaching its origin. There are eclipses when the sun, earth and moon are in line, which happens twice each year, one about every 173 days, or half a calendar year.

The earth is tilted around the plane of the ecliptic at 23.5 degrees, so with the moon's orbit at five degrees to ecliptic, its passage varies 23.5 + 5 degrees and 23.5 − 5 degrees north and south of the equator during the complete cycle of 18.6 years. As Dr Louis Thompson, Dean Emeritus of Iowa State University explains in a paper published by the Foundation for the Study of Cycles, this angle is called the 'moon's declination'; there was a minimum declination (18.5 degrees) in 1978 and a maximum (28.5 degrees) during August 1987. The next minimum should be in early 1997. The last time the declination was in the middle of the range at 23.5 degrees was in early 1992.

Thompson quotes work by Robert Currie, a researcher into cycles and weather records, who points out that the maximum tidal effects occurred when the moon's declination was 23.5 degrees and when the eclipse seasons were in the winter and summer. Currie went on to observe that the highest corn harvest yields materialised 9.3 years after the maximum tidal effect; this should mean an excellent corn crop with record yields in 1996–7.

Louis Thompson's timing is in line with Currie's, arguing that *highest* crop yields occur near the moon's minimum declination of 18.5 degrees, as happened near the years of 1904, 1922, 1941, 1959, 1978 and will occur again in 1996. Conversely, the *lowest* yields occurred four years after the moon's maximum declination in the years 1899, 1917, 1936, 1954 and 1973, and there should also have been poor yields in 1992.

The writers do not explain how these lunar cycles impact on our weather but they suggest that overlying events, such as volcanic eruptions or El Niños, could change the pattern as they obviously did in 1992, which was an excellent year for crops. Thompson also shows that since the very benign weather from 1958 to 1973, there have been a series of droughts in 1974, 1977, 1980, 1983 and 1988, each one progressively severe. He also shows that the year *after* El Niño is the time to expect a drought. In the early 1990s, El Niños extended for an unprecedented three years to 1994, which suggests that the next severe drought could be in 1995.

The Kuznets' US real-estate cycle

There might be a relationship between the lunar cycle just described and what Simon Kuznets, an American economist, called a 'US real-estate cycle'. Going back to the War between the States, he identified a rhythm of around 16.5 years taken over the period 1861 to 1972. This is essentially a construction cycle applying to housing and commercial buildings which one commentator sees as a natural rotation of family growth and capital investment feeding into the ability of the economy to provide jobs. Another explanation for this essentially American phenomenon is that waves of migrants to the US demand housing and work.

It could be tempting to relate real-estate investment with the lunar and crop cycle described earlier; after all, when food becomes more expensive there is less to invest in housing and people tend to stay in their present homes. If spending power is in a trough, then business activity is also down and less can be spent on office building or factories. The fit between the peaks and troughs of Kuznets' cycle and Thompson's lunar cycle is interesting, particularly outside the years 1940 to 1960 – which might, in any case, be classified as 'war years' for real-estate. There is no doubt historically that the US climate was particularly dry during the years when the yields were at their lowest, so perhaps there is a better fit with the lunar cycle at the Kuznet troughs.

Kuznet Peaks	Good Yields	Kuznet Troughs	Lowest Yields
1892	1897	1898	1900
1912	1915	1918	1918
1927	1934	1933	1937
1941	–	1944	1955
1959	1952	1960	–
1972	1971	1975	1974
	1988		1922

The Kuznets' Cycle's very existence was called into doubt after 1914 by the American economist W. W. Rostow, who questioned its validity after the waves of migration subsided. However, the cycle was still pertinent in the US during 1988 when the real-estate market was at its peak and perhaps in 1992 when near its low. Van Duijn reports in *The Long Wave in Economic Life*, that the building cycle in the UK was the inverse of the US up to the end of the Second World War. Britain, however, seems to have caught up since the 1970s, when the peaks and crashes of building activity and prices have occurred at similar times.

Raymond Wheeler's 18.3 rainfall and real-estate cycle

Working quite independently from the others, Raymond Wheeler identified an 18.3-year cycle of wet and dry, which he correlated with an American real-estate cycle going back to the year 1800. Although Wheeler's work does not extend beyond 1945 and Thompson's does not report the lunar cycle before 1892, the peaks and troughs for the years between 1897 and 1934 follow a similar pattern. For example, the low points in 1897, 1918 and 1934 fit quite well with the lowest yields and the highest prices, which bears out the suggestion that people tend not to move or build houses when their discretionary income is taken up with higher food prices.

Wheeler identifies the peaks and troughs of real-estate prices with how people feel in either wet or dry years. The reader will recall from earlier chapters that when it is wet and stormy individuals feel a greater sense of optimism, more people get married and the birth rate increases. Married couples need homes which increases the demand for dwellings. Conversely, when it is dry people feel less optimistic, fewer marry, the economy is depressed and housing activity declines.

CHAPTER 11

THE CYCLES COME INTO SHARPER FOCUS

There are many more short cycles than long ones, not by the predictable influences of the solar systems but through the whims of men. Edward Dewey, the first director of the Foundation for the Study of Cycles, identified no less than fifty-nine rhythms which had a duration of between nine and ten years so many influences must be at work. This chapter is concerned with only some of the more significant cycles that could affect the critical period we will be living through during the 1990s and beyond.

We have already met some of the most significant cycles – probably the most important being the seven- to fifteen-year sunspot rhythm, which is due to reach its average of 11.2-year minimum in 1995–6. It will be remembered from Chapters 2 and 3 that this is also the end of the Hale Cycle of 22.4 years, a period usually associated with drought conditions – in part caused by a decline in the westerly winds. The year 1995 could also be associated with volcanic activity from the low point of the Chandler Wobble, a 6.4-year disturbance of the earth's crust that is closely associated with volcanic action.

One cycle that could be dominant during the 1990s is the Juglar Cycle named after a French economist who in the 1860s was the first to identify that booms and busts came in a series with a duration of nine to eleven years. When Joseph

Schumpeter was writing about the Kondratieff Cycle in his great work on business cycles, he fitted six Juglars into one K cycle. He then fitted three of a much shorter rhythm called the Kitchin Cycle into one Juglar. This chapter will be primarily concerned with the Juglar because of its possible impact on the great credit bubble of the mid-1990s, which will be discussed further in Chapter 20.

The nine- to eleven-year Juglar Cycle

Clément Juglar became interested in how the rise and fall of interest rates and prices in London and Paris fell into a pattern with a regular rhythm of about nine to eleven years. He identified four phases of prosperity, crisis, liquidation and recession which had the form seen in Figure 19. What happens at each stage helps us to anticipate what lies ahead and to confirm what we already know but sometimes forget, which is that booms and busts do not last forever. This is how Schumpeter described each phase:

Prosperity
This is something that most people experienced in the 1980s and, if they can remember so far back, so did America in the 'Roaring Twenties'. Interest rates started low and raw-material prices were cheap, labour unions were not militant and inflation had been contained. There was a sense of increasing euphoria as business picked up, there was money to spend and profits to be made in the housing and stock markets. As the wonderful boom continued, people and business leapt at the chance of easy credit; they called it 'leveraging', using other people's money instead of their own to buy houses and stocks that were bound to go up in price – weren't they! Typically, the large banks and insurance companies woke up to the boom and invested heavily in housing mortgages, estate agents and commercial property. The old hands know that when the big players become involved, it is the time for them to sell.

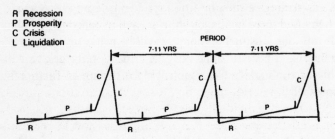

Figure 19. Phases of the Juglar investment cycle.

Crisis

This inevitably follows prosperity just as the boom of the Kondratieff Cycle is followed by a financial panic at its peak. Quite suddenly governments become alarmed at rising inflation and jam on the brakes by raising interest rates; the confidence that fuelled the boom evaporates and spending collapses. The additional debt that fuelled prosperity suddenly becomes a nightmare when companies and individuals find themselves without the revenue to pay the rising interest charges and have two choices: they can either declare themselves insolvent or come to some arrangement with their creditors. Those who anticipated the crisis sold assets to reduce their debt and kept their cash safe.

Liquidation

The panic to turn everything into cash accelerates as those who still have borrowings either dump what cannot be liquified or they fail. The Stock Market collapses as do interest rates when there are no longer any borrowers. This could be a good time to hold government bonds – if the governments have not destroyed their currency. In theory countries cannot go bust if they can avoid their debts by engineering a currency collapse – which is equivalent to defrauding their creditors. This is exactly what the Weimar Republic did to all those patriotic Germans who had bought and held government stocks to pay for the First World

War. (Those wishing a more practical guide to personal and business strategies during a collapse and depression should reach for *Meltdown* by the author – see the further-reading list.)

Recession

The bad credits and loans responsible for the liquidation phase are now wrung out during a depression that can destroy those businesses and individuals who believed the worst was over. During inflation the price of everything rose; now in deflation prices collapse as only the prudent have the spare cash to spend. Of course, this is the time to find bargains, whether one is looking for houses, companies, stocks or works of art. But life is not all bad, as *Meltdown* explains. The pace of life slows down during a depression when most of the bustling-about subsides and people have more time for others.

So far the Juglar is theory, but how does it work in practice?

The next chart shows how both the Kuznets' Cycle and the Juglar have worked in practice in the United States from 1920 to 1990. The series ends there for the moment but will be continued in Chapter 20; what is of interest to us now is how the Juglar Cycle has worked in the past and what we might see in the future.

Governments finance their spending either by raising taxes or borrowing. If they are prudent, their revenues from taxation match their spending which means they have no need to borrow – as in Britain at the tail end of the 1980s. When governments are forced to borrow, this immediately means they absorb some of the cash that would otherwise be invested in companies through the stock or commercial-bond markets. An increase in government borrowing is also inflationary because even more money has to be raised to pay for interest. It is estimated that the US government has to raise over $700 million per day just to pay interest on their borrowings.

One of the ways governments borrow is to issue what are known as bonds, or gilt-edged stocks in Britain. These are pieces of paper (called 'instruments') that promise to pay the holder a certain coupon or interest once or twice a year until the expiry

date some time in the future; these 'maturities' as they are
known can vary from only a few months up to twenty or thirty
years. However, once issued, the bond's value varies according to
how the market perceives future inflation. If inflation is set to
rise, the rate of interest required by the borrower will rise also
and the price of the bond will fall; conversely, when inflation is
expected to fall then the price of the bond will rise.

The US bond market which trades bonds of different maturities, is the most liquid in the world, with $20 or $30 billion
exchanging hands almost every day. But holders of bonds have
had an uneven ride, as Figure 20 shows. The interrupted line is
the yield of the thirty-year US bond called the 'Treasury Bond' –
or T-Bond. The bond yield rocketed upwards during the inflationary panic of 1918–19, then subsided almost continually until
1942, with a temporary blip upwards before the Crash of 1929.
The 1920s and 1930s were wonderful times to hold the T-Bond
whose value increased three or four times during the two decades.

After the Second World War, the T-Bond's yield started to rise
when inflation followed the rapid expansion of output. There
was a small inflationary blip in 1960 and then another in 1970,
probably caused by governments wishing to expand their
economies ahead of some important election. The rapid rise in
yields in 1973–4 was due to a bottoming-out of the Kuznets'
Cycle described earlier when rising commodity prices forced a
rapid rise in inflation. However, inflation was not dead because
after a dip it rose rapidly in the late 1970s, reaching a peak of
13.5% yield in the early 1980s – at the time of the second commodity explosion. This means that the value of any loyal
citizen's T-Bond holding in 1950 would have more than halved if
still held into 1980. Since then the value of bonds has easily
doubled, the yields having dropped to below 5.8% in 1993.

The dotted line is the rate of interest offered by the US
government for a short-term instrument called the 'Treasury
Bill' – or T-Bill. Instead of paying interest, the T-Bill is issued at
a discount so that the holder is paid par value when he redeems
the bill; for example, if interest rates are 10%, then a ninety-day
bill might be issued at 97.5 cents so that the holder might receive

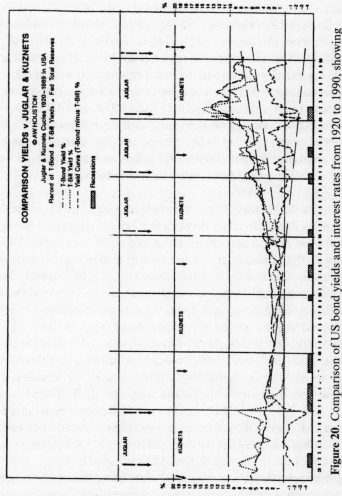

Figure 20. Comparison of US bond yields and interest rates from 1920 to 1990, showing the turning-points of the Juglar and Kuznets' Cycles.

$1 approximately three months later. This means that the American central bank, the Federal Reserve Bank (Fed), can use the T-Bill as one way of adjusting interest rates depending upon whether it wishes to expand the economy by reducing rates or clamp down by raising the discount.

The bill yield rocketed in 1920 to quell the inflationary blip; it then dropped during the 1920s before a rapid rise just before the Crash of 1929. The yields dropped to well below 1% during the 1930s in an effort to stimulate the depressed economy, only rising a fraction in 1937 during a rapid rise in commodity prices. Short-term interest rates were raised in 1960 and 1970 to follow the brief rise in bond prices before rocketing to a post-war high in 1974, responding to rapid commodity-led inflation. There was another huge increase in 1981 when interest rates rose to over 15%. Since then the T-Bill yield has declined to around 3% in 1994.

Figure 20 shows one more important line called the 'yield curve' – or the difference between the T-Bill minus the T-Bond yield – which tracks whether the Fed wishes to expand or dampen the economy. It was heavily negative in 1920 and 1929 when the brakes were applied, then very positive during the 1930s in an effort to revive the economy. Since then the yield curve has seesawed up and down in progressively more violent swings as the Fed has attempted to control the economy.

The Kuznets and Juglar Cycles now stand out quite clearly. They both combined in 1920 to produce the biggest interest-rate 'spike' for decades, the Juglar Cycle ended in 1919 and there was a modest impact of the Kuznets' Cycle in 1937. The impact of neither cycle could be seen during the 1940s and 1950s but the Juglar appeared every ten years after 1960 and, as we have seen, the drought associated with the bottom of the Kuznets was responsible for rocketing commodities in 1974.

Although the chart ends at 1990, neither cycle operated either in 1991 nor in 1992, which casts doubt either on the validity of the cycles or whether the effects of both have somehow been delayed and will return with greater force later. This important issue will be considered in Chapter 20.

Other significant cycles of less than ten years' duration

There are four other cycles which may be of significance, with other short-term rhythms that have been described earlier:

A 9.2 to 9.6 earth-rotation cycle

Martin Kokus has written in the *Cycles* journal about a cluster of rhythms which all occur within a 9.2 to 9.6-year time frame; these relate to temperature, rainfall, lake levels, tree rings, wildlife abundance, agricultural production and other indicators. The article suggests that the cycle is half the 18.6-year lunar rhythm described in the last chapter which somehow affects the earth's speed of rotation; this creates a torsion around the equator compared to higher latitudes which is likely to create volcanic action on tectonic plates.

The 6.4-year Chandler Wobble

This was described in Chapter 2 as beat frequency or rumble of two shorter rhythms that affect the relative movement between the earth's mantle and crust. A very high correlation between the cycle and major volcanic eruptions is reported with the next peak forecast early in 1995.

The three-to-five-year kitchin or inventory cycle

Joseph Schumpeter suggested that there is a shorter-term cycle lasting around three years which relates to the Juglar. Van Duijn describes a process whereby manufacturers and retailers go through a three-to-five-year cycle of stocking and de-stocking in the normal course of business. There are some interesting figures relating to the post-war years but it is probable that there are different rhythms for different trades which seem not to show up in interest-rate changes. Another factor for questioning the cycle would be the rapid strides made in computer-controlled inventory.

A forty-one-month cycle in industrial stock prices

In 1912, a group in New York hit upon a forty-one-month cycle in stock prices after hearing that Rothschilds in London had discovered a rhythm in Consols which they were applying to investment decisions. A paper printed in the *Cycles* journal during 1961 shows graphs of a regular rhythm going back to 1871, which bears quite a good relationship to stock prices but not enough to make accurate forecasts. The paper suggests that with such a short duration, other cycles are likely to be involved.

CHAPTER 12

CYCLES, FACT OR FICTION?

No, the world is not coming to an end quite yet; you might think so from the converging mass of cycles, but out of all this has to come a rational pattern that we can monitor and test over time. In the first place, it is a physical fact that the sun retrograded on 20 April 1990 and that the following years saw the highest sunspots since the 17th century, the time of the Maunder minimum. We can also be certain that sunspots will reach their minimum in 1995–6, implying that the climate will become cooler; but whether the end of the Hale Cycle also brings drought has yet to be seen.

There are numerous individual cycles at work during the 1990s ranging from 500 years to forty-one months. Some are inferred from historical records, as in most of Raymond Wheeler's work, others are more specific. Some of the cycles confirm each other, such as the coincidence of Fairbridge's 180-year planetary cycle and Browning's 179-year rhythm; some negate others, particular over the shorter time scales when there is a question of which rhythms are at work – something difficult to sort out, even with modern analytical techniques.

What do all these cycles mean, can they be relied upon either to predict what is likely to happen or, more important, when? Several influences are at work. First, there are the predictable movements of the solar system and their probable effect on sunspots and on volcanic action – both of which impact on the earth's climate and – indirectly – us. Next, there are cycles that have been deduced using historical sunspot and temperature evidence from records, such as tree rings and ice cores; confirmatory data can be found in historical records, such as ship's logs, accounts of battles, crop yields, monastic archives and the like. Finally, there are those cycles like the nine-to-eleven-year Juglar which, although possibly related to sunspots, are almost wholly to do with mankind as a political and economic animal.

Although the study of cycles themselves often involves very academic investigation into such sciences as astronomy, meteorology, climatology, physiology and geology, the ultimate impact will be their effect on people and the environment. If the weather is indeed to become cooler and drier, then some areas on the globe will no longer be able to support life and those living here will either die or be forced to move; it has happened in the past, so why not now? If people are to move, where will they go and if their destination is already overcrowded how will their hosts receive them?

As shown in previous chapters, history cannot be relied upon to reproduce itself just because one or more cycles have completed and others have begun. It is much more a question of understanding the available evidence, then looking out for the signs that will either confirm or deny the repetition of past events. For example, Raymond Wheeler's forecast – that the end of this 500 years will result in sweeping away corrupt governments and institutions that have outlasted their usefulness – looks probable. But this in isolation should not be relied upon because so many more influences are at work – the chance of Wheeler being correct will be considerably increased if at the same time it becomes cool and dry.

One is forced to admit how relatively little control mankind has over his own affairs. This ability will be put to a severe test in the 1990s when so many cycles all reach their low point – something that has not happened since the years around 1500 AD. Before moving on to how specific cycles have controlled such important practical matters as interest rates and commodity prices, it is useful to rehearse briefly what has gone on before by summarising the earlier rhythms in their probable order of certainty, as a prelude to the final chapter.

The 180-year planetary cycle

There seems little reason why we should not be in for a period of exceptionally low sunspots and increasing volcanic activity after the planetary upset of the sun's retrogration on 20 April 1990. Already we have had the longest era of high sunspots since the 17th century which could rebound to an unusually cool period similar to the other minima described in Chapter 2. How this will affect modern society is a matter of acute interest but at least we can be guided by the way people have behaved in the past.

Do we behave differently in hot and cool climates?
Almost certainly yes, based on the 180-year cycle described in Chapter 7. When it is cool people become restless, they resent the incompetence of politicians and revolt against governments. As the climate becomes warmer and more humid people's vigour is directed not at destroying what has gone before but creating something fresh under benign new rulers. Unfortunately, the creativity is often turned to wars of expansion and, in a subsequent warm-dry period, benevolence becomes tyranny. The cycle ends when, once again, there is a cool period and people seek their freedom.

The warm periods in Chapter 7 are really quite distinctive. First, there was the Gothic period in the early 13th century, then the Italian Renaissance two centuries later; this was followed by the English Renaissance in the 16th century. The next warm period included the Industrial Revolution which began in Britain before spreading across Europe and the USA. The final warm period started with the booming post-First World War decade of the 1920s which turned to tyranny, depression and wars of aggression during the hot dryness of the 1930s.

Cool periods are also distinctive; not only do they break up the existing order but very often something happens which makes possible the advance in the next warm spell. One example was the terrible famine in northern Europe followed by the Black Death in the 14th century; although many died, this ended serfdom in England as the survivors could demand their independence. The next cool period provided the impetus for Ferdinand and Isabella of Spain to expel the Moors and to be the first, with Portugal, to seek overseas possessions; the Tudor dynasty in England which led to the Elizabethan Renaissance started in the same cool spell. The English Civil War and liberation of Europe from Napoleon happened in the next cool periods which coincided with the Spanish and Brazilian colonies in South America declaring independence early in the 19th century.

The Kuznets' real-estate and Hale Drought cycle

The Kuznets' Cycle was evident in America until 1914; it was then downgraded until Louis Thompson pointed out a lunar-procession rhythm of 18.6 years which marries quite well with the last two falls of real estate and housing in 1974 and 1992. There could also be a relationship between the poor growing seasons of 1919, 1937, 1955 and 1974. There was not a poor season in 1992 probably because of the El Niño described in Chapter 3.

The Hale is another important rhythm of around twenty years which is a double 11.2-year sunspot cycle associated with drought years. It was held responsible for the Dust Bowls in the Mid-West of the United States in 1930–1, the dry weather in 1952 and 1974, and is due again in 1995–6.

A cluster of cycles around ten years

One of the most reliable rhythms is the sunspot cycle of 11.2 years which is believed to be responsible for the strength of the westerly winds, which bring moisture to the western US, Europe and parts of Africa. Sunspots might coincide with the Juglar investment cycle which, as Chapter 11 has shown, worked well in peace time from 1920 – perhaps García-Mata and Shaffners were right when they suggested that low sunspots actually do affect people's confidence. However, like the Kuznets in 1992, the Juglar failed to materialise in 1990 but does this mean the cycle is dead or just delayed? Other cycles may also be operating. There is held to be a growing cycle of half the lunar rhythm of 18.6 years, a tidal cycle of 8.85 years which can trigger volcanoes and another volcanic cycle of 6.4 years, called the Chandler Wobble.

Does the Kondratieff Cycle work?

There seems to be a forty-five to sixty-year economic cycle which has tracked the booms and busts of economic and political life at least since 1789, but the rhythm almost certainly goes back much further. Some statisticians are dubious about the way Kondratieff himself analysed his material and others have tried to explain the waves as driven by innovation or investment, although the climatic explanation is also interesting and could be conclusive. Of greatest importance is what might be expected at the top of the upwave, and towards the bottom of the down-wave .

Top of the upwave
The upwave of each cycle has ended with an inflationary blow-off as the pent-up pressures of the previous boom boil over with high interest rates and commodity prices; in this way the early 1970s were much like the early 1920s, the 1860s and the period around 1817. Doubters might argue that each top coincided with the end of a war – which is inflationary anyway. Another reason for the high commodity prices could be the overlap with the peak of the Kuznets described in Chapter 10.

The world's reserve currency has come off the gold standard

at the peak of every cycle. Britain went off the gold standard at the end of the Napoleonic Wars, only to return in 1817. America did the same during the Civil War when 'greenbacks' were issued unbacked by gold. Britain came off the gold standard in 1914 and returned for six years in 1925 at an unrealistic valuation. Finally, President Nixon uncoupled the dollar from gold parity in August 1971; it has not yet returned.

The bottom of the downwave

The events from 1789 onwards fit a pattern of collapsing credit, falling prices and steeply declining economic activity until all the excess and bad loans are finally wrung out of the system. The question is, will it happen this time or have our clever politicians and central bankers finally ended the rhythm that has cleansed the financial system since biblical times? The other alternative suggested is that the cycle has not been suppressed, but postponed to strike with vengeance later in the decade!

Raymond Wheeler's 500-year cycle

Something important seems to happen every 500 years – although it is not always possible to pin this down to specific weather changes. In every half millennium since the 6th century BC, an empire has either risen or fallen, or someone was born who would deeply affect succeeding generations. For example, Confucius and Buddha were born 500 years before the birth of Jesus Christ. Rome was sacked in the 5th century AD, Byzantium split from Rome around the year 1000 and was to fall to the Ottoman Turks 500 years later. The 1990s will end an era that began with the Reformation and the rising domination of the West; it will almost certainly end with quite a different set of priorities and notions of power.

Is there evidence for an east-west power switch every 500 years?

Probably not, although this is more discernible in the West than in the East; it could be because China's history of the rise and fall of empires, interwoven with rebellions, warlords, destruction and recovery, marches to a different drumbeat. For example:

500 BC to AD

This 500 years belonged to the West. By 300 BC the glory of classical Greece had declined with the disintegration of Alexander's empire but a new force was rising. Rome dominated the Mediterranean by the birth of Christ, and then went on to dominate much of Europe with the most sustainable legal, military and administrative system the world had ever seen. Meanwhile in China, the Ch'ing Empire flourished after the 'Warring States' had fragmented the country to be replaced by the Han.

AD to AD 500

Wheeler believed the East dominated this period but the honours are probably even. Rome reached its zenith before it too became lost in bureaucracy and was sacked by the Visigoths in 410. China prospered under the Han but this dynasty was replaced by the Hsiung-nu; this warlike tribe from the north came from the same stock as the Huns who started the devastation of Europe and the fall of the Roman Empire.

AD 500 to 1000

Again honours are probably equal if the Middle East is taken into account. While Europe was in the Dark Ages, the Muslim armies drove west into Spain to create the most dazzling court west of Constantinople at Cordoba on the Guadalquivir, housing half a million Muslims, Christians and Jews; further east on the Tigris, the capital of Caliph Harun al-Rashid, Baghdad, was probably the greatest city in the world. In China the T'ang Dynasty spread aggressively westwards to be beaten by Muslim warriors at the Battle of the Salas River. But despite this setback, the T'ang built a modern city at Ch'ang-an laid out on a grid and housing two million people.

AD 1000 to 1500

Honours are probably also even. The half millennium started

with a split between the Roman and Byzantine Churches, a divide that gave new vigour to the Orthodox faith. It was to be an unhappy time for the West, with periods of renaissance sandwiched between the Mongol invasions, the Black Death that destroyed a third of the population, and the Hundred Years' War between Britain and France – many believing in the coming of the four Horsemen of the Apocalypse: famine, wars, plagues and death. China suffered even more from the Mongols than Europe but eventually the Ming Dynasty was founded which started to repair the Mongols' vandalism.

AD 1500 to 2000

The West dominated this 500 years with voyages of exploration, conquest, acquisition, plunder and colonisation. Spain and Portugal led the ocean passages followed by the Dutch, French and the English. In a succession of wars fought by sea and land, Europe and later the USA created empires throughout the world even as far as China, where an aristocracy that despised the West was in no position to resist foreign trading enclaves. The period ends with no clear identification for the next 500 years.

There could be evidence for a religious cycle

Momentous philosophical or religious events have started and ended each of the past 500-year cycles: Confucius and Gautama were born in the 6th century BC and Jesus Christ 500 years later. The next 1000 years are less clear, with the Edict of Milan granting Christianity toleration in the Roman Empire in 313, the transfer of the capital to Constantinople twenty years later and the sack of Rome in 410. After the birth of Christ the most important event was the birth of the Prophet Mohammed in 570 and the First Jihad after his death.

The 500-year rhythm is clearer from 1000 to the present. Byzantium split from the Roman Church in 1054 and the eastern empire collapsed nearly 400 years later when the Ottoman Turks captured Constantinople. Christendom was again split in 1517 when Luther nailed his ninety-five theses to the castle church at Wittenburg. Modelski argues that much of the vigour shown by the Dutch, British and Americans was generated from the increased individualism released when Protestant countries split from Rome.

Evelyn Garriss in the *Browning Newsletter* dated June 1944 has identified a 180-year religious cycle, linking the remarkable rise of Christian fundamentalists in the United States to the Great Religious Revival of 1824 to 1850 in the North-East and Mid-West; she might also have linked it to the rise of the Puritans 180 years earlier.

It was said that Puritans arose naturally from Calvinism but Henry Hobhouse in *Forces of Change* believes in part this was a reaction against syphilis infection imported by sailors into Europe from the Caribbean. The first priest died from the disease in 1496, the first bishop in 1506 and the first pope in 1516. There is no guessing how it was caught, occurring as it did in the middle of the 'Little Ice Age'. People become more self-reliant when times are hard; the reaction led to a much stricter observance of religious and sexual ethics if whole nations were to avoid being wiped out. Whatever its cause, the stern Puritan ethic strongly influenced the Pilgrim Fathers and other settlers in the New World.

By 1810, the Napoleonic Wars were in full swing running parallel to the War of 1812 – both of which disrupted Europe and the United States at a time when the climate was becoming cooler. Britain had benefited from the missionary work of John Wesley who had revived the Church of England in the late 18th century, which many believe was responsible for the work ethic that made the Industrial Revolution possible.

It was a time of high food prices in the United States when the move westwards had started to break down the hierarchical society that still remains. Garriss describes it well: 'It was a time of opportunity and despair, as moral and social certainties crumbled, and the masses in society had to adjust to new demands'. This led to the Great Revival, particularly in Massachusetts, Pennsylvania, New York and the Mid-West – the areas under the most climatic pressure. Church membership became more intense and localised, there was a revival in civic responsibility and virtue, and political movements preached abolititionism, temperance, labour reform and white male suffrage.

Now 180 years later, we can recognise similar symptoms of order breaking down in the inner cities, AIDS, scandals and corruption at the highest levels, and a pervasive liberalism that is invading established principles. We have yet to discover whether it will again become much cooler but if it does we can expect a powerful extension of the present religious revival and a return to the Ten Commandments in Christendom and to the Koran in Islamic countries.

The 100-year weather and nation cycle

Both Wheeler and Modelski came to the conclusion quite independently that a 100-year cycle could be identified going back at least before 1500 AD. This may, however, be a better analytical than predictive tool because it was difficult to determine when one of Wheeler's warm and cool periods would begin or end. Wheeler's cycle starts cool and dry, becoming warmer in the middle; this initially makes for creative vigour, which subsequently turns to tyranny. The rule of despots and dictators collapses as once more it becomes cool and people revolt. Modelski's cycle follows a similar 100-year rhythm with one nation becoming dominant, then having to fight a major war before a period of peace. It is interesting that both men timed their cycles not at the end of a century but somewhere in the middle, coinciding with a cool period.

The birth of national supremacy

Modelski is on solid ground when describing his research into the rise and decline of national supremacy; as described in Chapter 8, only four nations out of the near dozen empires that flourished in the last 500 or 600 years ever reached his criterion of durable states which dominated for 100 years or more. The qualities exhibited by these nations is important because they provide a clue as to how any new power might emerge in the 21st century.

There are several reasons why Modelski believes that some states become dominant, while others have only a short reign of brilliance like a shooting star. First, they should be difficult to invade – a factor which rules out most Continental countries. Second, they should achieve a form of democracy that unites the will of the people. Next, the country should have the economic ability to sustain and win a war through global reach – the ability to impose their will overseas.

Now we need to look for the spark that will trigger the next country to achieve domination after the forecast decline of the United States early in the next century. Modelski describes how these changes may happen but at the end of a 500-year cycle there may not be a dominant nation but an Idea. For example, the Muslim empires were created not by revolting against a dominant power, but by nations touched by the Word. Whatever the trigger next time, one could look for an Idea which creates the next power and sustains it through to win a major war when challenged.

Achieving independence is the spur that fired many national ambitions. It was the impetus that gave Spain the vigour to defeat the Moors, the Portuguese to win independence from Spain, Holland to break free from Spain and the thirteen colonies of the newly formed United States to separate from Britain.

Unification is another spur. Germany achieved its greatest strength and threat to its neighbours when Bismarck created the First Reich. China has also blossomed under a benign leadership which allowed the natural strength of its peoples to develop. However, unity is not the sole criterion as Russians found under the tsar or the Soviets; there has to be a genuine freedom of expression and individual independence before the whole is greater than the sum of the parts.

A new regime created France's domination and expansion under Louis XIV and the Tudors provided new impetus for England. In Japan the Meiji took control after the humiliation of the Shogunate, when the country was unable to resist Admiral Perry's demands in 1853.

Religion motivated the Ottoman Empire, possibly the most

remarkable of all those described in Chapter 6. Inspired by the Koran, the Seljuk Turks gained control of the caliphate in the 11th century; absorbing the Ottomans, they then overran Anatolia, crossed the Dardanelles and captured Constantinople; they went on to control the Balkans, Hungary, southern Russia around the Black Sea, then east to the Caspian. They also occupied the old Byzantine territory in North Africa. Although totally undemocratic, the caliphate allowed considerable local autonomy for further conquest or fighting invaders; the local sultans could almost do what they liked, provided taxes were collected and remitted to the centre.

– and the forces of decline!
Some countries have worn themselves out either through war or internal decline. The Portuguese suffered from an ill-fated foreign venture and the Spanish took over their throne. The great empire that Louis XIV created became enfeebled after supporting the American colonists against the British and succumbed to the Revolution. Britain never really recovered from the First World War and although it played an important part in winning the Second World War, the country was more content to accept the easy life of socialism, then revive itself – as did the losers, Germany and Japan.

Another cause of decline seems to be the remoteness of rule and the domination by bureaucrats which inevitably leads to corruption. Roman rule became remote and corrupt, China has suffered the same fate several times and perhaps this too will be the downfall of the European Union and the United States.

Could we be due for another 'march of the barbarians'?

One must pray not, but Iben Browning in *Climate and the Affairs of Man* identified an 800-year climatic cycle based on tree-ring analysis which tallies with the major migrations in history when it became impossible for nomadic people to stay in their homeland. We have already identified the Hun invasion of Europe and China in the 5th century AD and the Mongol attack 800 years later. Browning believed this was part of a series.

Around 2000 BC the Indo-European people dwelling in southern Russia poured through the Caucasus. Joined by the Hittites, they spread west to Greece and southern Italy, then east to Turkey and Persia, where they became the ancestors to the Medes and Persians. The same peoples known as the Shang or Yin spread through China, just as did the Hsiung-nu around AD 400. It is thought that the Hyksos people who occupied Egypt for several hundred years from 1750 BC were from the same Semitic stock.

There was another mass movement from the Caucasus when men, women and children left their homeland and came south for food. Those living in the Levant or Egypt called them 'People of the Sea' because, although land-based, when they came to the sea they launched themselves to settle islands like Cyprus and Crete. These peoples also infiltrated latter-day Palestine where they became the Philistines; they were stopped at Egypt by the armies of Ramses III. It was a time for other people to move as well; the Etruscans moved into Italy, the Celts invaded England and, around 1195 BC, Moses led the Jews across the Red Sea in their flight from Egypt.

In around 400 BC the founders of the Hallstatt culture which had settled in Eastern Europe were pushed west and south by Steppe nomads, mounted warriors from north and east of the Danube. The Hallstatts, known as 'La Tene', went to the Ukraine, south to Turkey and south-west to Spain.

If we are now entering a particularly cool period, peoples in Central Asia and Mongolia could still provoke the tough Turkic tribes who live in the region to move again both south and west. As they have done in the past, they would push westwards the probably hungry people in Russia, Ukraine and Eastern Europe but it would not be a migration of mounted warriors, as in the past. This time many states could be armed with at least a few nuclear weapons which could be used, unless the world was able to operate a relief operation on a scale never before attempted.

CHAPTER 13

MOST DISASTERS ARE NATURAL BUT MANKIND USUALLY MAKES THINGS WORSE!

Climatic changes have played a considerable part in shaping history and also in many of the disasters which have beset mankind. At certain periods in history, volcanic action and sunspots cool the climate, so affecting areas normally able to grow crops. Apart from people behaving differently in varying temperatures, food shortages inevitably lead to more violence and this chapter contains a section on the devastation of famine. Of course, shortages occur equally when it is very dry or wet; for example, there were crop failures after the Tambora eruption, not through too little rain but too much, exactly the same conditions that depleted the US corn harvest following the July flooding of the Mississippi in 1993.

Those living in the immediate vicinity of earthquakes and large volcanic eruptions are also at risk from shattered houses, raging fires and personal tragedies. Some of the accounts described later show the scale of the destruction, and the horrendous cost of repairs and rebuilding. Sometimes there is an associated tidal wave, as with the Lisbon and Tokyo earthquakes, but most deaths are caused by masonry falls or fires. As we have seen from earlier chapters, volcanoes generate huge quantities of ash, and tidal waves from an eruption like Krakatoa overwhelmed tens of thousands of people. Only nuclear explosions come anywhere near the force of a major volcano.

Mankind's ability to destroy his fellow creatures has been impressive in the last two centuries, probably running equal to the toll of nature. Atomic bombs or man-made fire storms have been devastating but even worse has been the systematic extermination of race or class ordered by dictators. Against this, man's ability to defraud others has been relatively mild, concerned either with crashes and swindles or eliminating a whole nation's savings through destroying the value of the currency.

Although not life-threatening directly, a major swindle or fraud can do terrible damage to people's livelihoods or the expectation of pensions. The chapter describes three types of swindle: the first is the collapse of a financial empire and the second is probably the biggest fraud ever perpetrated by bank officials on their customers. The third is how modern politicians can and do defraud their fellow citizens of their savings on an unimaginable scale, and never themselves be brought to justice.

Famines haven't gone away

The beginning of the food chain for the animal and human kingdom takes place continually around the clock in plants. In a process called photosynthesis, carbon dioxide in the air together with water absorbed through plant roots are converted into sugar nutrients and oxygen in the presence of the sun's energy. The process occurs primarily in leaves, which is why plants and trees grow so as to maximise the surface area exposed to the sun.

Each leaf carries tiny pores, called 'stomates', which during the day regulate the carbon dioxide entering the plant and the discharged oxygen; at night the process is reversed, oxygen is absorbed and carbon dioxide released. Just below the stomates are the 'chloroplasts', which contain chlorophyll, the complex organic substance which converts the sun's radiant energy to a chemical form that links the carbon, hydrogen and oxygen atoms to produce glucose. The plant uses this substance in several different forms to build growth cells, circulate chemicals and take up minerals from the soil.

This sounds straightforward and most of the time the plant can receive enough solar energy, and draw enough moisture from the soil and carbon dioxide through its pores. If fact, the post-war 'green revolution' has been extremely successful in improving the efficiency of all three processes. Botanists have improved the 'architecture' of plants so that the leaf area exposed to the sun has been increased and they have developed strains to suit differing climatic conditions. New irrigation programmes have increased the water supply so a greater density of plants can be grown for a given area, and improved farming techniques and fertilisers have more than doubled the yield per acre in many areas.

All this has been essential to accommodate the world's exponentially rising population, made possible by man's increasing ability to reduce mortality. People need around fifty different substances, called 'nutrients', to be healthy. Each of these has a specific function alone, or combined with others to service the body functions. If people do not either consume enough food or eat the right kind of nutrients, they become ill or die. Nutrients fall into six categories:

Carbohydrates

These are the prime source of energy, composed almost entirely of carbon, oxygen and hydrogen – not dissimilar to the substances that keep plants growing. Most energy is consumed from crops like wheat, rice, corn or rye; vegetables like potatoes, beans, tubers and legumes also provide starch, and sugar is almost pure carbohydrate. If the body lacks carbohydrates, it first raids the stored fat from flesh tissues before energy declines.

Fats and lipids

These are the concentrated stores of energy the body needs in the form of fatty acids that contain several vitamins. This reservoir of energy comes from animal products such as butter, fatty fish, meats, eggs, milk and cheese; but plants such as olives, coconuts, peanuts or soyabeans also supply fats. Lipids have similar properties to fats – one of these is cholesterol which is needed by the blood but in excess can be seriously damaging.

Proteins
Made up from nitrogen-rich substances, these are essential for life and growth, performing essential functions such as building and replacing body tissues, regulating the water balance, creating the enzymes vital for digestion and building up the body's immune systems. People in developed countries absorb most of their protein through animal products although nuts, peas or beans are also valuable. If the body does not receive enough protein it draws upon its own tissues which is why the starving have wasted muscles. Children in underdeveloped countries are in real danger of protein deficiency.

Vitamins
Only discovered as an essential food early this century, these act as organic catalysts to promote health, long life and mental alertness; they also help the body to absorb proteins and resist infections. Vitamins are categorised by their solubility and their particular use. For example vitamin A works to resist infection and promote sight, vitamin C reduces the risk of scurvy, while a lack of vitamin D in children induces ill-formed bones, enlarged joints and shrunken chests. People in developed countries either manufacture or grow a diet that supplies enough vitamins for healthy living.

Minerals
Calcium, phosphorous, sodium, potassium, sulphur and magnesium are in the body in relatively large amounts; for example calcium, magnesium and phosphorous are largely present in bones and teeth, and are essential for children to reach their physical potential. Other minerals such as iron, iodine, copper and zinc are also necessary in small quantities. Those who eat a mixed plant and animal product diet seldom lack their required minerals.

Water

This is second only to oxygen in importance for human survival; we can exist for weeks without food but only days without water. In temperate climates a body loses various factors: approximately two pints a day through excretion, expired air and perspiration which must be replaced – a loss of 10% being fatal. A combination of high temperature and a low water intake quickly creates heat cramps, exhaustion, and a severe drop in mental and physical energy.

Although so much is known about healthy living, man is not the master of all things and climatic tragedies can occur, as they have done in the past. However, a severe crop failure or drought now could be extremely serious because the world's population has grown so fast with medical advancement in reducing mortality. Any natural disaster on a huge scale such as the Mississippi flooding in 1993, the 1930s Dust Bowl or the drought in 1988 could spell disaster for millions.

William Dando in *Geography of Famine* quotes William Shurtleff's description of famine during the 1970s:

> During the 1970s, fifteen million died each year of starvation and malnutrition-caused diseases. Seventy-five per cent of these who died were children. This is 41,000 deaths each day and over 1700 an hour. Malnutrition causes millions of premature deaths each year and in some societies 40% of the children die before the age of five; the survivors often suffer such severe and chronic malnutrition that their physical and mental growth is permanently retarded. The vicious circle soon becomes a downward spiral as malnutrition leads to poor work, education and health which in turn generates more poverty and malnutrition.

Dando identifies three stages of famine:

The first stage of malnutrition or hunger is exemplified by nervous excitement, extreme irritability, loosening of social bonds and lessening of morale. Food riots, violent protests, social strife and individual anti-social acts generally occur at this stage. (Note: this particular type of aggression was shown in the bread riots during the French Revolution which followed the drought caused by Lakigagar's eruption in the 1780s.)

The second stage of malnutrition or severe hunger can be seen as individual apathy, mental depression, nausea and inability to concentrate. There is lack of ambition, melancholy, submissiveness and little interest in sex. Males and females begin to lose some aspects of their sexual differences; males begin to resemble females by loss of beard, enlargement of breasts and development of smooth, soft skin.

The third and final stage of acute under-nourishment or starvation leads to the break-up of the human personality and internal disintegration of the body. Self-preservation and mental control are lost, scruples and inhibitions disappear, followed by madness, stupor and finally death.

European famines
There were terrible stories of famine during the particularly cool period before the Norman Conquest when people were forced into cannibalism. William Dando recounts conditions in 1068–70 in England 'when so great was the famine in Northumberland that men, compelled by hunger, devoured human flesh, also that of horses, dogs and cats'. Others sold themselves as slaves, so that at least someone else might have an interest in preserving their existence – others just died. 'It was horrific to behold human corpses decaying in the streets . . . for there was now no one left to bury them'.

- As has been noted in an earlier chapter, there was the terrible famine of 1317–18 when rioting serfs were put down with much brutality. People in a weakened condition were in no state to resist the Black Death when around one-third of the population perished.
- There were famines in the cool period of the early 16th century.
- There were famines and civil disturbances across the whole of

Europe during the mid-17th century. Wheat prices reached a peak from the drought and the ravages of the Thirty Years' War. During 1697, church archives at Torryburn in Scotland recorded that the number of funerals increased over five times.

- Simultaneous to the French bread riots of the Revolution, a famine was reported in southern England. Wheat prices again reached a peak in 1810. In Lancashire there were food riots, now remembered as the Peterloo Massacre, in 1819, after the great Tambora eruption.

- There were food shortages in the 1830s which forced the repeal of the Corn Laws in England, when the unrest was in part responsible for the Great Reform Act of 1832.

- The 'Hungry Forties' were a time for food shortages throughout Europe, culminating in the riots of 1848. Particularly horrendous was the Irish Potato Famine described below. It reduced the population of Ireland by death or migration by one-third in five years.

Famines in Russia

In the last 1000 years one might expect famines to have been in the peak of the cold and dry periods described in Chapters 6, 7 and 9. To some extent, these dates tally with Dando's table of Russian famines:

- There was a drought in most of Russia in 1309 during the time of the Great Famine.

- There was a drought in Muscovy in the early 16th century, when it was very cold elsewhere.

- There were several famines in the mid-17th century.

- There were five famines in various parts of Russia during the 'Hungry Forties'.

- There were three famines during the 1890s after the great volcanic eruption of Krakatoa.

- There was a particularly bad drought and famine in 1919–20 at the peak of a Kuznets' Cycle which increased the viciousness of the civil war after the Revolution.

The Irish Potato Famine of 1846

The potato was originally a native of the Andes, a staple food of the Incas and capable of growing some 8000 feet higher than corn (maize), also a staple food. It has been observed that the Incas' true contribution to the world was not the gold and silver plundered by the Spanish but these two plants. Francis Drake is thought to have brought the potato to the British Isles; having missed the Spanish treasure fleet, he picked up stores from one of the Caribbean islands before returning home (see *The Seeds of Change* by Henry Hobhouse).

The potato was a godsend to the Irish because their extremely wet climate and rocky soil make it difficult to grow bread-making grain anywhere except in the south-east and around Dublin; many Irish had to be content with a heavy bread or cake made from hardier oats or barley. Crop cultivation was also crude. Although the harness had been introduced into Europe for ploughing around the 7th century AD, the Irish were still making furrows in the 16th century by securing the plough to the horse's tail – a strangely insensitive and inefficient method.

Ireland also suffered from a social structure that was based not on land but on fiefdom controlled by a local clan or 'king'. By around AD 1100 there were some 150 kings for an estimated population of 500,000 without any overall unifying force, and the country was locked in tribal skirmishes. They could unite to resist invaders, however, when an army led by Brian Boru defeated a combined force of Scots and Norsemen at the Battle of Clontarf. Most Irish lived well off a diet of oat cakes, cheese, curds, meat, milk, eggs; game abounded and the rivers were full of fish. There were no towns before the Viking invasion and the unit of value was a cow, one unit being a 'set' which gave the value for other tradeable items, such as gold, bronze, tin, horses or slaves.

As a further background to the famine it is important to have some understanding of the Church in Ireland. Founded by St Patrick in 432, it lacked the settled townships of many other parts of Europe and grew up as a uniquely Celtic institution founded on monasteries and retreats, not parish churches. The ministry was through bishops (over 1000 reported in the 6th century) and priests using the Gaelic tongue. Surplus clerics were encouraged to evangelise in Scotland, Lindisfarne in north-east England and in Wales. They also went as far afield as Hungary, Iceland and Poland. Despite the power of the Word, invaders of Ireland such as Norsemen and Vikings destroyed what they could of the Christian heritage – unlike the Gothic invaders of Europe who were absorbed into the remnants of the Roman Empire.

The real divergence between England and Ireland occurred after the Reformation, although before then, as we have seen, the Celtic Church had grown quite differently from the Roman faith practised elsewhere. Encouraged by the Pope, the English urged the Irish to set up counties and pay tithes to Rome; after the Reformation, Henry VIII dissolved monasteries and gave the land to Irish and Anglo-Irish nobles.

The policy was reversed by Mary, continued by Elizabeth and reversed once again by Charles II. All this might have been containable but for James I (of England) transferring Scots (and some English) to Ulster to relieve the famine in Scotland. The greatest damage to Celtic traditions was inflicted by Oliver Cromwell, who was incensed by the number of Irish fighting on the side of the king in the Civil War and by the subsequent attempts by Charles I to encourage the Irish to return him to the throne. It is estimated that the population of Ireland diminished by one half through emigration, deportation, starvation and slaughter,

Meanwhile the potato was increasing in importance for, in the absence of a tied system of landlord and tenant, English settlers were able to take over the best land, pushing the native Irish towards more unhospitable areas. A method of planting known as lazy-bedding proved the most practical way of growing potatoes. A lazy-bed could be made anywhere, on a mountainside or in a bog, by laying manure along a stretch of land which was then covered by scooping a trench on either side and planting the tubers. A strip of 500 to 800 yards was enough to feed a family with the supplement of milk, pork, bacon and cheese. The family would live close in a turf cabin with perhaps a cow and pig.

Thus the potato flourished, being adaptable to poor growing conditions, a cool climate and easy cultivation. The trouble was that it only took less than fifteen weeks a year to prepare the crops and there was no work for the rest of the time, unless the peasant could be employed by tenant farmers or a landlord to pay off rent, the set-off being known as 'truck'. Without the capacity to earn, poor families received very little cash. The Irish actually prospered after the restoration of the Stuart monarch and the population doubled from 500,000 to 1.25 million by 1688. But supporting a losing Catholic monarch was a mistake because the Protestant King William exacted penal laws, which made Ireland virtually an English colony.

Catholics were barred from joining the army, navy or holding public office and were denied the vote; neither could they hold land (or own a horse), ensuring that unless a landowner became Protestant, his estate would be sold. Catholic education was made illegal, the religion proscribed and priests were hounded. The Catholic aristocracy fled to settle in France or Spain, the merchants became Protestants to survive and the peasant Irish learned to lie, cheat and be cunning. As all trade was to be conducted through England, the Irish also learned to smuggle their excellent wool to the Continent; crops that were surplus were sold abroad as there was no money in Ireland. Despite the drawbacks the Irish population increased from 1.5 million to nine million from 1760 to 1840.

There had been food shortages in the second and third quarters of the 18th century but matters became serious in 1820–1, some five years after Tambora erupted, when about 250,000 died from starvation. Between 1820 and 1849 the Irish suffered distress for fourteen of the twenty-nine years. By the time of the 'Hungry Forties', described earlier, there were food shortages all over the northern hemisphere and any surplus grain was sold for the best price. The last straw for millions of Irish was the fungus *Phytophthora infestans* which appeared in the Isle of Wight in June 1845; it took only two months to reach Ireland, where it recurred intermittently until the 1920s.

Good husbandry can avoid a repetition of the disease by rotating the crop cycle every six years, not using diseased tubers for seed, and boiling the potatoes fed to cattle whose manure would be used for next season's planting. This was nearly impossible for people living in poverty and on the edge of starvation. When the disease struck, a promising field might show a few plants which turned brown and died, but the fungus spread so rapidly that within a week the whole crop would be black and stinking.

The aftermath was terrible. It is estimated that at least one million people died from starvation or diseases like typhus or cholera; some fled to Australia and New Zealand; the majority went to America, where they formed a powerful anti-British lobby around Boston and New York. In all, some 5.5 million people had emigrated by the First World War, reducing the population of Ireland by two-thirds from 1840.

Could a famine on this scale happen again? Already millions die every year and often nothing can be done, because civil wars ensure that either the grain is prevented from arriving or it is hijacked and sold for the highest price. The real danger for the world is if a situation arises similar to the 1840s when there is literally not enough food to go around; those without either move in pursuit of food or steal whatever they can.

The peril from volcanic eruptions

The volcano is one of the most powerful forces known to man, the larger ones creating devastation many times greater than atomic bombs; fortunately, unlike nuclear targets, most eruptions are some distance away from populated areas. As was explained in Chapter 3, all eruptions occur around the tectonic-plate margins – particularly those areas where the sea bed (oceanic crust) is disappearing below the land mass, called the 'terrestrial crust'.

The pressure caused by millions of tons of matter grinding away against existing rock creates very high temperatures and enormous strains which melt the rock to form pockets of lava in what are known as 'magma chambers'. The stresses also cause pressures which force the molten rock towards the surface. It then only requires a trigger, such as an exceptional high tide or an internal fissure, for an explosive release of the material. Two further examples show just how devastating such eruptions can be:

Mount Pelée on the island of Martinique in the Caribbean began to be restive on the morning of 8 May 1902, showing the usual signs of earth tremors, grumbles and small discharges of sulphur, gas and lava. People in nearby St Pierre began to be worried but the mayor forbade people to leave town until the forthcoming elections; it was not a sensible decision. Soon afterwards the volcano erupted in what is descriptively called a '*nuée ardente*', a radiant cloud of hot, glowing particles and gas, which spilled over the lip and raced down the hillside at 100 miles per hour, engulfing St Pierre within minutes. Out of 8000 citizens apparently only one survived, a drunk who had been put in the jail's dungeon the night before to cool off!

Krakatoa (meaning the 'terrible one') went off on 27 August 1883, supposed by many to be the most distinguished upheaval on record. They were wrong. As we have seen in Chapter 3 Tambora was probably ten times bigger but there were fewer people around to witness the immediate results. Krakatoa is part of a chain that runs down through Sumatra, then continues eastwards to New Guinea; at the time of the explosion there was only one island, now there are four.

The authorities had thought the mountain volcano was extinct, an opinion not shared by the locals. However, in May 1883 the area quivered from time to time; this was followed in August by two submarine eruptions that went off with a deafening noise that shattered the residents of Batavia (present day Jakarta), some seventy miles away, and could be heard 2000 miles away by South Australians – who took it to be rock blasting. By the early morning of 27 August, the magma chamber beneath the crater had been completely discharged, carrying with it the material above it. The dust was ejected some twenty miles into the stratosphere where it was responsible for the amazing sunsets described in Chapter 3, visible as far apart as Spitzbergen and Brazil. Such was the volume of material that the day after the explosion Batavia at midday was as dark as midnight.

The immediate local effects were spectacular. In place of the mountain there was a huge hole 1000 feet deep, which filled with thousands of tons of seawater. This in turn created a tidal wave, a Tsunami (described earlier); the 140-foot-high crest swept up the Straits of Soenda between Sumatra and Java, inundating several towns and killing at least 40,000 people. The tidal wave was observed as far away as Cape Horn and the sea temperature 300 miles away rose by 10°C.

The second phase of the eruption started at two minutes past ten the same morning, when over half of the land mass fell into the magma chamber creating, it is said, the loudest explosion ever recorded, and another tidal wave. The two explosions erased all traces of life in a matter of hours, leaving behind a primeval landscape with layers of lava 300 feet thick in places.

As was explained earlier, the ash and pumice made for the excellent growing conditions that were found by a scientific expedition which ventured to the site in October 1883. The first plant life to colonise the area was a green and blue algae which in three years formed a layer like gelatine over the tephra. Next to come were seeds either washed up by waves or carried by birds and, seventeen years after the eruption, the islands were once again covered by a youthful forest that provided a home for such creatures as lizards and snakes. By the first years of the 20th century, Krakatoa looked little different from many other tropical islands in the area.

Earthquakes are more dangerous to cities

Earthquakes are a much more local disturbance than volcanoes and, being more numerous, often claim greater fatalities than eruptions in highly populated areas. Long before seismology became an accepted science, primitive people blamed earthquakes on animals which lived deep within the land or in the oceans; it was thought to be the mole in India, a whale in Latin America and catfish in Japan. Later the Greeks believed they were caused by tempests in subterranean caverns. It was only in the latter part of the 19th century that geologists thought they were due to slippage in tectonic plates.

Faults or slips occur regularly in geology when a mass of rock slips relative to another, easing the enormous strains that build up during movements in the underlying strata; some of these movements can be acute. The slippage can either be along the surface horizontally, or vertically, which is called a 'normal fault'; a normal fault on a gigantic scale occurs when the ocean slab is forced under the land mass. There are other reasons for earthquakes: one of them is from the gradual cooling of the earth, which introduces rock strains released by an external trigger such as high tidal forces. Another could be a phenomenom called 'isostasy', where different rock formations exert varying vertical pressures on the earth's crust, which at some point adjusts to cause earthquakes. Like volcanoes, it is estimated that 80% of earthquake energy is released from the shores circling the Pacific.

Earthquake shocks away from the immediate fault are felt at different times because the impulse travels along varying paths in the earth called the 'P-primary' and the 'S-secondary' waves. Both waves are important for measuring the power or severity of an earthquake at specially equipped seismic stations. The P-wave arrives first, providing the first reading, the S follows, and depending upon the distance, the severity can be measured on a scale derived by the American seismologist, Charles Richter.

Another scale, called the 'Mercalli', is more descriptive, measuring the severity on a scale from one to twelve. A Mercalli one would be a tremor that was hardly felt – rising to six when frightened people leave their houses, masonry cracks, china is rattled, pictures fall and bells ring. Finally, a twelve is total destruction.

These are short accounts of notable earthquakes:

Lisbon on 1 November 1755
Perhaps the most devastating earthquakes on mainland Europe happened at 9.40, 10 a.m. and noon one Sunday, which was All

Saints' Day when many people were at church; each shock lasted several minutes. Within six minutes of the first tremor, 30,000 were killed in public buildings, many of these being worshippers. Like other earthquakes that have hit cities, probably the most damage was from the fires that took six days to extinguish and overall 12,000 buildings were demolished. The shock was felt all over Europe, with damage reported as far away as Fez in Morocco, and Seville, Cordoba and Granada in Spain. The resulting Tsunami overwhelmed those living close to the shore and by the time the wave reached Martinique in the West Indies it was still some thirteen feet high, travelling at around 250 miles per hour.

New Madrid, Missouri in 1811 and 1812

Fortunately there were few people living near New Madrid in southern Missouri when the greatest earthquake on record struck the US on 16 December 1811, then again on 23 January and 7 February 1812. The area worst affected comprised around 40,000 square miles, including parts of Tennessee and Arkansas when a region thereafter called the 'sunken country' dropped three to nine feet and was quickly filled by river water. The soil was broken open, sulphurous vapours were emitted, forests ruined as soil washed away from roots, and domes and depressions were formed in the soil. The earthquakes were powerful enough to shake down chimneys in Cincinnati 400 miles away.

San Francisco on 18 April 1906

At 5.12 a.m. the San Andreas fault split along some 270 miles from Upper Matole in Humbold County to San Juan in San Benito County. At the moment of release, the energy stored in the rocks before the deformation suddenly resumed a new position in some places twenty-one feet from the original alignment, sending a huge shock along and around the fault, causing damage 300 miles away.

Although only a few lives were lost compared with Lisbon (700 to 30,000) the greatest damage was from fires caused by fractured gas mains, compounded by the ruthless demolition programme introduced by a US army squad commanded by Brigadier General Funston to create fire breaks. Rats, flushed out from the wharfs and Chinatown area bordering the docks, were also a problem; looters were warned they would be shot on sight – and some were.

Overall the damage from shock was estimated at nearly $25 million and from fire $400 million which sent shock waves through the insurance markets; although several reinsurance centres reneged, Lloyd's of London paid up – earning it continued business in the American market. The earthquake also made A.P. Gianninni the owner of the Bank of America. When none of the other banks was open, he removed the assets to secure locations outside the city and set up banking booths on pavements outside the wreckage. (There is a fascinating account of what happens during a major earthquake in Thomas and Morgan-Witts' *The San Francisco Earthquake*.)

Tokyo on 1 September 1923
The death toll was almost the highest ever when nearly 150,000 died or were missing from thirty seconds of earthquake which occurred at noon, when fires were lit as people were preparing their midday meal. As in San Francisco most of the damage, estimated at $2,500 million, was caused from fires that ripped through the traditional wood and paper construction. Tragically, most people died from the conflagrations, including 30,000 herded into a park designated as a refugee centre, where such was the overcrowding that people were jammed upright. In the short but violent eruption, 54% of brick buildings collapsed, also 10% of those built with reinforced concrete; in some places the movement was so violent that potatoes were literally ejected from the ground.

The epicentre was in Sagami Bay to the south-east of the city, where the main fault line runs through the Izu Peninsula. The tremor swept destruction over the Kanto Plain which included Yokohama as well as Tokyo and in the bay itself some parts experienced depth changes of three quarters of a mile. The tremor also triggered a Tsunami; the wave, thirty-six feet high, swept many out to sea and destroyed hundreds of homes.

Japan sits on the cusp of four tectonic plates, including the huge Pacific plate, which extends to California. There are three others: the Philippine plate to the south, the Eurasian plate to the west and the American plate to the north. Not surprisingly Tokyo has had forty-five recorded large earthquakes since the 9th century AD, of which 1923 could have been the largest. The next worse loss of life in Japan was probably during the Second World War, when bombing caused a fire storm from which over 80,000 died. The latest earthquake, on 11 July 1993, quite high on the Richter Scale, was on the island of Okushiri in the Sea of Japan some distance from Tokyo. There have been major earthquakes around Tokyo every seventy years or so from at least the 17th century, so one can only hope this last tremor was the *big one*.

Swindles – man destroys man

Desperate men have often indulged in swindles when their empires were about to be toppled or when a government decided to devalue the currency by printing money when policies had failed. The Maxwell fraud to raise cash in support of a falling share price by selling pension funds is just the latest in a long line of financial swindles or frauds. As several cycles suggest that we may be coming up to a position similar to 1929–30, it may be interesting to examine three examples of swindles or frauds.

One of the best-known London frauds was committed by a company financier and promoter, Clarence Hatry. In September 1929 he was convicted of fraudulently forging certificates when trying to assemble the finance to buy a large steel conglomerate that he would later float on the Stock Market. The second is a swindle carried out by officers and employees of the Industrial Union Bank at Flint, Michigan to enrich themselves by stealing customers' deposits to speculate on the New York Stock Market. Finally there is an account of how the German government of the Weimar Republic swindled their fellow countrymen out of their savings.

The collapse of the Clarence Hatry financial empire in 1929
Clarence Hatry's first enterprise was in 1912 when he devised a plan for helping Central European emigrants to reach the United States and Canada; his agents would help the newcomers avoid rejection when they reached the New World. After the First World War, Hatry formed British Glass Industries through a series of acquisitions which later failed in 1926, the year of the General Strike. The strike was over in seven days and Hatry set about merging his General Investment Trust with Debenhams and launching his Corporation and General Securities by issuing £37 million bonds.

Hatry then turned his attention to a much bigger prize, which was the capital of the United Steel Corporation for £8 million by agreement with the shareholders; he could then use this as a base for acquiring other independent steel companies which would then be floated as a single issue. If it worked it would be a stupendous coup, earning considerable capital gain. The financier was farsighted, he knew that power stations would be built to supply ever-increasing demands for electricity, and the demand for cars was also on the increase. Hatry could raise £1 million from his own funds and a further £3 million from his City contacts; he hoped to raise the rest from the merchant bankers Samuel Montague through his contact, Lord Bearsted. In discussions with the bank, the financier believed the funds would be available. He had not reckoned on a change of government.

By 1928, the Conservative government led by Stanley Baldwin was coming to the end of its five-year term and a general election was called for 31 May of that year. The party was split over Indian independence, with Baldwin supporting the policy while a group led by Winston Churchill opposed. In the end, the Labour party with the Liberals won a majority and Ramsay MacDonald became Prime Minister; fearing socialism the Stock Market tumbled and confidence within the City crashed. The day after the election Hatry again met Bearsted to be told that the loan was no longer available.

Gravely disheartened, Hatry discussed the position with his chief of staff, Edmund Daniels, and together they worked out a plan for raising the funds elsewhere. Working long hours, Hatry's team tried every available source of funds but felt these were discouraged by Montague Norman, then Governor of the Bank of England; Norman was said to disapprove of Hatry's methods because the financier was overstretching his resources. However, by 23 June they were within £900,000 of their target of £4 million but at their wits' end to find the rest until, at a fateful meeting, Daniels suggested that they borrow the remainder on the security of the loans involving another Hatry company.

It was not a good time to be raising money because of concerns over the new socialist government. Hatry was already using some of his remaining funds to support the value of his company's shares in the declining Stock Market (just like Maxwell sixty years later); the time for completing the steel offer was running out. Reluctantly Hatry agreed on a plan proposed by Daniels and his aide, an Italian called John Gialdini; the swindle, a criminal offence, involved raising loans from banks on the security of shares that had never been sold. But before implementing the fraud he made one last attempt for help from Norman at the Bank; it failed and the swindle went ahead.

By 19 September, the value of Hatry's companies had plummeted on the Stock Exchange and the financier was summoned to the accountants Gilbert Gaunsey, appointed by Lloyds Bank to investigate the dealings. There was nothing for it but to admit failure, as only £789,000 of the £1.6 million of stock issued had been received for genuine sales; an audit showed that Hatry's companies had only £4 million assets for £19 million liabilities. The accountant advised the financier to confess everything to his lawyer and telephoned to arrange a meeting with Sir Archibald Bodkin, the Director of Public Prosecutions. It being late in the day, a meeting was arranged for the next morning at 10 a.m. in Bodkin's office.

It was not a happy interview. The Director kept the malefactors waiting and then made them stand while their confessions were duly delivered; that over, a detective was called in and the men put in his custody. It was an unusual arrest because as the detective had no warrant to hold them he advised them to repair to the Charing Cross Hotel where they had an excellent lunch; in a few hours they were behind bars. On 16 December 1929, Hatry and his associates were committed to trial at the Old Bailey where he was sentenced to ten years' imprisonment. He was released in 1939 and spent a number of years again as a financier before his death in 1965, aged seventy-six.

The collapse of the Hatry empire was considered by some to be the precursor of the Wall Street Crash of October 1929 but this is unlikely because the seeds of that disaster had already been sown in the rampant mania of speculation described in *The Day the Bubble Burst* by Gordon Thomas and Max Morgan-Witts, and in *The Great Crash, 1929* by Kenneth Galbraith. About the same time that Hatry was committing a fraud on one side of the Atlantic, another was being hatched in the United States of America.

The Union Industrial Bank, Flint, Michigan 1929

One evening some of the officers and staff of the Union Industrial Bank met informally to plot a gigantic swindle that involved using depositors' cash to speculate on the New York Stock Exchange; the members, who included John de Camp, the senior vice-president, and other bank officers, had different reasons for wanting more cash; one had a sick wife and a family to bring up, another had heavy gambling debts.

Ivan Christensen, the assistant cashier, and his wife Betty had adopted a high lifestyle way beyond his salary of $375 per month and were building a $75,000 mansion in a fashionable part of town. The main stockholder and chairman of the bank was Charles Mott, a senior operating officer of General Motors; the vice presidents were also shareholders. The president was Grant Brown, a leading citizen in Flint, whose personal reputation and ability had increased the depositor base of the bank to $32 million in ten branches; Brown's son Robert was also in the racket.

Christensen was one of the first to see the potential for stealing cash, investing it in the Stock Market, making a modest profit and returning the cash. Encouraged, he tried it again but this time lost, until further 'loans' eventually gave him a lucky break. Some time in 1928 he found that others were doing the same and, the secret out, Christensen became leader of a group that systematically plundered their customers' savings – over $2 million was stolen to play the market.

The embezzlers used depositors' money which was ostensibly sent to New York to earn interest, then immediately repatriated to Flint for speculation; as before, any profits were used to replace stolen money plus interest; losses meant further thefts. Another method of raising cash was through raiding customers' safe deposits. It was also possible to raise cash through what was known as the 'faked noted scheme' – or FNS. Like many institutions, the Union Bank was involved in transferring bills and drafts around the country, including share certificates. Instead of these being transmitted, the 'league of gentlemen', as they pleased to call themselves, forged promissory notes to local personages but the associated loans were duly 'borrowed'.

One problem was the bank examiners, who were known to visit the bank 'unexpectedly' after lunching in a local hotel. When warning of their coming was given by a local informer, the 'league' reckoned they had three hours to adjust the books before the officials arrived. Such was the skill of the embezzlers that everything was in perfect order by the time of their arrival.

By May 1929, the 'league' had succeeded in paying back half of the $2.5 million they had stolen with well-placed investments in RCA Radio and in a food stock, whose acquisition had been underwritten by the banking house J.P. Morgan. Other investments had gone well and by August the embezzlers now only needed $62,000 to replace the fortune they had stolen earlier. But when one of the directors informed the chairman about Christensen's grand new house, suspicions were aroused and the strain on the league nearly reached breaking point.

The problems were compounded when an investment into a hot tip lost $300,000 and a further bad break another $400,000;

by the end of the month, news of the Clarence Hatry failure had taken the market down still further and the losses were topping $1.5 million. By the end of September 1929 Christensen was receiving broker's demands for more cash if the positions taken by the league were not to be closed. They were near to despair when a big investment syndicate stepped in to support the market. But the respite was only temporary and by 24 October, five days before 'Black Tuesday', the embezzlers were down £2 million.

The end came at 2 p.m. on 29 October when the conspirators estimated that they owed the bank $3 million (it was actually nearer $3.6 million); the bottom had fallen out of the market and there was no way the money could be paid back. One of the leaders, Frank Montaigne, asked to speak to the bank president privately and told him the truth. Grant Brown called a meeting in the board room and one by one the embezzlers came in, including Brown's son Robert; the president telephoned the chairman Charles Mott to report a 'problem'.

By 5 a.m. Mott had received a full confession and the resignations of the league who had spent all night in the boardroom; he then summoned Flint's public prosecutor, Charles Beagle, and turned the case over to him. Charles Mott, however, was a man of honour. Instead of declaring the bank insolvent, he travelled to Detroit and drew $3,592,000 from his private account which was then driven to Flint escorted by armoured cars. On 3 December 1929, the embezzlers were given custodial sentences ranging from six months to ten years in the Michigan State Prison where it was reported they were model prisoners, sharing adjacent cells and working together to bring the jail's records up to date.

The Weimar Republic destroys the mark

By the mid-1990s it is now almost commonplace to read that politicians have made their currency worthless; since the Soviet Union was dissolved the rouble has crashed to a thousandth of its value against the US dollar, likewise the Ukranian and Serbian currencies. They have many examples to follow, the most striking being the collapse of the German mark after the First World War. It seems odd that the German currency should have been so vulnerable to manipulation when the DM is now regarded as the pinnacle of financial rectitude.

The problem really started during the war when the government decided that the conflict would not last long and they could safely borrow to pay for the enormous increase in expenditure. It was a mistake – not for the government who received the cash, but for the patriotic German citizens who bought 156 billion marks. To achieve this, the government removed the gold backing from a third of all notes issued and let the currency float against others. Germany had lost the war and the disbanded armed forces, who believed they had not been beaten in battle, came home to half the pre-war living standards, the cost of food demanding three-quarters of a family's average income (compared to one half earlier). The mark which had parity with the schilling, the franc and lire in 1913 had shrunk to one quarter of its value by 1919.

The demobilised soldiers and sailors returned home to find their country in turmoil from the wave of communism sweeping the Continent after the Russian Revolution in 1917; it split the nation and precipitated industrial unrest. However, for internal stability, the most dangerous issue facing the nation was the crippling war reparations imposed by the Treaty of Versailles; this required Germany to pay the victors, primarily France and Belgium, a sum equivalent to around one quarter of total German exports and a high proportion of all German taxes.

Germany did not have the means to make the payments, for their tax collection was a joke; anyone rich enough could evade the liability and in any case their nationalised railway system was heavily into loss. The reparations remaining unpaid, the French occupied the Rhine ports in the hope of diverting the production and trade in lieu of payments. It was an unwise move, for the German workers simply downed tools.

If this made life difficult for those on strike it was desperate for the government which lost a considerable proportion of its income from loss of revenue. They had resorted to printing money before but the presses had to be kept running continuously to pay for state expenditure which now included the Rhine dockers. In the three years prior to 1922, notes in circulation increased nearly six times to 200 milliards (thousand millions) and on the foreign exchanges the mark plummeted.

By September 1922 most alert people were learning how to deal with hyperinflation where the money supply increased by 10% in as many days. Despite interest rates of 25% it was pointless to hold cash and instead the wisest investment was to buy tangible items such as wheat, a herd of cattle, copper or gold; obviously the more portable the investment the better, with the yellow metal at the top of the list. Academic ability counted very little in these circumstances, while guile and muscle enabled an individual to duck and weave to survive.

New trades arose and new forms of currency were introduced. The most numerous were the *Winkelbankiers*, the back-street currency speculators; they could borrow millions of marks at low rates of interest and buy dollars which four months later could be sold; the bank paid back and a new loan could be taken out for fresh speculation. A new currency was introduced based on 125 kg lots of rye, called the '*Roggenmark*', which could be redeemed three years later with 25 kg interest. As in Russia today, farmers refused to accept marks for their produce and turned to barter trading.

Export industries thrived in these conditions but the government finances benefited little because only a foolish manager would keep anything of value in marks. Paying employees, however, became a problem because money lost its value so quickly wages were paid twice each day, the notes being carried away in mail sacks or – as the tradition went – in wheelbarrows. Collecting taxes became a nightmare when assessments made at one mark value would be collected a year later at perhaps a thousandth of the value.

In January 1923, Germany again being in breach of their reparations, the French occupied the Rhineland, the industrial heart of Germany, which devastated the German economy and as the workers refused to co-operate, the Weimar government felt obliged to support them. By March 1923, the chairman of the Reichsbank, Dr Rudolf Havenstein, proudly announced that note production was keeping thirty paper mills, 150 print works and 2000 presses working three shifts. This prodigious output was able to increase the amount of money circulating by two-thirds in only a few days.

By the autumn of 1923, five million people were out of work and the country was disintegrating with the communists and fascists creating disruption and civil disorder; looting was widespread and farms were raided. As in the French Revolution, food hoarding was a criminal offence punished not by the guillotine but by long periods in jail. The government was totally out of control with expenditure exceeding income by a factor of 1000; in despair it declared martial law when several states demanded secession. An attempted putsch in Bavaria by the future Führer was seen off by a group of local militia and the ringleader jailed; it was then that Hitler wrote *Mein Kampf*, which, had anybody taken him seriously at the time, would have saved the world a disaster.

The solution was proposed and later implemented by Dr Hajlmar Schacht, president of the Boden Credit Bank. His plan was to issue a new unit of currency called the '*Rentenmark*' (equivalent to one gold mark) backed not by the yellow metal but by German assets such as mortgages, property, commercial bonds and debentures (a fixed interest stock having security over a company's assets). The rate of exchange would be one rentenmark for every trillion (that is a million million) old marks.

Incredibly it worked but the withdrawal symptoms were horrendous because inflation had wiped out the savings of the middle classes who were left with almost nothing, from selling just about everything to stay alive. The Stock Market fared better than many other investments but even that had not caught up with the collapse of currency. The government was almost totally discredited and quite unable to raise any long-term loans after their abysmal record of imprudence; they could only exist on short-term borrowings from abroad. This was one of the factors responsible for the banking crisis in Britain and America in 1931, when Germany reneged on her interest payments. As with France after the collapse of the *Assignat*, in the resulting chaos the German people welcomed a dictator as the solution for their ills.

CHAPTER 14

THE IMPACT OF CYCLES ON WHEAT AND CORN PRICES

Previous chapters have concentrated on the relationship between cycles and history as the only result of climatic variations. Changing people's attitudes and behaviour is one thing; what it all means for important matters such as commodity prices, interest rates and stock prices, which impinge on business and economics, is quite another. There will now be six chapters covering the following:

Chapter 14: how two of the major commodities, wheat and corn have varied with climatic cycles.

Chapter 15: the driving force behind gold and silver prices which from 1660 to 1971 were the basis behind monetary stability and political probity.

Chapter 16: the cycles underlying commodity prices.

Chapter 17: the relationship between commodity prices and bond yields.

Chapter 18: some of underlying cycles behind bonds, short-term interest rates and stock prices.

Chapter 19: the underlying cycles behind real-estate and construction.

About cereals

Wheat is one of the seventeen plants that provide 90% of man's food supply, grown on nearly three-quarters of the earth's tilled area; another cereal is rice that feeds around 50% of the world's population. Botanists estimate that these and other crops developed from the 300,000 plants which grew naturally. In the course of time only around 300 (0.1%) are regularly eaten and only fifty are actively cultivated.

Cereals give the body two essential foods: carbohydrates provide energy and proteins supply the amino acids which keep cell structures in good condition. In the West only 20% of carbohydrates are eaten directly through bread, cakes or breakfast food; the rest is consumed indirectly through animal products, such as meat, milk or eggs. In the developing world cereals are eaten directly, with proteins supplied by sweet potatoes or cassava.

Plants live by converting carbon dioxide and nitrogen in the air with water drawn from their roots into sugars in the presence of sunlight. The waste product of photosynthesis is oxygen which sustains life in the animal and bird kingdom. In the course of time, scientists have improved the conversion efficiency by breeding species with, for example, increased leaf area and have introduced fertilisers to improve the land yield.

So successful have these innovations been since the Second World War that the so-called green revolution has improved agricultural output regularly by 5% per year in countries such as China, India and Pakistan. However, the increased output of wheat and rice will have to continue if the three billion extra mouths expected from 1990 to 2015 are to be fed – this may not be easy, as the growth potential may be slowing down.

Unfortunately, after a reaching a peak in 1977, some 5% of arable land has been taken out of production for various reasons: some has been consumed by industrial and road expansion which could yield greater economic returns in the long run; towns also take available land. What could be more disturbing is that some land is becoming unfit for tillage through lack of moisture; it has become too cool or the soil has become excessively salty. For example, there are areas in Pakistan which cannot raise crops because the land has been soured from salts in the pumped water. The worst case is the Aral Sea east of the Caspian which is nearly dry because Soviet planners diverted the rivers Amu and Syr to irrigate cotton production.

Plants use huge quantities of water because the proportion of water actually available for photosynthesis from rainfall is actually very small. It is estimated that globally two-thirds evaporates, another quarter runs off, leaving only some 10% for soaking in the land. Even when water reaches the plant, different species require different quantities to function. This is illustrated by what is called the transpiration ratio, the water consumed for every ton of harvested weight of grain: a ton of wheat requires 517 tons of rainwater, rice around 650 tons and corn (maize) needs 350 tons.

Water consumption presents a problem in the 1990s because of freak weather conditions in many parts of the world. There is also a danger that aquifers, the huge natural underground storage areas that have irrigated production for many decades, could be in danger of being pumped dry. The best known is the Ogallala formation lying under the American states of Nebraska, Kansas, Colorado and Texas which has been gradually pumped out since filling after the last ice age.

Of all the cereals grown, wheat accounts for some 28% of the total tonnage, corn is next with 27%, rice third with 25%, then barley at 10%; the balance is made up of sorghum, oats, millet and rye. Sorghum, with millet, grows best in the inhospitable hot-dry, mainly sub-tropical areas like the Sahel region of Africa and is the staple crop for that area.

On the other hand, oats and rye are hardy plants able to grow in higher latitudes where they withstand cooler growing temperatures than wheat. Oats are mainly made into oat cakes and porridge which is reputed to account for the Scots' rude health; containing no gluten, it cannot be made into bread. Rye, however, does contain gluten and is often made into a thin, bread-like pumpernickel; it is staging something of a comeback after production declined nearly 20% in the decade to 1981.

Wheat

Wheat itself may have been the first cereal crop to be cultivated by our ancestors 12,000–18,000 years ago in the irrigated lands of the Tigris and Euphrates – not long after the last ice age receded. It must have been difficult to harvest the first crops as the seeds naturally split and scattered when ripe. But some strains would have retained the seeds in the 'spike', which our forefathers learned to harvest either directly from the stem or by threshing after cutting the straw.

Even though it might have been possible to harvest more than one crop a year, wheat must have been an ideal concentrated food crop and easily portable for travellers or armies. The straw also could be used, providing useful bedding for cooler winter nights, a fuel, a binding for making buildings and a raw material for making baskets or mats.

It is almost certain that the Egyptians were the first to grind wheat into flour, then bake bread, so enabling life to be sustained for so many centuries along the Nile. Wheat also made the Industrial Revolution possible because it was more nourishing than the thin soup previously available to those living in the countryside.

However, wheat cannot grow when it is either too wet or too dry. Just as Joseph predicted in the Old Testament, there was famine in the land when the Nile failed to flood. Endless rain seems to have been the cause of the terrible famine of 1317–18; the Tambora eruption in 1815 caused similar flooding and probably provoked the hungry crowds to riot before the Peterloo Massacre in 1816. Wheat is a tough crop but even it will not grow in extremes of drought or temperature.

Wheat grows best in temperatures around 25°C, with a range between 4 and 32°C, although lower temperatures are possible. The annual rainfall should be between ten and twenty-five inches, which means that Ireland and Wales are not the best places to grow the crop. The great plains of the US and Canada are excellent for wheat, provided there is adequate rainfall from the westerlies or from the Gulf of Mexico; the shoots are generally protected by snow during the winter but a frost at flowering time can be fatal.

Wheat also flourishes at many different altitudes – as low as the Netherlands and up to nearly 10,000 feet in the Chinese highlands.

Wheat's versatility has developed in recent years as plant genetics have enabled strains to grow in drier and cooler conditions. The new strains also make more efficient use of moisture and the available sunlight, reducing growing periods for spring wheat down to 100 days or less. A particularly interesting hybrid of wheat with rye is triticale, which, it is hoped, will have the qualities of wheat with the hardiness of rye. The great flexibility of wheat is shown in the variety of its uses.

The majority of wheat is the hard red winter strain grown in the US and Canada which has the high protein and gluten content ideal for breadmaking. Yeast is added when the bread flour is made into a dough and the mixture is ideal for capturing the carbon dioxide which, when baked, makes an open structure and a good crust. White bread is made from flour that has undergone extensive milling to remove the grain's protein-rich outer layer of bran.

The softer varieties of wheat grown in Europe are more suited to making cakes, biscuits, pastry and are used in cooking. French bread is made from a similar flour but it has a lower protein content and its small grain size provides a crisp crust. Unfortunately, French bread becomes stale quite rapidly which accounts for the many small bakeries in that country.

Another strain is durum wheat which ranges in colour from white to orange-yellow to red which makes it much in demand for semolina, and in the preparation of pastas such as macaroni and noodles.

The cycles of wheat

One of the most remarkable long-term studies of wheat prices related to weather was carried out by Raymond Wheeler. By plotting temperature and rainfall from tree-ring data with wheat prices at Exeter (in England) going back to the year AD 1260, he reported the unusual result that there is a direct relationship between high rainfall and high wheat prices; conversely, wheat prices were subdued when rainfall was unusually low.

Wheat and the 180-year cycle

Another interesting correlation is around the 180-year cycle and a peak in wheat prices. For example, prices were high in 1812, there were a series of peaks around 1650, a small price rise in 1480 and the highest price for around 200 years during the Great Famine of 1317 – all these dates are near the high points of the 180-year cycle.

Although it is *generally* true that high rainfall goes with high prices, the peaks described earlier were all during periods of exceptional *dryness*. For example, it was dry and cool in 1810 (after exceptional wetness), in 1650, in 1480 and in 1317. It seems that wheat is susceptible to both exceptional high and low rainfall, with the really poor seasons coinciding with unusually cool and dry weather.

Wheat and the Kondratieff Wave

Wheat also follows a forty-five–sixty-year cycle confirming that at least in part the Kondratieff Waves are climatically driven. The evidence for this is in Figure 21, showing nearly 200 years of wheat prices from 1800. The first peak coincided with the 180-year cyclical high point described earlier, the next was in 1870 after the American Civil War, when commodity prices rose to their highest point for sixty years. The next peak was in 1920 just after the First World War when massive post-war inflation was made worse by a low point in the Kuznets' Cycle – see Figure 20. Finally the last peak was in 1974, also the high point of the Kuznets. The next low should be around 1997 with the Kondratieff Cycle – unless there is another cool–dry period following the retrogration of the sun on 20 April 1990.

The corn cycle

We met this crop before in Chapter 13, when Sir Francis Drake returned from an abortive raiding session on Spanish treasure ships with only two plants to show for his trouble; one was the potato, the second was corn (or maize). Botanists confirm that

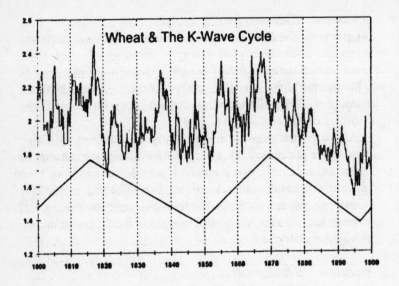

Figure 21. The price of wheat and the Kondratieff Cycle.
(Courtesy of the Foundation for the Study of Cycles.)

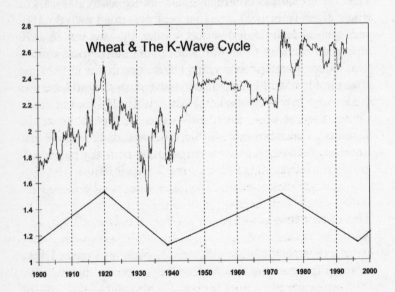

corn stemmed from a native grass, called 'tiosinte', found in certain parts of Mexico and Central America. When the first settlers arrived in North America in the 17th century, they found the native Indians cultivating what is now known as flint corn as far north as the St Lawrence estuary. This was a new crop to the settlers and they had to seek help from the Indians in its cultivation. Whatever its origins, William Cobbett, the author, agriculturist and farmer in the early part of the 19th century, described the plant not only as the 'greatest blessing of the country' but also as 'the greatest blessing God gave to man'.

Indeed, corn does seem an amazing crop, producing at least twice the abundance of output per acre compared with wheat. It also can be hybridised to grow from sea level to 13,000 ft up in the Andean mountain ranges of Latin America and from as far north as fifty degrees in Canada. It is found as far south as Argentina and Chile and in the warm weather of the early 1990s, the crop was also grown in southern England.

The efficiency compared to wheat stems from a better internal system of converting carbon dioxide, nitrogen and moisture to nutrients in the presence of sunlight – photosynthesis. From this comes a much lower requirement for water than wheat, with a transpiration of 349 tons of water required for one ton of harvested corn – nearly 50% better than wheat.

The Indians found it easy to cultivate the crop by hand-forming a mound free from weeds before planting. They could also plant seeds in woodland with the minimum of soil preparation. The settlers found the same; they could plant corn between rows of trees before the land was completely cleared. Now production is highly sophisticated with a machine combining the functions of spreading fertiliser and pesticide, then tillage and planting in a single pass. Harvesting is equally efficient.

However, there are drawbacks: one is that corn cannot stand frost at any time of the growing season. Another is that if the weather is very hot and dry at flowering time, the tassel called the 'silk' at the end of a cob can dry up and wither which severely damages the yield. Like many crops corn is susceptible to flooding both in root damage and in preventing farmers operating their sophisticated harvesting machinery. In July 1993 an area just smaller than France was flooded by the Mississippi, reducing the total crop by at least 30%.

Unlike wheat, corn contains no gluten, so the flour can only be baked into what the Mexicans call 'tortillas', flat cakes similar to the Indian chapatti. In North America, over 80% of corn is consumed by animals on the farms where it is grown; it can also be fed as cattle food after fermentation in the presence of organic acids. Corn is eaten directly as popcorn, sweetcorn, breakfast food, grits and flour; the corn kernel has a high proportion of starch which is a source of carbohydrates for alcohol, either for drink or for industrial application.

Its best known use is in bourbon whiskey in the US and rye whiskey in Canada; a typical mash might contain 75% corn and 15% rye plus 10% malt to convert starch into fermentable sugars. Apart from drinks, fermentations produce citric acid, antibiotics, vitamins and a fuel ethanol.

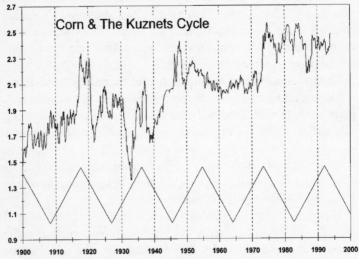

Figure 22. The price of corn and the Kuznets' Cycle. (Courtesy of the Foundation for the Study of Cycles.)

Normally planted in May, corn grows steadily during the summer towards a September harvest provided the weather is suitable. As well as being sensitive to frost during the planting and growing season, corn cannot tolerate waterlogged ground and hot drying conditions when flowering. This sensitivity tends to make the crop conform to the Kuznets 18.6-lunar and the 22.4-year Hale drought cycles – see Figure 22. Although not a cereal, soyabeans, grown for animal protein, have a similar rhythm to corn.

As might be expected, corn prices peaked in 1920, 1937, 1954 and 1974. There were two anomalies: first in 1948 there was the spike in prices that usually follows a war and secondly, more importantly, a failure of the Kuznets' Cycle in 1992. This could mean the cycle no longer applies and we can anticipate falling prices. Alternatively, it could be that the expected drought was aborted by the El Niño of 1992 and was delayed until 1995, the year after the last El Niño in 1994. This would time the next dry season for 1995, the same year as the expected low point of the 22.4-year Hale drought Cycle.

CHAPTER 15

THE LURE OF GOLD
AND SILVER

The precious metals of gold, silver, platinum and more recently palladium have fascinated and been used by man for thousands of years. They have been a means of exchange between people who had no other common yardstick; they are almost impossible to corrode, which is why all the gold that has ever been extracted or mined is still in existence – thought to be in excess of 110,000 tons. Gold and silver have been used for ornaments and jewellery from the time of their first discovery because they are highly malleable and have a wonderful lustre.

They also have industrial uses. Silver's excellent electrical conductivity makes it valuable in electronic circuits where the current values are low; it is also widely used in photography. Platinum and palladium are used in circuitry for their resistance to corrosion, and in dentistry because they can both be cast into precise shapes. Gold is the heaviest of the metals per unit weight and, as we shall see, has been the best yardstick for the control of inflation ever devised.

The cycles of gold and silver prices have run in parallel over time whenever they have both been used as a currency and store of value. Gold has an overall sixty-four-year cycle, meshing in with shorter rhythms, all of which suggests that the next high point in gold will be around 1997–8 when the four cycles converge. Ever since silver was demonetised by the US government in 1873, it has generally followed the Kuznets' Cycle. However, if gold reaches a new peak later in the 1990s, then silver and the other metals will surely follow.

Gold, the inflation fighter

It is thought that gold (and silver) were first used by Mesopotamian merchants around 3000 BC in their business dealings at home and also by the Egyptians who had also discovered the metal in the Nile delta. The Romans used gold coins but the currency ran into disrepute when greedy emperors tried to make coins go further by shaving off slivers (hence the origin of milled edges) or forming alloys with other metals such as copper. Devaluing the coinage has been the cause of empires collapsing or the rise of dictators for centuries.

The gold content of the earth's crust is minimal, which is why the metal is found in areas of high volcanic activity, where material from the mantle has been brought to the surface. This explains the concentrations on gold mining initially by the Incas, then the Spanish in the Andes; the Klondike gold rush in the 1850s and the South African and Australian finds in the 1890s. It is estimated that in the 110 years before AD 1600, the Spanish either mined, looted or stole the equivalent of eight million ounces of gold, which if cast as one would make a eight-foot cube. In the latter part of the 20th century at least 50% of the world's gold is mined in South Africa, with Canada, Russia, the United States and Australia also significant producers.

Unlike almost any other metal, gold can only be dissolved in a solution of concentrated acids called *aqua regia* made up from three parts of hydrochloric acid to one of nitric acid – an unusual combination which explains why gold is very often found in its natural state. 'Placer mining', as it is called, replicates the panning of the 'forty-niners', who sought gold in the gravel of rivers where the other metals in the original host rock had dissolved. Gold is also extracted from deep mines where huge quantities of rock are extracted for processing later on the surface. Many patents have been taken out for obtaining gold from sea water where the concentration is a tiny 0.1 milligramme of gold per metric ton of water.

Gold can be easily rolled, worked and cast, which explains its attraction as an ornament, but its very versatility makes the metal open to alloying, which is why strict purity standards have been set. One-hundred-per cent gold is rated twenty-four carat; the British standard is twenty-two carat or 91.67% purity alloyed with 8.33% copper; American, German and Italian coins are rated 21.6 carat. Other usual alloys are silver which reduces the depth of the colour, and platinum or palladium which is the jewellers' 'white' gold. A cheaper white gold can be made from an alloy of 50% gold with nickel, copper and zinc.

Gold in England

After the Romans, gold and silver became a serious coinage once again following the Norman Conquest, when one pound sterling was equivalent to a pound of silver with a purity of 92.5%. An interesting chart produced by David Williams and published in the *Cycles* journal September 1993 shows how the value of the pound devalued against gold during the period from 1343 to 1980. It started at an index of eighteen but, as the pound declined in value, rose during the Hundred Years' War to twenty-two and then increased to thirty-five before Queen Elizabeth's Great Recoinage Act of 1560 devalued the currency even further to seventy. Then in 1669 Sir Isaac Newton as Warden of the Mint firmly established Britain on the gold standard during the reign of Charles II at a new index of 100 where it remained until 1931.

It was a remarkable policy decision. As William Rees-Mogg points out in *The Reigning Error*, the pound sterling was tied, and freely exchangeable, with gold at the rate of £3.17 shillings and 10.5 pence until 1931 with two exceptions: the Napoleonic and the First World Wars. This parity value saw Britain through the Wars of Spanish Succession, the seven-year Prussian War and American Independence. The UK came off the gold standard from around 1800 to 1819 when, for a brief period, the weakness index peaked at 180 in 1813. Britain came off the gold standard again in 1913 when the index weakened to 270 in 1920; there was a brief period from 1926 to 1931, when once again gold reached 104.

Except for the two pauses described earlier, the British currency was freely convertible into the equivalent weight of gold – the supply of which was increasing annually at about 3%, enough for a steady expansion of the economy. This did not mean that prices were stable during that time because other factors described in the next chapter intervened. Its greatest importance was the curb it applied to politicians: if the government tried to inflate the economy before an election, then foreign holders of sterling could change their notes into gold and the reserves would quickly drain away. Likewise if the economy was too restricted, then gold would flow back to the Bank of England and the government knew it could ease interest rates or whatever controls had been applied.

Since 1931 the pound sterling has been at the whim of politicians but supposedly tied to the US dollar until that too came off the gold standard in August 1971. Anybody trusting enough to hold their savings in sterling rather than gold sovereigns since the Second World War would have seen the value of their cash decline to a thirtieth relative to the gold price in 1980 and by a twentieth from the mid-1990s.

Gold in America

A gold and silver coinage was adopted by Congress in 1792 with gold priced at $19.36 per Troy ounce; it remained there until the war of 1812, when specie payments (a description for metal convertibility) were suspended in August 1814. The price reached $23.07 in 1815 before specie payments were resumed on 20 February 1817. The price was raised to $20.67 per ounce until 31 January 1934, when it was further raised to $35.

There were three other suspensions: the first was during the panic of 1837, the next was also during a brief flurry in 1857 and the next during the Civil War. As the British suspended the gold standard during the First World War, so did the Union on 31 December 1861 when 'greenbacks' were issued and the price

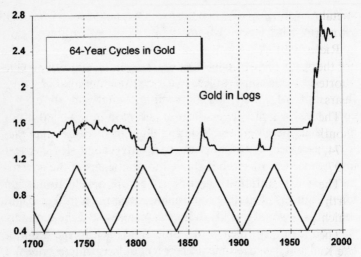

Figure 23. Sixty-four-year cycle in gold. (Courtesy of the Foundation for the Study of Cycles.)

nearly tripled to $59.12 per ounce. The war over, the price of $20.67 was resumed on 1 January 1869. Specie payments were finally suspended for individuals in 1934 after the Roosevelt administration made it a criminal offence to hold gold.

The US treasury amassed three quarters of the world's total gold holding until the late 1950s, when foreign holders of dollars started converting their cash into the metal. The process accelerated in the 1960s when the Kennedy administration began to inflate the economy and created money to pay for the Vietnam War. The drain on gold reserves became so severe that the US was eventually forced off the gold standard on 15 August 1971 by the then president, Richard Nixon.

The experience of America and Britain shows that gold has been the traditional hedge against inflation which stopped governments printing money while their currency was linked to that precious metal. It happened several times to both the dollar and pound during the 19th century and with a vengeance after the Second World War. Anything on the scale of a major commodity-price scare caused by a steep climatic change could send the metal rocketing upwards once again. But gold cycles have their own drumbeat.

Richard Mogey, the Executive Director of the Foundation for the Study of Cycles, has identified several gold rhythms. The shortest one of note is forty months, the longest is sixty-four years:

The forty-month cycle is similar in duration to the forty-one-month stock rhythm described in Chapter 11. It made a high in 1974, another in 1980, in 1988 and the next peak is expected in 1997.

There is a 5.6-year cycle that could be associated with the earth's disturbance of the Chandler Wobble (every 6.4 years) which rises to the next high point in 2000.

The next is an 18.14-year cycle with a not dissimilar pattern to the Kuznets. The last high point was around 1974; it reached a low in 1990 and the next high point is expected in 1998.

There is a sixty-four-year cycle shown in Figure 23 from AD 1700 to 2000. There is a high point around the seven-year Prussian War, the next at the time of Napoleon and the next during the American Civil War. There was a peak during the banking crisis and devaluation of 1934, and the next high is expected around 1998.

Silver is the whitest metal of all

Silver and gold have been monetary running mates for at least 5000 years as one civilisation after another has married the two currencies in different proportions. The earliest known ratio was one of gold to five of silver. The rates varied between 8.93 to one and fifteen to one up to the fall of Rome and remained there until the fall of Constantinople in 1453. The first US coinage law in 1792 fixed the ratio at fifteen to one where it remained until the US demonetised silver in 1873. The price languished for many years but then hit a high with the Kuznets' Cycle in 1920, only for the price to collapse in 1932 when its ratio to gold rose to seventy-two to one. Gold nearly reached its old ratio of fifteen to one at the peak of the 1980 inflationary crisis, but the ratio again crashed below that of 1932 to eighty to one in 1992.

Silver, like gold, is a highly ductile metal and is treasured for its brilliant white colour; it is so malleable that one gramme of the metal can be drawn to a thread a mile long. It has also a much higher electrical conductivity than most other conductors, such as copper, zinc, tin – or even gold – which has created an industrial use apart from its application to photography. There is also a steady demand from countries like India where it is highly prized.

Although Europe has had a small supply of silver from a mine at Kongsberg in Norway, the metal became available in quantity when the Spanish treasure ships started arriving from Chile and Peru in the 16th century. Although the greatest output now comes from Mexico and the US, a large proportion of silver is extracted with copper, lead or zinc workings – making production more economical if the market price collapses.

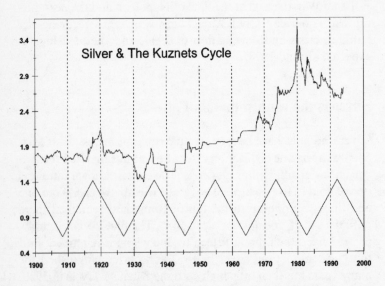

Figure 24. Silver related to the Kuznets' Cycle. (Courtesy of the Foundation for the Study of Cycles.)

Silver price fluctuations

The silver price remained at about $1.32 per ounce until it was demonetised by the US in 1873 when the metal was dumped on the market and the price fell to around fifty cents. There was a strong demand for the metal in 1919 and the price rose to $1.35 per ounce when the British government bought 300 million ounces to mint silver rupees in India and the Chinese were allowed to buy the metal on the open market. Silver then crashed to twenty-five cents per ounce in 1932, when the Indian government demonetised the rupee and, once again, the reserves were dumped on the market.

Figure 24 shows how silver has broadly tracked the Kuznets' Cycle, marking the high points in 1920, 1936, 1974 and with a scheduled new peak in 1992. However, like the price of corn, this new high point did not materialise, suggesting that silver could move with gold later in the 1990s.

CHAPTER 16

COMMODITY-PRICE CYCLES

Throughout history man's ability to grow crops has been dependent on the elements providing the essential sun and moisture.
Although we have made some contribution with adapted
hybrids, improved fertilisers, better irrigation and much more
sophisticated management, none of these can compensate for
poor weather conditions. This was evident when the cycles of
wheat and corn were considered in an earlier chapter, and
although precious metals respond to man-made wisdom or folly,
they also follow weather-related commodity prices.

Our knowledge of some crop and commodity prices goes
back a long way. The British economist William Beveridge was
the first to deduce the series of wheat prices going back to AD
1260. Two Americans, George Warren and Frank Pearson, pro-
fessors at Cornell University, extracted the prices of a wide range
of materials purchased for the British army and navy going back
to the days of Samuel Pepys. Bavarian crop-price data in
Munich and Augsburg going back to AD 1450 were published in
a paper written by J.M. Elsas in 1936.

Warren and Pearson's list incorporates many of the items
needed to keep a ship and its company at sea. To cut down theft
or fraud from the victualling depot, careful records were kept for
such items as corn, tobacco, cotton, wheat, butter, coffee, mess

pork and beef, tallow, molasses, salt, sugar, hides, leather, sheeting, wool, coal, pig iron, tin plate, linseed and whale oil, tar and turpentine.

Elsas' paper is no less interesting, itemising items from Munich which included rye, oats, wheat, barley, rice, peas, honey, oil, salt, straw, wax, hides, bricks, fustian, ticking and scarlet woollen cloth. Augsburg had a similar list but added such things as carp, lard, lumber, lime, beef, suet and cheese. The report also detailed the wages for labourers including such trades as mowers, straw cutters, rakers, carpenters, masons, bricklayers, ditch diggers, drivers and loaders. In those days pay usually lagged behind commodity prices except during a major upset. Wages increased rapidly during the Thirty Years' War, also in Spain during the last years of the 16th century when the country was hit by the plague. In those days most people worked on the land but even in the year 1900, over 41% of the American population was employed in agriculture. In the 1990s the figure is nearer 3%.

From all this information the Foundation for the Study of Cycles has compiled a record of commodity prices going back centuries for some of the basic items. For example, they have computerised data for cattle going back to 1749, coffee to 1797, copper to 1784, corn to 1720, cotton 1732, gold to 1560, hogs to 1749, petroleum to 1890, silver to 1273, soyabeans to 1924. This has been sufficiently representative to assemble a data base which broadly matches the most widely followed series of commodity prices – the Commodity Research Bureau (CRB) futures index which started in 1956.

The CRB futures is an index covering twenty-one different commodities under six headings: grains, soft and industrial commodities, meats, precious metals, imported products and miscellaneous. As these are the most widely traded items on the Chicago and New York exchanges, they can be instantaneously computed and transmitted electronically. The composition of the CRB broadly matches the Foundation's data base:

The grains comprise 28.6% of the total index, including wheat, corn, oats, soyabeans, soyabean oil and meal.

The next largest section is industrial commodities, which include copper, cotton, lumber, crude oil, unleaded gasoline which together add up to 23.8% of the total.

There are three groups which each comprise 14.3% of the total: the precious metals of gold, silver and platinum; cattle, hogs and pork bellies; imported coffee, cocoa and sugar.

Finally, orange juice contributes 4.7%.

The exchanges calculate all the futures prices for the months ahead (closing prices published daily in the *Wall Street Journal* and mostly in the *Financial Times*); then an arithmetical mean is worked out. All the means are then multiplied together and the twenty-first root of the twenty-one average prices is calculated continuously to provide the CRB futures index (1967=100). Reuters and the *Economist* also publish indices. For example, the *Economist* breaks down thirty commodities into three groups: foods, industrials and non-food agriculturals; in addition there is an overall index – all of which are published weekly. Unlike the CRB futures, where commodities are equally weighted, the *Economist* applies varying factors.

Commodity cycles

As might be expected from the cycles governing wheat and corn, there are similar rhythms dominating a collection of commodities which the Foundation has designated as a surrogate CRB. The first is the relationship with the Kondratieff Wave. Figure 25 shows the index peaking in 1816, declining towards 1848, then rising to the next peak during the American Civil War. After the decline to 1896, the graph keeps rising until commodities blow off in 1920 before bottoming out once more in 1939. Although we cannot be sure of the precise timing, the peak of the K-Wave was in 1974, with the next low point expected in 1997–8.

Commodities also relate to the Kuznets' Cycle. Figure 26 shows the cycle peaking in 1919–20 and the panic of 1937. There is no evidence of a commodity rise in 1955, although it became very dry but the next peak was in 1974 when there was a massive rise in prices. There should have been a peak in 1992 but, as explained earlier, this could well have been postponed to 1995–6.

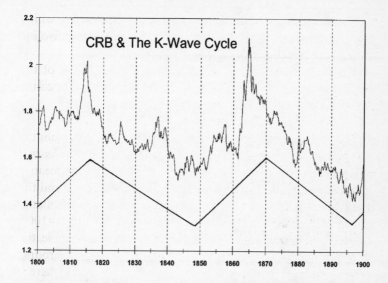

Figure 25. Relationship between an index of commodities and the Kondratieff Wave. (Courtesy of the Foundation for the Study of Cycles.)

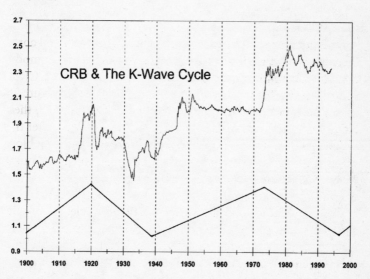

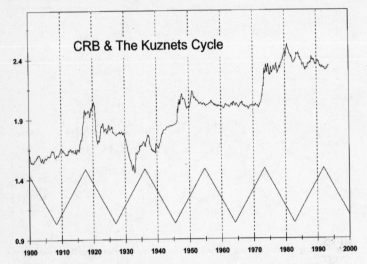

Figure 26. Relationship between the CRB and the Kuznets' Cycle.
(Courtesy of the Foundation for the Study of Cycles.)

CHAPTER 17

BOND YIELDS FOLLOW COMMODITY PRICES

All spending institutions depend upon cash. Central and local governments achieve this by raising taxes, but if their spending exceeds their income they have the power to borrow the money from banks and other investors, such as insurance companies. Most governments until the First World War were on the gold standard, which forced them to balance income with expenditure and such matters as the balance of private savings. For example, the US government had only $3 billion of debt by 1917 when the total national income (or gross national product: GNP) was $40 billion – a ratio of 7.5%. By 1994, the ratio of government borrowings was in excess of 70% but the US was not the most indebted nation: Belgium had borrowings of 130% of its national income and Italy's ratio was 110%.

The money needed by governments will come through the sale of bonds or fixed-interest stock whereby it raises funds from major institutions such as banks, insurance companies, pension funds etc. This is the same source that commerce and industry need for loans and share capital; thus the state is in competition with private enterprise for money. If the state's demands are excessive, interest rates are pushed up – a situation called 'crowding out'. When a stock is issued, it will always have a tag of the interest payable (its coupon) and when it will be bought back (redeemed), if ever.

Britain issued the first irredeemable government stock in 1729, which were later converted to 3% consolidated annuities (Consols), yielding 3%; the interest held until 1888, when it reduced to 2.75%, then 2.5% in 1903, where it has since remained. Debt financing for firms started to become popular in the 19th century, when utilities like railways, canals, water boards and later gas companies issued debenture stock which not only paid a fixed coupon but gave the borrower first charge over the assets of the company in the event of failure; commercial firms like breweries, which had a large asset base, also issued debentures.

Bonds were also a favoured method of raising funds for the US – often in Europe – for individual states, and also for canal- and road-building companies. Despite some setbacks during the war of 1812, the boom continued until the country was approaching the panic of 1837, which led directly to the debt repudiation of 1843. Richard Mogey in the *Cycles* journal of February 1994 notes that this was a very difficult time for the US, as it coincided with a government policy of repaying the national debt between 1830 and 1835; this meant that no bonds were issued between 1835 and 1841 because of declining collateral.

This payback should have meant more available cash but the panic of 1837 and the coming Depression forced banks to fail; the state of Michigan repudiated its debts and as bond yields rocketed, the value of other states' debt collapsed to only a few cents in the dollar. The panic forced the price of early railroad bonds to decline by more than 80% from 1836 to 1843 and the value of most foreign loans to the US either fell heavily or were repudiated. By 1839, the European market for US securities no longer existed.

The years up to the 1860s were more serene for Britain and America, budgets were balanced and the euphoria was encouraged by the first gold rush in the early 1850s. The boom accelerated in the Union during the Civil War, which was paid for by the issue of 'greenbacks', which forced the yields of note-denominated bonds lower despite rising inflation. The problem was compounded by the National Banking Acts of 1863–5, which allowed bank notes to be backed by government bonds, not gold. This created a demand for bonds which lowered their yield even more. Once again those who trusted the integrity of governments lost heavily – just as they did in the French Revolution and in the Weimar Republic; the value of greenbacks collapsed by 40% in three years.

However, despite the Civil War and the rolling depression of the 1870s, the US national income rose with prosperity and as noted earlier the total US federal debt was only around $3 billion by 1917 (the same volume was issued in three days in 1994). The early part of the 20th century also saw rising European prosperity until the outbreak of the First World War.

Britain came off the gold standard in 1914, and funded the war by raising taxation and issuing an irredeemable war loan. This originally had a coupon of 5% but was subsequently downgraded in 1931 to 3.5% when the government deemed that bond holders should suffer similar pain to employees who had to bear lower living standards in the slump. In America, the government issued longer-term redeemable stock to pay for Roosevelt's New Deal; it originally matured for redemption at twenty years but this was subsequently increased to the present thirty-year T-Bond. Companies tried all means of reducing debt during the Depression and investors could be offered attractive terms for swapping their debt into equity holdings.

After the Second World War, the British government wanted to increase public spending to such a degree that it could no longer issue irredeemable stock; although some redeemable bonds had been issued previously, it was obliged to offer investors maturities ranging from a few months to over twenty years. Companies also started issuing their version of redeemable bonds, called 'loan stock'. Unlike debentures, these were not directly secured on the company assets and consequently commanded a higher coupon; they also had other attractive features, either making them convertible into shares at a given value or with a variable coupon tied to the bank rate.

After the Stock Market crash in 1974 many banks were in trouble with excessive losses from the collapse in real-estate prices and raised the cost of lending to their customers. As a number of American companies had better credit ratings than the banks, they found loans could be raised more cheaply in the market place. Accordingly a new money market was created in New York, dealing in company IOUs with a maturity of three, six and twelve months. By the mid-1990s very few of the larger companies raise loans from banks.

The failure of a number of companies during the 1970s and early 1980s left investors holding valueless securities, prompting the need for a business, wishing to issue securities, to find an outside credit agency to give investors a risk assessment. Credit-rating firms such as Moody's, and Standard and Poor, had been in existence for many years but now their business expanded, when they would be paid to judge credit ratings for issuing bonds. These might range from an AAA rating for a company with a rock-solid commitment rating to those of a lesser grading, forcing a company to pay a higher coupon for any stock issued. Later agencies were asked to give country risk assessments when several in the developing world were in danger of default. Ultimately what were known as 'junk bonds' were issued during the 1980s which gave investors no protection from failure but the opportunity to make a considerable profit if the associated venture succeeded.

Bond yields v commodity prices

There is a direct relationship between a bond yield and the rate of inflation, which is often signalled by rising or falling commodity prices. In fact, as the next chart shows, there has been a consistent relationship over nearly 200 years (with the certain exceptions described earlier), with commodity prices generally leading bond yields. The bond yields respond to changing inflation because once a bond or fixed-interest stock has been issued, the price in the market place will vary with the expected rise or fall in prices.

For example, a bond could be issued at 100 pence with a coupon of 6%, when the rate of inflation was, say, 3%; for the price to stay at 100p, investors would expect the rate of inflation to remain the same. If, however, rising prices increased the rate of inflation to 4%, then investors might look for a return of 7 or even 8%; clearly they are not going to pay 100p for the stock when they could earn 8% elsewhere. Hence in an open market, the stock would have to be offered at, say, 80p (reflecting the 25% increase in inflation) to find a buyer. Conversely if inflation dropped to 2%, then the value of the stock might rise to 130p. During the deflation of the 1930s, 2.5% Consols were actually being traded at the equivalent of 120p; compare this with a price of around 36p in the spring of 1994!

The next chart shows how bond yields have responded to the varying commodity prices over the last 200 years. Figure 27 compares the equivalent of the modern CRB index described in the last chapter with the yield of high-grade bonds which are a combination of British 2.5% Consols and then US stocks.

The chart shows a steady decline in both commodity prices and yields until the 1840s, with a rise in both lines during 1815–16 when Tambora erupted. Bonds diverged from the ruling deflation during the panic of 1837 to 1843 and then started rising with commodity prices until the American Civil War, when they diverged. While there was a peak in commodities, yields collapsed over the uncertainties with greenback-denominated bonds. Both commodity prices and bond yields collapsed during the deflation towards the end of the century.

The two lines ran in unison until both peaked in 1920 and then subsequently declined in the 1930s, with bonds collapsing the furthest because the US government was issuing quantities of debt during the Depression to pay for the New Deal. Commodity prices remained high after the Second World War to provide food for the millions displaced by the war, while yields were kept down by governments still trying to balance their budgets.

However, from 1960 yields started to follow commodities when the US administration progressively inflated the economy. There was a high point in the bond yields during the peak of the Juglar Cycle in 1970; both lines peaked at the Kuznets' Cycle

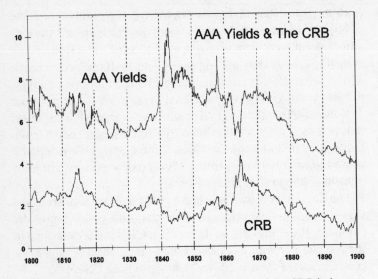

Figure 27. Comparison between the equivalent of the CRB index and AAA-rated bond yields. (Courtesy of the Foundation for the Study of Cycles.)

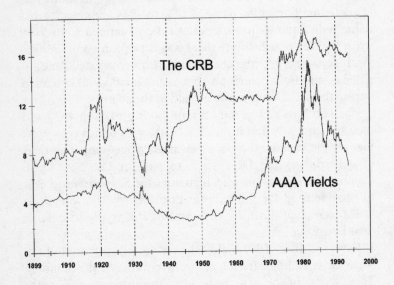

high point in 1974, and again with the Juglar inflation around 1980. The 1980s were a time of relative stability for commodity prices but the bond yields collapsed – possibly because the US was off the gold standard – just as it was in the 1860s.

Cycles in bond yields

It is not surprising, then, that if bond yields follow commodity prices they should obey a pattern similar to the Kondratieff Cycle shown in Figure 28. The long wave peaked in 1910, reached a low point in 1931, then reached the next high in 1974. The next low point is expected in 1997–8.

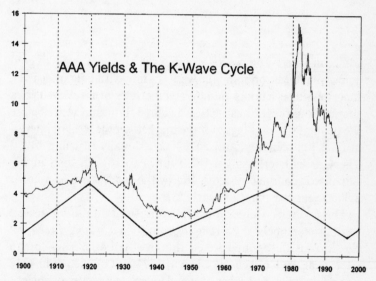

Figure 28. Comparison of bond yields with the Kondratieff Cycle in the 20th century. (Courtesy of the Foundation for the Study of Cycles.)

CHAPTER 18

POLITICIANS ONCE USED INTEREST RATES RESPONSIBLY

Charging interest on borrowed money is a custom as old as gold coins. While Mesopotamians were trading with gold and silver, they were also lending money – sometimes at rates even loan sharks would regard as excessive. Three thousand years before the birth of Christ, kings, not the market, set the level of interest at rates between 10% and 20% – occasionally reaching 140%! The Greeks later brought these down to 10% in their highly organised economic systems, and by the year AD 1 rates were at a 3000-year low point of nearly 5%.

The Church's views on usury (from the Latin *usura*, usage) were strict, namely: *it is wrong to profit from a brother's need*, yet the various faiths interpreted things differently. The Roman Church at the Councils of Lyon in 1274 and of Vienna in 1312 passed an edict outlawing money lenders as enemies of society. They were to be refused confession, absolution and a Christian burial until they had made proper restitution.

However, this left the field clear for the Lombards, the Italian financiers and money changers, to lend money to the Church and state, provided interest was kept below 50%! (It is said that the sign of the three golden balls takes its origin from the three blue spheres to be found in the coat of arms of the Medici family.) For 600 years, this allowed the Jews to extend credit to

Gentiles on interest but not to other Jews; Christians were generally forbidden to be usurous but it depended on who wanted the money. For Islam, the ban was complete but recently Muslims have been known to charge a higher price for goods or services bought on credit.

Richard Mogey, in an article in the January/February 1994 edition of *Cycles*, identifies a 500-year cyclical trend in short-term interest rates, which marches in step with the Wheeler rhythms explained in Chapter 6. They fell from 20% to 10% in 2000 BC, and to 5% just after 500 BC. Rates turned upwards about AD 50, reaching around 12% by the sack of Rome in the 5th century AD. Interest fell once again to 5% after AD 500, another turning point. However, they were on the move upwards by AD 1000 at 10%, reaching a high of 25% around 1500.

The taking of Constantinople by the Ottoman Turks, cutting the overland trade routes, was the turning-point. It compelled the Europeans to find an alternative source for spices; it also created rampant inflation when 400,000 pounds weight of gold were landed in Europe during the 16th century. The new trading opportunities forced first England, then other countries to shake off usury laws, opening the flood gates to demands from traders and the new breed of small manufacturers. Enterprising individuals realised that money could be borrowed and invested more profitably in trade than in land.

Interest rates played quite a different role once Britain made gold specie freely convertible in 1669. Varying the rate was used to encourage overseas holders of pounds to keep their cash in sterling bonds, not convert it into gold, despite upsets such as wars. It was a remarkably successful policy which kept Britain on the gold standard for two centuries.

We saw earlier how Britain left the gold standard in August 1798 during the Napoleonic Wars, which coincided with the war of 1812. The price of Consols declined to forty-seven but had recovered to ninety-six in May 1825 after Britain once more resumed specie payments; there was a further fall in Consols during the panic of 1825 and later in February 1831, when there was rioting against the Tory government.

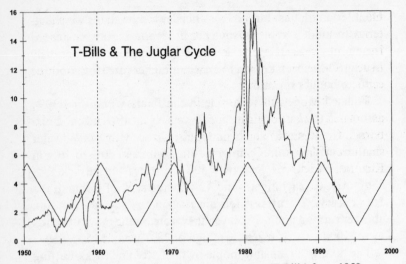

Figure 29. Cycles of short-term interest rates (T-Bills) from 1950 to 1994, associated with the Juglar Cycle. (Courtesy of the Foundation for the Study of Cycles.)

The government was obliged to import the equivalent of $240 million of food with gold when the crops failed in 1846, the year of the Irish Potato Famine. The rundown in the gold reserves created the panic of 1847, when the government increased interest rates to 8% and allowed the banks to issue additional notes. This prompt action stabilised the position, the panic subsided and gold flowed back. There was another upset during the Crimean War, interest rates being raised to 10% when the gold reserves ran down to the equivalent of $3 million. The Bank of England had to take similar action during the inflationary peak in 1866 after the American Civil War and again during the Franco-Prussian War of 1870.

With Britain off the gold standard in 1914 and again in 1931, the US dollar has had to bear the brunt of maintaining gold reserves. Chapter 11 showed how the Federal Reserve Bank was forced to raise the price of treasury bills as a means of quelling the inflation of 1920 and again in 1929 to dampen inflationary surges. The Treasury Bill (T-Bill) is a very short-dated stock of ninety days which is issued by the US authorities to raise short-term money; it does not actually carry any interest but instead is issued at a discount. For example, a 12%-yield bill might be issued at ninety-seven cents allowing the holder to make three cents over three months, 12% for the year.

The post-war history of interest rates is shown in Figure 29, associated with the Juglar Cycle mirroring the peaks in the bonds. The Juglar peaks are in 1960, 1970, 1980 and there was a small peak in 1990. The 1974 high point was caused by the Kuznets' Cycle.

CHAPTER 19

CYCLES OF HOUSING
OR REAL-ESTATE

At the peak of the Japanese housing boom in 1988, it was estimated that the total value of dwellings was six times the value of
the Stock Market – then valued at $4 trillion (thousand billion).
Of this, the land occupied by the Imperial Palace was said to
equal the worth of Californian estate, and the city of Tokyo
matched the whole value of real-estate in America. In 1992, the
Japanese debt per household was 108% that of income, making
housing valuations very vulnerable to a rapid rise of interest
rates if inflation were to increase steeply.

In Britain, the total value of housing was more than three
times the whole national product in 1993, taking the average
value of twenty million homes at £55,000. These are very large
figures and the housing market employs many people in the construction trades, as suppliers of materials, in estate agencies and
in funding institutions, such as banks and building societies.

Most work on housing or real-estate cycles has been done in
the United States where an 18.6-year rhythm has been identified
(see Chapter 10); it was believed that the waves of immigration
were partly responsible, coupled with a rotation of the labour
force, family formation and construction – all of which fed back
into national output and employment.

Richard Mogey in the May/June 1991 edition of *Cycles*,

identifies two main series affecting real-estate: the first is the Kondratieff, or long, Wave described in Chapter 9, the second is the Kuznets' Cycle explained in Chapter 10. Approximately three Kuznets fit into one Kondratieff. Mogey identifies several factors making up these two cycles.

The first is the average life of the housing stock, incorporating the age, style, cost and size, which is dependent upon the family number. Another consideration could be the suitability for a work-place at home in an area quite separate from the living space. Homes become obsolete or run down; in poorer areas, it is often more economic to build anew, not to refurbish an unsuitable or badly constructed building.

The cost of borrowing is another factor in deciding housing cycles. Mogey has identified all major lows in real-estate, coinciding with interest-rate floors. Over the years since 1850, the low points have been in 1898 and 1939, the bottom of the Kondratieff Cycles. Also, both real-estate booms in this period, 1888 and 1925, were preceded by a fifty-four-year top in interest rates.

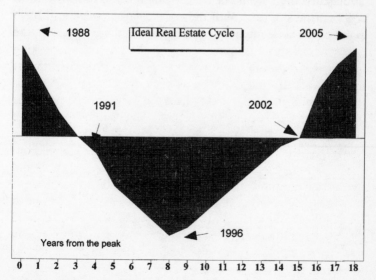

Figure 30. Idealised real-estate cycle drawn in 1991. (Courtesy of the Foundation for the Study of Cycles.)

Richard Mogey believes another factor in real-estate cycles are international battles, as defined by Raymond Wheeler's index. Wars diminish the demand for housing, while the end of the conflict triggers a boom from the returning forces setting up families. There were falls during the American Civil War in 1860, the Indian wars of 1880, the Spanish-American War of 1898 (also bottom of the Kondratieff Cycle), the First and Second World Wars, and the Vietnam War.

In the shorter term, housing in both Britain and America is very sensitive to a negative yield curve (when the value of short-term interest rates rises above bond yields – see Figure 20). The biggest crash since 1920 was when the yield curve in the US went negative in 1925 followed by housing values losing over 80% up to 1934. There were minor falls when the yield curve went negative in 1950, 1960, 1967 and 1970. There was a major crash on both sides of the Atlantic in 1974 and again in 1981.

Richard Mogey has suggested an idealised future for real-estate in Figure 30, which was drawn in 1991 when it was anticipated there would be a steep fall in prices in line with the 1992 Kuznets' Cycle. With the crisis delayed to 1996, the low point of the cycle might be reached later in the decade.

CHAPTER 20

CONFRONTING THE UNTHINKABLE

Continuous working of highly stressed metal causes metal fatigue, the fault that caused the crashes of the first jet airliner, the de Havilland Comet. Our study of cycles shows that the same thing can happen to nations. At some point the tensions that have built up over each 500, 180 or 100 years fracture the existing order, forcing people to rethink their institutions, priorities and sense of values.

Society has broken down before and no doubt will do so again. Britain dissolved into chaos after the Romans departed taking all their treasures with them; the sack of Rome in AD 410 ended centuries of order; the fall of Constantinople in 1453 ended one empire but encouraged the rise of European domination. Mankind is resilient; every setback was devastating at the time but others emerged to start afresh.

Now we could be faced by another discontinuity in the affairs of mankind which perhaps will be every bit as difficult as the ones before. For all our sophistication, this time we could find it immensely difficult to adjust as we have known only improving security and prosperity since the Second World War; we now consider it a *right* that this should continue to our children and grandchildren. If Raymond Wheeler and others are proved correct, we will be entering a cool-dry period when individuals could become restless and angry, quite prepared to throw off conventions or rulers that oppress or vex us.

The low point in several climatic cycles increases the risk of greater volcanic activity, associated with unusually low sunspots; both these would make the weather in the upper latitudes of the northern hemisphere unusually cool and probably also dry. Neither do they make for good crop-growing conditions in the mid-1990s and food shortages would provoke rising inflation – just when politicians thought they had won the battle. Climatic variations are not the only reason for examining historical parallels; we should also be contemplating the strong possibility of a financial collapse.

Since around 1960, many western governments – particularly the United States, Belgium, Italy and Britain – have been living beyond their means and increasingly have borrowed to maintain the spending level that politicians promised the electorate. The US in particular had to borrow at the rate of $1 billion per day in 1993 – funded increasingly by the central bank being forced into effectively creating money to buy government securities. This is the modern equivalent of the money-printing spree of the Weimar Republic which caused the hyperinflation and a currency collapse of the early 1920s. Either through arrogance or ignorance politicians never seem to learn from history, which is why Russia, Serbia and some Latin American countries have resorted to the printing presses to pay for even more government spending.

Either of these two events, a change in the climate affecting harvests and people's attitudes, or a financial collapse, would be enough to trigger the biggest ever crash. In combination they would be devastating. The lesson of the cycles is that both are likely to occur in the 1990s and we should understand what they mean and what we can do in preparation.

The advent of another climatic minimum
Earlier chapters have described the events of previous minima. Every time planets have disturbed the sun's motion, there has been a period of low sunspots and increasing volcanic action

which has cooled the climate, reduced crop yields and made people impatient of the existing order. We saw in Chapter 14 how wheat prices rocketed in the Maunder minimum of 1630, and in the Sabine minimum of 1810 we also noted the chaos of those turbulent times.

The world has actually done rather well, feeding the rising population for the last twenty years through the green revolution. As Figure 31 shows, output has kept abreast of consumption in most years, except 1974 and 1988 when, despite all the new techniques, a severe drought ruined the harvest. The production in the four years from 1989 has been exceptional – particularly in 1992, which should have been a poor cyclic year – although the impact is likely to be delayed, not avoided.

Crops can also suffer from too much rain and unfortunately 1993 was not a good year, when devastating floods in many parts of the American corn belt reduced output by 30% and lowered the volume of carry-over stocks proportionate to 1973–4. The mid-1990s are also likely to be difficult years if the end of the El Niño and the Hale Cycle create growing conditions similar to those of 1973–4 and 1988. If that happens we could expect commodity prices to rise very significantly – probably to double those of 1974, with the CRB index rising to a peak of 440 (see Figure 32).

How a climatic change of this scale might affect other arable parts of the world would depend upon the available moisture and warmth. In the conditions described by James Shirley in Chapter 2, one might expect the rain belts to move further south over North America and Eurasia, making growing conditions very difficult. Of these countries, the US and China would certainly fare better, with their long north–south geographic spread, than Russia which stops at forty degrees north – although any political agreement with the Ukraine could considerably increase potential food supplies.

If there are shortages, it should be possible to bring land back into production in Europe and the US, but this may not be practical in Russia or China because their land under cultivation has actually *diminished* from the mid-1970s by 18% and 23%

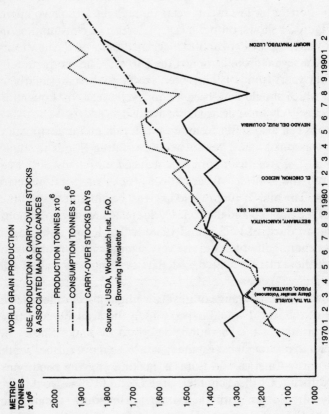

Figure 31. World grain production from 1970 to 1992, related to consumption and carry-over stocks.

respectively. Land can only be brought back into use if it is not too cool and dry for germinating seeds, and has not become contaminated, for example, by excessive salt; a period of exceptionally dry weather in the mid-1990s could cause terrible shortages – particularly in Russia, a country already reeling from chaos and neglect.

Are we heading for a financial collapse?

Poor harvests could have a devastating impact on any dollar-based world financial system, however governments respond to rising commodity prices. One alternative would be to contain any rises in commodity prices by lifting interest rates to quell inflation (one of the scenarios outlined in *Meltdown*). This could only be undertaken by confident politicians, for most households would be forced to spend a higher proportion of their income on basic expenditure, such as food, fuel and other fundamentals, and much less on other things. Countries would be plunged into recession.

Alternatively, politicians could 'accommodate' rising inflationary pressures by forcing ever more money into the financial system to keep interest rates low – just as the Weimar government printed money in the early 1920s. Governments have some control over short-term rates but the yields on longer-term bonds would rocket upwards in response to rising prices, so making it extremely expensive to raise any loans over, say, twelve months' maturity. Governments might take the risk of raising interest rates if their economies were booming, but when the dominant influence is still deflation in the mid-1990s, their most likely course is to continue the policy of cheap money, hoping they can contain the serious inflation and currency collapse.

Apart from dealing with inflation, western economies will be faced by rising unemployment from jobs made uncompetitive from increasingly cheap imports from emerging economies. Countries such as Vietnam are able to hire energetic labour at a fraction of the cost of the western equivalent; it is estimated that thirty-two Vietnamese or five Poles could be employed for one western semi-skilled worker burdened with excessive social security and welfare charges.

As international consultant Michael White points out, the 'cybernetic revolution', or the ability of firms to substitute intelligent processes (such as robotics or biogenics) in what is known as automation, is already upon us. It has already reduced 'blue collar' employment and still further reductions are being made by subcontracting or outsourcing processes to areas of cheaper wages in Eastern Europe and particularly in the Far East. This pattern is spreading to 'white collar' employment, where many clerical and middle-management grades are being taken over by computers and their like, and are disappearing for good.

Political pressures to protect home industries will become increasingly acute near election times. White suggests this will force governments to go in for trade blocs, such as the European Union or North America Free Trade Area to negotiate what is known as 'managed trade', deals made to protect home employment from 'unfair' competition. Any restrictions placed upon imports into high-cost trading blocs would reduce competition and increase inflation.

Overhanging rising commodities and restricted trade is the grossly over-extended credit system in the United States – and other countries. There have been financial panics in the past, but any upset to the financial balance now is likely to be much greater because of the crippling debts of the American and other governments, as in Belgium, Italy and Canada; there is also the incredible scale of what is known as the 'derivative financial markets' which is, at around $50 trillion, double the entire output of the world by the end of 1994.

The danger from derivatives

Apart from indebtedness there is the potential hazard of breaking down what are known as the derivative markets which are part of but separate from other exchanges such as foreign exchange, the stock and bond markets. Little information is available for this activity but the General Accounting Office of the US government was commissioned to make a study and this brief description is taken from a précis made by Anthony Robertson of Fastnet Associates.

Derivative trading covers four basic activities:

Forward contracts represent over 40% of the market which largely apply to foreign-exchange dealings. For example, an importer may be concerned that his country's currency will decline before a consignment is paid for; the risk may be off-set by enough foreign exchange to cover the whole or part of the delivery through the agency of a bank. Once the debt is due to be settled, the purchaser has the cash available. Of course, being perverse, the foreign-exchange market might go the other way and the importer could make a loss; to guard against this he might be well advised to enter an equal and opposite *futures* contract.

Futures contracts are really a sophisticated bet that two currencies will move relative to each other, they can also apply to other contracts, such as bonds or commodities. The deal requires an owner with a holding of foreign exchange, bonds, commodities or the like; for example, the holder of, say, one million DM, 5,000 bushels of soyabeans or $100,000-worth of US Treasury Bonds. Believing they will go up in value he is prepared to sell the rights to anyone who believes the contract will go down in value – the second party. The third is the broker who makes a market between buyer and seller in exchange for a commission. Hence for a sum worth a fraction of the value of the contract the buyer can control many times the size of his purchase. If the price goes down as he believes, the buyer stands to profit; conversely the seller will pocket the purchase price of the contract (less commission) if the price rises.

Option contracts The danger in futures trading is that the buyer of a contract may be required for what is designated as a 'margin call' if, as in the example mentioned above, the price in the contract rises not falls. The buyer faces a choice: either he can close the contract, thereby losing his purchase price or pay an additional deposit if he believes the price will ultimately fall. Margin calls can become very expensive if the price goes against the buyer. Alternatively, the buyer may buy an option at a fixed price at the time of the contract requiring no margin calls, irrespective of whether the price rises or falls. Options, however, have an expiry date when the contract closes. Futures and options constitute 18% and 13% respectively of this huge derivative market.

Swops (or swaps) are an ingenious method of raising loans in another country when no collateral is available. For example, an American company wishes to raise a loan to buy a business in Germany; without collateral it can offer its own security through an intermediary, such as a bank, to a German company aiming to raise a loan in America. On the face of it there is a matching obligation and both principals achieve their objective. Swops can also apply to interest rates where the parties to matching contracts swop liabilities and benefits. By mid-1994, the swops market is estimated to be over $10 trillion, nearly double the size of the United States national product.

Inevitably what started as legitimate business attracts the attention of speculators and traders helped by the Fed. When the Bank aggressively reduced interest rates during the early 1990s many banks, already under pressure from huge real-estate losses, had their deposits reduced as lenders could receive a much better return from the booming bond and stock markets. Undeterred, many bankers (and others), rather than lend money, saw this as an opportunity to use the existing financial instruments to speculate. For example, an American bank might use the swaps system to buy German bonds; another might use futures trading to speculate on American bonds increasing in value. George Soros probably used futures to sell sterling shortly before Britain left the Exchange Rate Mechanism.

In effect, what was initially sound commercial practice was used as a profit source, which worked well provided US interest rates continued to fall. The Fed itself made use of the conditions by encouraging the banks to 'ride the yield curve' to help pay for the government's burgeoning deficit; this meant giving the banks a source of low-interest funds to buy higher yielding bonds. There were benefits all around, the US treasury received its cash and the banks were able to rebuild their reserves after suffering terrible losses from real-estate during the recession. All seemed to be well – except the financial bubble continued to grow exponentially.

Then there was a hiatus. Instead of continuing to rise, the bond market started to downturn, probably discouraged by governments having to borrow even more funds or deterred by rising commodity prices. On 4 February 1994 the Fed raised interest rates by 0.25%, signalling its concern about the speculative bubble. As the bond market reacted negatively, some derivative players banking on interest rates remaining low started to lose money and were forced to sell their contracts. The downturn became a rout and the losses grew. Fastnet lists fifteen public and private institutions which together are known to have lost nearly $75 billion from derivative trading, including Metallgesellschaft ($4 billion) and Kidder Peabody ($3 billion).

The initial losses have shown how an external shock, such as rising commodity prices or a revolution in Russia, could pose huge potential dangers to American banks and institutions with an exposure worth many times their capital. For example, in 1993, Bankers Trust had derivative exposure worth $61.8 billion – roughly thirteen times shareholder equity; a loss of $4.75, minuscule compared to the market, would wipe out the bank. Additionally Chemical Bank, Citicorp, J.P. Morgan and Chase Manhattan all had derivative exposure 250% in excess of their equity.

The situation is even more dangerous when it is understood that the potential liabilities are off the balance sheet, implying that third parties have little or no knowledge of the risks in lending to any one institution. It is also widespread, with 40% of state governments, public retirement and private pension funds using some form of derivatives. Finally, 41% of all trading was between dealers, considerably increasing the risk of a domino failure effect of one bank, broker or institution on others.

Anatomy of the crash

The scale of the likely financial crash and how it could come about is shown in the next chart, Figure 32. The reader will recognise several features from Figure 20 in Chapter 11 which singled out the phases of the Kuznets and Juglar Cycles from 1920 to 1990. The yield on the thirty-year Treasury Bond, reflecting inflationary trends in the US, will be familiar – as will be the yield of the ninety-day Treasury Bill which central banks use to regulate their economies short term by making credit either cheaper or more expensive.

The yield curve is the difference between the two rates; when it is positive the central bank is trying to stimulate the economy, when negative it is slowing it down. The reader will have noticed in Figure 22 that every time there has been a Juglar or Kuznets crisis since 1960, the amount of interest rate needed to quell inflation was progressively greater. This next chart will go some way not only to explain the trends but to identify how these might move in the future.

The two added curves are the CRB index, an amalgam of twenty-one different commodities aggregated together. Finally, there is the US Federal Reserve credit – something which needs a short explanation. The Fed, like several other central banks, is by law independent of the federal government; as the banker to the government, it receives state revenues and provides cash for paying its liabilities. The Fed also issues notes, regulates the banking system and has a duty to keep inflation under control. Previous chapters have shown how the Fed has reacted to earlier peaks in the Juglar Cycle by increasing short-term interest whenever inflation appeared to rise.

Until 1960, around 60% of the central bank's assets were supported by the gold held by the reserve bank at Fort Knox to provide a stable base for the leading currency – just as the pound sterling had been underwritten from 1669 to 1914. President Kennedy was elected in 1960 with a programme to expand the economy, so that the Fed was encouraged to issue an increased number of notes without the traditional gold backing; at the same time some of the gold stocks were sold – so reducing the historical stability even further.

Relative to an index of 100 for the purchasing power of the US dollar in 1913, the currency's worth had declined to 30% by

1965; by 1990 it had fallen to 8% – a drop of over 70% in twenty-five years. The citizens of other countries were defrauded even more than the Americans by their politicians; for example, the purchasing power of the once rock-solid pound sterling had fallen 95% from 1945 to 1990.

The policy to expand the economy might have been contained but it was the decade of the Vietnam War; this the American government financed not by raising taxes but by increasing the note supply – not unlike the German Imperial government in the First World War. It did not actually print notes directly but was more subtle. When the US Treasury needs to issue more securities than would normally be accepted by private institutions, the Fed then steps in to buy bonds for its own account paid for not by its own cash but by writing a cheque to the US Treasury which is then deposited in some bank – which can itself then buy government securities.

The assets of the Fed, once 100% gold, are now well over 80% government securities which it has bought from the Treasury to finance America's persistent (and growing) deficit. As a counterbalance to the assets, the Fed's main liabilities are notes issued, which are effectively printed when the receiving bank accepts the Fed's cheque, the new money either being spent by the government or lent by the bank. This creates a very dangerous position because if the Fed continues to issue notes without the backing of gold, the whole edifice could collapse, effectively making the currency, and everything denominated in it, worthless – exactly what happened to the German mark in 1924. Unfortunately, as described later in the chapter, this could easily occur if the government decided to counter rising commodity prices by flooding the market with even more liquidity in an attempt to keep interest rates low.

The chart in Figure 32 shows there was a modest Juglar financial crisis in 1970, a rather larger one in 1974 when the Kuznets peaked and an even larger one in 1980 after a bout of rapid inflation. By this time, the Fed was buying more and more securities, and the credit line was a rising curve, suggesting that they too were obeying some sort of parabolic law.

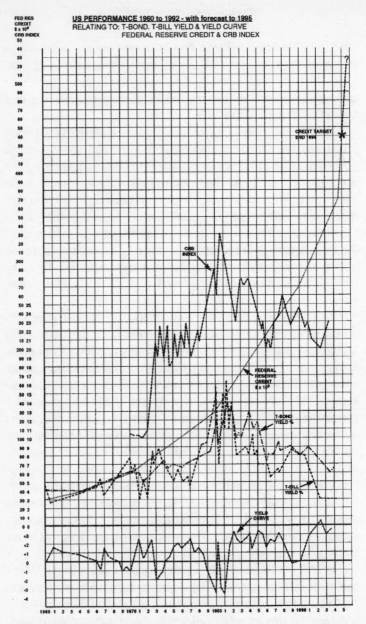

Figure 32. US performance since 1960, showing the relationship between the CRB index, the Treasury Bond and Bill Yields, and the federal-reserve credit.

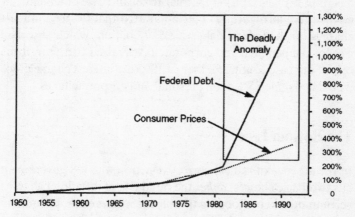

Figure 33. The Deadly Anomaly: growth of federal debt and consumer prices. (From J. Pugsley's *Interest Rate Strategy*.)

Then in 1982, the lines diverged. As Figure 33 shows, inflation, as measured by the Consumer Price Index (the CPI), tracked the government debt curve until 1982, when instead of following the curve upwards it went sideways, showing that for the time being the relationship between debt and inflation no longer held. This is what John Pugsley in his *Interest Rate Strategy* calls the 'Deadly Anomaly'. At some point either consumer prices rise to meet the federal-debt curve or the debt collapses to meet the CPI line.

Some of the factors that could trigger a collapse have already been considered. The first is the problem of rising commodity prices and the reaction of the government; the next is the possibility of inflation from rising tariff barriers to reduce unemployment – particularly in the politically sensitive middle classes – the group that elected President Clinton. Finally, there is the sheer scale of government borrowing. If the level of debt continues to rise exponentially, then by the end of 1994, the federal-reserve credit could reach over $440 billion and by the end of 1995 the curve would be rising almost vertically.

A similar point was made by Harry Figgie in his book

Bankruptcy 1995, showing how the total US government debt has risen with a graph very similar to the increase of US federal-credit curve in Figure 32. Figgie reported that in 1992, interest charges on the federal debt were $293 billion, which absorbed 52% of the personal and corporate taxes raised that year; if the rate of increase continued, then in 1995 the interest charge alone would consume 85% of all personal and corporate taxes.

The Bottom Line

In the absence of radical corrective action, the US government has two basic choices: *either* the rapid rise in inflation has to be accommodated by flooding the market with even more liquidity to keep interest rates down; *or* the government increases interest rates to dampen the flames of rising prices.

In the first case, bond yields would rocket and the dollar collapse as investors fled the currency. It still might be possible to retain value in the Stock Exchange but commodities, particularly precious metals, would soar in the absence of government cutbacks. In the end the Fed would be forced to borrow from abroad and interest rates would move rapidly upwards towards the rising credit curve to attract foreign funds. Eventually, like Germany in 1923, it would not be possible for the US to raise any more government debt, and the official bonds and bills would become worthless. The US and other countries would then be plunged into the deepest recession ever and in the ensuing collapse and despair, even the strongest nation could turn to a dictator.

A more likely scenario would be the break up of unions and federations as nationalism eats away at federal ties, as it did in Germany in 1923–4. Then, Saxony, Prussia and the Rhineland tried to secede from the federation but were prevented by the imposition of martial law; Bavaria could also have separated if the attempted putsch led by the future Führer had been successful. The strain is showing in the 1990s with the break-up of the Soviet Union, Yugoslavia and parts of the Russian Union wanting to secede. In the West there are growing political parties wishing to divide Canada, Italy and even Britain. Federations such as the United States could come apart as individual states questioned the need for a powerful and expensive federal government. There could also be dangers within even stable unions from aggressive minorities wishing to form their own ethical or political enclaves.

Alternatively, the US government would be forced to raise short-term interest rates to quell inflation and at the same time cut its expenditure drastically to balance its budget. If that were to happen, there would be no need to issue more securities and the credit line would stop rising. This action, however, would plunge the US into a deep recession, probably accompanied by a return to the gold standard, with a devalued dollar at a rate of over $3000 (present dollars) per troy ounce. The Stock Market would collapse but any new gold-backed bonds issued would become very valuable – as they were in the 1930s. The medicine would be extremely painful not only in the US but in all countries but the seeds would be sown for a democratic revival.

Which will it be? One would like to feel that present-day politicians had the stature and authority to take the second course. However, as Raymond Wheeler points out, the end of a half-millennium marks the demise of institutions that have outgrown their relevance and we could be faced with the first alternative as the quickest path to destroying the old system and creating the new.

Life after the crash: what will it be like?

Piecing together a situation in which there are few modern precedents is always risky, but going back to the history of earlier climatic 'minima' should enable us to sketch out at least some of the landmarks. It is easier to outline what might be in store for us than actually predict how many of us would react to an extremely difficult situation where life as we know it was falling apart; we might also wonder whether we had the energy to adapt, persevere and whether we have the inner strength to help others.

Raymond Wheeler has already provided us with at least part of an agenda of what might be expected at the end of a 500-year cycle or a climatic minimum. He identified the main changes that would involve a collapse of existing institutions, a liberation of the individual and a power shift from the West to East. If he had been a businessman he might also have suggested how businesses could be kept running and personal capital preserved.

A collapse of existing institutions

Wheeler was probably right when he predicted a major discontinuity every 500 years starting in the 6th century BC. We are now near the end of the millennium and should be able to pinpoint how any collapse would come about. The public institutions of most nations rely heavily on state spending which has been lavished on citizen-support programmes taking up an ever greater proportion of national wealth and manpower.

This was introduced in the belief, fostered by politicians, that in rising prosperity the state should support individuals rather than encourage independence. For example, Britain pays nearly £7 billion per year into the coffers of the European Union, of which almost 60% is given to farmers to keep food prices artificially high; families in Europe spend well over £1,000 a year more on food than they need compared to the rest of the world. There have been programmes for keeping the price of food artificially high before. The British government introduced Corn Laws in 1815 to keep out imported grain until the domestic price reached eighty shillings a quarter. Further tariffs were introduced in 1823 but the policy was repealed in 1846 during the famine of that year when the government was forced to import cheap grain.

A great many will suffer from a cutback in government expenditure, not least the bureaucrats running the vast machine of benefits and entitlements. Numbers of people will become highly resentful, even violent against the politicians who had promised support in the past and can no longer deliver. The following headings might form an initial agenda for what should be done:

Government's ability to spend

The main casualty of both the alternatives spelled out earlier would be governments' ability to continue their social and other support programmes. Yet for fear of angering the electorate, these would be the last to be scrapped by politicians seeking re-election; unfortunately, this is just another reason why weak governments would chose inflation, not deflation as a response to rising prices – as did the Weimar leaders before them. Of course, the end result will be much worse; countries suffering a major inflation, then a devastating collapse into a depression, will be in no position to raise any long-term debt, and find their ability to raise taxes severely curtailed.

Whether any politician would be able to survive such a debacle is doubtful; possibly only someone outside politics would be acceptable as a potential leader. It happened at the time of the English Civil War when Oliver Cromwell, who before the war was a farmer, rose to lead the New Model Army to victory. After the king's execution Cromwell was himself declared Lord Protector to rule while both Parliament and the monarchy were suspended.

Scale of government cutback

The largest peacetime decline of tax revenue happened in the US, when the gross national output declined around 30% from 1930 to 1934; although the decline was acute, it was not catastrophic; the government was able to borrow the considerable shortfall to fund Roosevelt's New Deal public works, and work-creation programmes. Should there be an equivalent crash now, many nations would suffer a decline of at least 30%, probably nearer 50% – a shortfall that could no longer be made up by even more government borrowing.

Assuming that US taxed income would fall by 50%, this would reduce federal revenue from $1075 billion (1992 figures)

to $537.5 billion; of this $293 billion (55%) would still be needed
to pay the interest on the national debt – that is, assuming it had
not all disappeared with inflation. This would leave $245 billion
to be split between social-entitlement programmes (running at
$766 billion in 1992) and then military spending of $313 billion, the two largest budget items. The total federal budget was
nearer $1500 billion in 1993, with the other charges proportion-
ately greater.

Using 1990 figures, a 50% decline in revenue in Britain would
reduce the available income to around £95 billion, of which £18
billion (19%) would be swallowed up in interest, leaving £77 billion for other budgeted items. In 1990, these included £56 billion
for social security, £22 billion for defence, and £26 billion for the
Health Service. The government spent a total of £289 billion in
1993–4 (up £65 billion from 1990) and increased the deficit to
£50 billion; this huge rise threatens the whole basis of the welfare
state should there be a crash on the scale anticipated.

Clearly governments cannot abnegate defence spending,
although the armed services can expect considerable cut-backs –
particularly the administrative and civilian 'tail'. In 1933 the
US defence budget was cut nearly 30% to $531 million, the army
taking a 50% reduction – as did also veterans' benefits. This
time the only hope of avoiding a social collapse would be to
delegate the responsibility for most health and education expenditure, plus a much-reduced contribution for social security and
unemployment payments, to local communities.

In Britain a cut-back on this scale would allow central or local
government to employ only a fraction of the current 3 million
people, excluding the armed services, which amounts to more
than 10% of the working population. This means that for the
state to continue functioning, a great deal of public expenditure
and administration would need to be devolved to individuals
licensed by the government – so relegating a highly competent
core of public-sector employees to an important monitoring role.

This delegation of responsibility would be not unlike the
arrangement made to dispense the first English Poor Laws introduced in 1597–8. A poor rate was raised from members of a

parish, and administered by the churchwardens and substantial property owners. Needy adults were found work either in their own homes or in the community, and their children were apprenticed to learn a trade. So successful was this programme in England that other countries in Europe adopted a similar system.

Because a government has been made insolvent it does not necessarily follow that all other institutions will also fail. Although the Weimar Republic was morally and financially crippled in 1924, most companies remained solvent and were the driving force for the recovery during the latter part of the 1920s. It is likely in any future collapse that corporations – particularly the smaller ones – will be the mainspring for organising the many local communities described later in the chapter.

Problems of rising unemployment
Any collapse on this scale could only accelerate the cybernetic revolution not only in business but to every area of public administration described earlier. This would mean that only around 30% of the working population would be skilled enough to look forward to any sort of personal security. Of the remaining 70%, a proportion would be skilled tradesmen or professionals working on a contractual basis, leaving probably around 50% with apparently little hope of a secure future.

No civilised nation could contemplate the possibility of up to 50% of their fellow citizens leaving school at sixteen with only the prospect of short-term, unskilled jobs ahead of them. As Michael White points out, those running countries and industries know little of history, believing that we still live in an industrial age when in fact the cybernetic age is already upon us. Whether or not there is a collapse on the scale described, there is very little prospect of returning to a time when the majority of school leavers can see anything but endless uncertainty ahead and a collapse of their previous expectations.

What can be done?
Unfortunately there is little any government can do directly in the face of severe budget restrictions. A nation unable to offer

any sort of a future to their young men and women is in grave danger of disintegration unless those with brains and imagination can address the problem of their fellow citizens, not as an act of charity but in their own self-interest either individually or through a company. There is no way that the successful can distance themselves from their neighbours in a modern society without the severe danger of social disorder.

Several solutions have been suggested. Michael White has proposed a government-run employment agency which hires out people on short-term contracts; unemployed individuals would be paid a minimum wage and given training. Sir Ralph Howell, a Member of Parliament, suggests a similar idea where the government acts as an employer of last resort, putting people to work on local projects. Unfortunately both these and other programmes assume that the government will be able to fund such plans, when in reality this is unlikely.

Any solution should take into account Raymond Wheeler's insight that cool periods encourage individuality. If indeed it is to become cooler, then it may be possible to harness the same professionals' home-working techniques to those less gifted or naturally able to work for themselves. After all, the power and marketability of individuals and small groups have been enormously increased in the last decade with the advent of computers and machinery. Franchising could make a whole range of new small businesses available to people who had the energy and initiative to work for themselves according to a plan.

A new definition of community
With the declining influence of full-time central and local government, the responsibility for mutual support will be in the community just as it was by the craft guilds 400 years ago in the Elizabethan age. Communities are likely to react in certain ways. Some will adopt the approach of a Kibbutz, where almost everything is held in common ownership.

Other communities will retain personal ownership but be prepared to pool resources for such matters as security, schooling, health and municipal maintenance; they will also appoint groups to help support those setting up on their own and providing useful local work for those with nothing to do. As state-run services decline, the more enterprising households are likely to use modern technology to increase the level of personal health care, and both adult and child education.

Unless funded by local enterprises, most communities will only have limited state funds and will probably rely on different forms of barter systems to pay for the services outlined earlier. Bartering was widely used during the Weimar Republic, and is in use today in places like Russia and the Ukraine where currency has become worthless. Modern systems such as the Local Employment Trading System (LETS) initiated by Michael Linton of Courtenay, British Columbia, have been adapted to work in many countries; LETS is computer-based, simple in operation and has a built-in marketing programme for helping people setting up on their own.

Bartering will be particularly important to help the many retired people whose state pensions will have been severely reduced by a reduction of government revenue. Most communities have a large, untapped reserve of older, experienced people who could make a considerable contribution to such matters as the administration of new businesses, organising the unemployed within the community, or teaching adult skills.

Liberating the individual

Earlier chapters have described man's reaction to an environment changing from cool to warm, wet to dry and so on; people become more energetic as it gets cooler, and anxious if there is a food shortage; recall the anger at the time of the Peasants' Revolt when the king refused to end serfdom. Whatever the disruption that lies ahead, there will be considerable anger and resentment when people discover their expected security is an illusion and their savings rendered worthless from the collapsing currency.

What, then, are the qualities needed to survive a major collapse? Can any conventional education help one to ride out a
tempest similar to the Weimar Republic hyperinflation?

The meaning of the individual
Philosophers throughout the ages have disputed whether reality can be known through the senses or from some greater and
ultimate meaning which reduces human experience to mean-
ingless trivia. The great writers Boccaccio and Petrarch started
the Italian Renaissance by liberating a world that had become
clogged with the rituals and rigidities of an unreformed
church. The first humanists revived interest in the classical
Grecian glories and showed that man can not only observe
and think for himself but that he could also be enormously creative; there were also some in the Church who were in favour of
this discovery.

The Renaissance was followed by the Reformation which continued the work of liberation from a powerful and, at times,
corrupt Church. But the undermining of the worth of the individual was already beginning. In his book, *The Ominous Parallels*,
Leonard Peikoff explains how the German philosopher
Immanuel Kant downgraded the Enlightenment by arguing that
man could not possibly know reality, could not know 'things as
they are'. It follows that an individual's understanding of reality
is of little value unless it can be subordinated to a group, the
community or a country. Peikoff shows how every socialist or
fascist tyranny can be justified once the personal will is downgraded to the good of others.

Peikoff's mentor was the American objectivist, Ayn Rand,
whose keynote book, *Atlas Shrugged*, is still the manual for
those wishing to survive difficult times. Rand answers Kant by
declaring that 'man is blind, because he has eyes – deaf, because
he has ears – deluded, because he has a mind – and the things he
perceives do not exist, because he perceives them'. Rand holds
that 'man's mind is the basic tool of survival, Life is given to
him, survival is not. His body is given to him, its sustenance is
not. His mind is given to him, its content is not. To remain alive,

he must act, and before he can act he must know the nature and purpose of his action . . . To remain alive, he must think.'

The key to survival

Guile and muscle counted for more than academic ability to survive the great Weimar inflation. To thrive people must be totally realistic – to be what Rand calls 'selfish', which means not a disregard for others, but a clear-sighted regard for reality. She goes on to urge people to use their brains, not to surrender judgement to others; it means facing reality at first hand, not as a leap of faith. After all, who using their own judgement would have taken a Weimar politician's advice to buy mark-denominated fixed interest bonds when the currency was crashing?

A person with a code of rational self-interest upholds the virtues of independence, integrity, honesty, justice, productiveness and pride, and dignifies others with the same qualities. It can only exist where there is political as well as economic freedom, and where others, when they are at all capable, have the right and duty to exercise the same qualities that one has oneself. Ayn Rand asserts that people must not rely on others for sustenance but that everyone, where physically or mentally possible, should struggle to reach their own potential.

So, how are we to adapt to discontinuity?

For most with considerable difficulty, because if Rand is right most people will need to dig deeply into their own resources; there will be precious little state cash available for supporting the less well-off. What, then, are the qualities for survival?

Flexibility seems an essential ingredient because in rapidly changing conditions, people should be able to turn their hand to many things and do several things at once – accepting different remuneration if needed. Women are generally more able to do this than most men, which is why their unemployment rate is lower. Flexibility also means an ability to learn new skills, without formal training if necessary, when one's training either becomes obsolete or can be done more cheaply by someone else.

To make wider use of their talents, people are forming

networks which can be enriched and expanded over time. The best networks only bring value to participants where individuals bring qualities of mutual support, information or contacts.

The best games-players and the most successful businessmen are able to 'read' what is going on for themselves without needing an army of advisers; it is well known that if the big 'players' come into a market, such as property, then it is usually the time for the minnows to go elsewhere. This is the quality of opportunism, the capacity to discern a chance and act swiftly. Reading the situation also requires good communications both for receiving and transmitting ideas in a wide variety of media.

Having status may be important in a settled stable environment but could be a disadvantage when survival turns upon an individual's being able to undertake quite different, or even quite menial jobs for a short while. It is reported that the only way innocent people were able to remain sane and hold on to their standards in Stalin's Gulags was to pretend they were on a prolonged and disagreeable holiday or adventure which would eventually be over.

Most of us will be travelling through unfamiliar territory without help from many of the trusted principles and landmarks that no longer apply. Most of the middle class who lost everything during the German great inflation found that previous certainties, such as trusting the currency or entering a profession as the key to a secure future, were overturned as the mark collapsed and there was little market for conventional skills.

Apart from those who relish change as the breath of life, most of us will need to create a new set of values to discern what is and what is not important, when all around is in disorder. Finding this identity might perhaps come more easily to a person of faith, with a belief and hope that their God will help them to bring out the best in themselves – not only for their own comfort and strength but also for others. This need has already stimulated fundamental sects in the Muslim and Christian worlds which are growing rapidly in their search to learn and practise the will of God. Difficult times make people aware of their own vulnerability, which is why the Bible and holy scriptures are read seriously in times of uncertainty.

A large proportion of the population will need the self-reliance to work for themselves. There will be no difficulty for those who are naturally independent; the transition will be particularly painful for those used to the routine repetitive work associated with most public service. The new cybernetic business organisations will increasingly need talented sub-contractors, but for the majority the new franchises that should become available will be the best way to learn self-reliance.

The new world order

From the perspective of the mid-1990s, it looks as if Raymond Wheeler's 500-year East–West cycle may come about. He believed that the centre of economic and political power would move from West to East for the next 500 years, while the West regained its sense of values and priorities. However, this has seldom been a precise cycle, and although several nations, such as the Singaporeans and Taiwanese as well as the Japanese, have already overtaken Britain in output per head, the spirit of enterprise would need to incorporate the Chinese for the move East to be conclusive.

From his perspective of the 1950s, Wheeler believed that India would become the leading nation in the 21st century; it is a democracy, there are a growing number of educated people and, given the right political encouragement, more Indians could be successful as businessmen and traders. Despite their long cultural history the Indian nation has seldom been aggressive outside its own borders and, like a number of other nations, India could still be riven by religious extremism.

There is little doubt that the cybernetic revolution described by Michael White's report, *The World in Flux*, will change for good the way companies (and probably governments) are managed. The combination of replacing manual operations and many decision-making processes by computers started in Japan, and has taken firm root in the Pacific's western rim. Cybernetics also implies outsourcing many of the production processes previously, and as Japan and other countries become increasingly uncompetitive, firms will progressively buy components and assemblies from low-cost producers such as China, Indonesia, Malaysia and Vietnam. Soon European and American customers will become less important to this growing region as standards of living increase.

Finally, there are the 700- and 800-year religious and people cycles which could provide the latter-day power focus, as did the Mongols and Ottoman Turks nine and ten centuries ago. The peoples living in Turkey along Central Asia to Mongolia could still be a potent force when displaced by a significant food shortage. If these people were forced to move to more fertile pastures, the domino effect on Europe and China would be devastating.

Saving one's business and keeping capital intact

Those who were running a business or managing inflation in 1973–4 will remember mounting inflation, wild swings of interest rates, company collapses and spiralling commodity prices; banks failed, prices had to be revised every quarter and currency exchange rates girated. Something similar could lie ahead if the delayed Kuznets' Cycle returns in 1995–6. If the rules of the mid-1980s no longer apply, how can new principles be devised, tested and implemented?

Riding the switchback: an earlier part of this chapter suggested two scenarios. Governments could deal with a rise of commodity and food prices in two ways; either they could 'accommodate' surging prices by continuing to pump money into the economy, keeping interest rates low, or they could raise the cost of money to keep down inflation.

Scenario one
Increased commodity prices would trigger a rapid rise in bond yields as suggested by Pugsley earlier in the chapter. As money

was taken out of fixed-interest stock, several things could happen: central banks would be forced to monetise borrowings at an increasing rate, forcing up even more steeply the federal credit curve in Figure 32. The cash released from bonds could either go into the Stock Market or into tangible assets, such as commodities or related stocks. Wide-awake investors could leverage their investments in the full knowledge they could pay back the principal in debased currency.

Finally, the currency would fall as investors sold a weakening currency – just as investors sold the mark in the early 1920s. In those days just the German and Austrian currencies were affected, but if similar events occurred today no one denomination would be safe and most investors would buy gold or silver as the safest refuge. The German Stock Market performed well in the early 1920s, despite the crash in bonds, but it was three times more profitable to hold gold; the relative fall was so great that the entire market value for all stocks was £271 million in 1923 compared to a pre-war figure of £1767 million.

Housing and real-estate values could also rise while interest rates were held down but would be sold rapidly in the event of a liquidity squeeze. As inflation reached its peak, the frenzy of speculation would be so great that the exchanges would be forced to close, making it no longer possible to sell securities or deal in the rapidly expanding 'hedging and swap' techniques used so widely by investors and speculators. Eventually, the authorities would be forced to allow rising interest rates to attract foreign cash which could soar to well over 30% in the USA. Pugsley's deadly anomaly in Figure 33 would be nearing completion.

The spiral of money creation can only end in the most horrific crash when companies can no longer afford extremely high interest rates and are forced either into failure or to liquidate anything of value just to stay solvent. As credit dries up there will be a selling avalanche of houses, companies, securities and *objets d'art* – anything to pay off debt and raise cash. Unfortunately, it will be too late for many; their politicians once again will have succeeded in destroying the currency – just as in Germany in 1924. Pugsley's anomaly would be complete.

Of course, running a business or making money from investments will still be possible but will require a new style of
thinking where the old principles are jettisoned and new rules
worked out. If the inflationary signal anticipated by the commodity cycles appears, then every board or investment fund
should set up a separate unit to devise, monitor and implement
strategy; something on the lines of a military intelligence staff
unit would be appropriate.

Scenario two
The second alternative assumes that rising commodity prices
would create a 'cost-push' inflation forcing governments to raise
short-term interest rates. There would be an immediate fall of
the bond and stock markets as investors moved out, feeling their
cash would be safer on deposit. The political reaction would be
immediate as individuals and companies were forced to reduce
the prohibitive interest on their loans and mortgages. Like the
first scenario the liquidity squeeze would depress the value of all
assets, including housing, as high borrowers dumped every surplus item to avoid collapse.

The economy would be plunged into a deep recession as
spending power is squeezed by higher food prices and many
companies would fail either through their market collapsing or
from excessive debts. The government would be forced to trim its
own spending and with less need to sell securities, the reserve
curve in Figures 32 and 33 would fall.

Scenario two would not imply a happy outcome but at least
the currency would be saved – as would many institutions –
something unlikely in the first alternative. Economies would
also revive more quickly because it would still be possible to
issue government debts although, with a new alignment of currencies, the coupon might be lowered – just like Consols during
the 19th century.

So how could businesses be run?
Only by rigorously applying the principles of the cybernetic revolution described by Michael White and converting every

available item of fixed costs using the 'Third Generation' ideas suggested in *Meltdown*. The businesses that should do particularly well are low-cost food processing and distribution, those applying cybernetic techniques and, most importantly, ideas and equipment helping people to become independent. Any organisation should ensure that all debts are paid off in both scenarios before the crash; however, in the first alternative it might be worth delaying the payback in devalued money as late as possible. The strategic-intelligence group suggested earlier is even more important for industrial and commercial companies than investors, because of their longer time lags.

International trading

It is difficult to see how any governments would be able to continue free trade or other agreements when so many of their countrymen were out of work. Initially, the world will probably split into three trading blocs, the Far East, North America and Europe, where it will be essential for international firms to operate as if they were a domestic company. But the strains will tell in either of the two scenarios as one nation after another demands a relaxation of the club rules to make itself more competitive. It is hard to see the European Union surviving as anything other than a free-trade area when cash shortages arrest the Common Agriculture Policy and community-support programmes.

The message of hope

Every other period of climatic stress has always rewarded those who had the capacity, endurance and wit to see it out. From the horrors of the Black Death came the Renaissance, from the rapid changes of the 1500s emerged western trading, and then industrial expansion. Is it really so appalling that in the new golden age an individual will find a new sense of freedom, responsibility, personal values, faith and a capacity to find success – just as Raymond Wheeler predicted back in the 1950s?

SELECT BIBLIOGRAPHY

American Institute for Economic Research, 'Stand Still, Little Lambs, to be Shorn!', Princeton Economics, 1993

Armstrong, Martin, 'The Greatest Bull Market in History', Princeton Economics, 1986

Barry and Chorley, *Atmosphere, Weather & Climate*, Methuen & Co. Ltd, London, 1968

Beckman, Robert C., *Crashes*, Grafton Books, London, 1990

Briggs, Asa, *Iron Bridge to Crystal Palace*, Thames & Hudson Ltd, London, 1979

Burroughs, William J., *Weather Cycles: Real or Imaginary?*, Cambridge University Press, 1992

Carcia-Mata and Shaffner, 'Solar and Economic Relationships', Foundation for the Study of Cycles*, 1st edition, 1945

Chaunu, Pierre (ed.), *The Reformation*, Alan Sutton Publishing, 1989

Dando, William, A., *A Geography of Famine*, V. H. Winston & Sons, 1980

Dent, Harry S., Jr, *The Great Boom Ahead*, Hyperion Press, USA, 1993

Dupuy, R. Ernest and Dupuy, Trevor, N., *The Encyclopedia of Military History*, Macdonald and Janes, 1970

Fairbridge, Rhodes, *Planetary Periodicities and Terrestrial Climate Stress*, Columbia University, 1984

Fairbridge, Rhodes and Shirley, James, 'Prolonged Minima and the 179 Year Cycle of the Solar Inertia Motion', *Solar Physics*, 1987

Fastnet Associates, 'Financial Derivatives', pub. 1994. Available from 39 St Peter's Square, London W6 9NN

Feavearear, A. E., *The Pound Sterling*, Oxford Clarendon Press, 1931

Figgie, Harry, Jr, *Bankruptcy 1995: The Coming Collapse of America and How To Stop It*, Little, Brown and Company, Inc., Boston, 1992

Galbraith, John Kenneth, *The Great Crash, 1929*, Penguin Books Ltd, London, 1988

Gariss, Evelyn (ed.), 'The Browning Newsletter'. Available from PO Box 494, Burlington, Vermont 05402, USA

Handler, Paul 'United States Corn Yields, The El Nino and Agricultural Drought 1867–1988', *International Journal of Climatology*, University of Illinois, 1989

Herman and Goldberg, *Sun, Weather and Climate*, Dover Publications Inc., New York, 1985

Hobhouse, Henry, *Forces of Change: Why We Are the Way We Are Now*, Sidgwick & Jackson Ltd, London, 1989

——, *Seeds of Change: Five Plants That Transformed Mankind*, Sidgwick & Jackson Ltd, London, 1985

Huntington, Elsworth, *Climatic Changes*, John Wiley & Sons, London, 1922

——, *Mainsprings of Civilisation*, John Wiley & Sons, London, 1945

——, *Seasons of Birth*, John Wiley & Sons, USA, 1938

Kirkland, William and Douglas, *Power Cycles*, Professional Communications, 1987. Available from PO Box 7585, Phoenix, Arizona, AZ 85011, USA

Kondratieff, Nicolai, *The Long Wave Cycle*, Richardson and Snyder, USA, 1984

Lamb, H.H., *Climate, History and the Modern World*, Methuen and Co. Ltd, London, 1982

——, 'Volcanic dust in the atmosphere; with a chronology and assessment of its meteorological significance' (266A:425–533), Royal Society of Philosophical Transactions, 1970

Landsheidt, Theodor, *Sun–Earth–Man*, Urania Trust, UK, 1988

Linton, Michael, 'Local Exchange and Trading Systems (LETS)'. Available from 1600 Embleton Crescent, Courtney, V9N 6N8, British Columbia, Canada

Mitchell, Wesley Clair, *Business Cycles and Their Causes*, University of California Press, Berkeley, 1972

Modelski, George, *Exploring Long Cycles*, Pinter Publishers Ltd, London, 1987

——, *Long Cycles in World Politics*, University of Washington Press, Seattle, 1987

Modelski, George, and Thompson, William, 'Kondratieff Waves: The Evolving Global Economy and World Politics: The Problem of Coordination'. Presented at the N.D. Kondratieff Centenary Conference in Moscow, 17–19 March 1992. Available from Foundation for the Study of Cycles[*]

Patterson, Robert T., 'Why Gold?', American Institute for Economic Research, Great Barrington, MA, USA, 1963

Peikoff, Leonard, *Ominous Parallels*, Stein & Day, USA, 1982

Rand, Ayn, *Atlas Shrugged*, New American Library, distributed by Penguin Books Ltd

Rees-Mogg, William, *The Reigning Error: The Crisis of World Inflation*, Hamish Hamilton Ltd, London, 1974

Rostow, W.W., *Why the Poor Get Richer and the Rich Slow Down*, Macmillan Publishers Ltd, London, 1980

Schumpeter, Joseph A., *Business Cycles: A Theoretical, Historical and Statistical Analysis of the Capitalist Process*, Porcupine Press, Inc., Philadelphia, 1980

Shirley, James, 'When the Sun Goes Backward', March/April 1989. Available from Foundation for the Study of Cycles[*]

Simkin, T. (ed.), *Volcanoes of the World*, Hutchinson Ross, Inc., USA, 1981

Sloan, Alfred P., *My Years with General Motors*, Sidgwick & Jackson Ltd, London, 1965

Smith, Adam, *The Wealth of Nations Books I–III* (ed. A. Skinner) English Library, Penguin Books Ltd, London, 1982

Steiger, Brad, *A Roadmap of Time*, Prentice-Hall, USA, 1975

Stone, Norman (ed.), *The Times Atlas of World History*, Times Books, London, 1989

Stoskopf, N.C., *Cereal Grain Crops*, Reston Publishing Co., USA, 1985

Tannehill, Ivan, *Drought, its Causes and Effects*, Princeton University Press, 1947

Thomas, Gordon, and Witts, Max Morgan, *The Day the Bubble Burst*, Penguin Books Ltd, London, 1980

——, *The San Francisco Earthquake*, Stein and Day, New York, 1971

Thompson, Louis M., '186 Year Lunar Cycle: Its Possible Relation to Agriculture', *Cycles Journal*, March/April 1989. Available from Foundation for the Study of Cycles[*]

van Duijin, J.J., *The Long Wave in Economic Life*, Allen & Unwin Publishers Ltd, London, 1983

Warren, George, and Pearson, Frank, *European Commodity Prices*, John Wiley & Sons Ltd, London, 1933

Warren, J. P., *The 50-Year Boom-Bust Cycle*, Warren, Cameron & Co, UK, 1982

Wheeler, Raymond and others, 'Weather Science Foundation Newsletter'. Available from Foundation for the Study of Cycles*

White, Michael, 'The Cybernetic Age', pub. 1994. Available from 57 Lynn Fells Parkway, Melrose, MA 02176, USA

——, 'The Fifth Epoch', pub. 1994. Available from 57 Lynn Fells Parkway, Melrose, MA 02176, USA

Windelius, Goran, 'Large Volcanic Eruptions and Earthquakes in Pace with the Chandler Wobble', *Cycles Journal*, September 1993. Available from Foundation for the Study of Cycles*

Winkless, Nels, and Browning, Iben, *Climate and the Affairs of Men*, Fraser Publishing Company, USA, 1975

Zahorchak, Michael, *Climate: The Key to Understanding Business. Cycles*, Tide Press, New Jersey, 1983

* Foundation for the Study of Cycles
900 West Valley Road
Suite 502
Wayne, PA 19087-1321
USA

INDEX

Note: Illustrations are indicated by italics